Social Class in Scotland: Past and Present

To my mother

Social Class in Scotland:
Past and Present

Edited by
A. Allan MacLaren

JOHN DONALD PUBLISHERS LTD
EDINBURGH

© John Donald Publishers Ltd.

All rights reserved. No part of this publication may be reproduced in any form or by any means without the prior permission of the publishers, John Donald Publishers Ltd., 8 Mayfield Terrace, Edinburgh EH9 1SA, Scotland.

ISBN 0 85976 013 8

Printed and bound in Great Britain by Morrison & Gibb Ltd., London and Edinburgh

Acknowledgements

I should like to take this opportunity of formally thanking the contributors for their collaboration in bringing this volume to fruition. I must thank especially Marc MacLaren for her steadfast support throughout — particularly in the compilation of the index. Finally I must record my gratitude to Cecile Fleming for her friendly and efficient secretarial assistance.

A.A. MacLaren

Contributors

A.A. MacLaren, M.A., Ph.D., is a lecturer in Sociology, University of Strathclyde; author of *Religion and Social Class: the Disruption Years in Aberdeen* (Routledge & Kegan Paul, London, 1974).

Enid Gauldie, M.A., B.Phil., is visiting lecturer in the School of Architecture, Dundee; author of *Dundee Textile Industry* (Scottish History Society, Edinburgh, 1969) and *Cruel Habitations* (Allen & Unwin, London, 1974).

T.C. Smout, M.A., Ph.D., is Professor of Economic History, University of Edinburgh; author of *Scottish Trade on the Eve of the Union* (Oliver & Boyd, 1963), and *A History of the Scottish People 1550-1830* (Collins, 1969).

Malcolm Gray, M.A., is Reader in Economic History, University of Aberdeen; author of *The Highland Economy, 1750-1850* (Oliver & Boyd, Edinburgh, 1957).

Ian Carter, B.Sc.(Soc)., M.A., is a lecturer in Sociology, University of Aberdeen; author of various articles on the Scottish highlands, and on rural culture.

R.Q. Gray, B.A., Ph.D., is a lecturer in Social History, Portsmouth Polytechnic; author of a number of articles on aspects of social stratification and of a forthcoming book on the labour aristocracy in the Victorian class structure.

J.G. Kellas, M.A., Ph.D., is Senior Lecturer in Politics, University of Glasgow; author of *Modern Scotland* (Pall Mall Press, London, 1968) and *The Scottish Political System* (Cambridge University Press, 1973).

Peter Fotheringham, M.A., is a lecturer in Politics, University of Glasgow; author of an article on the American party system.

John Scott, B.Sc.(Soc.), is a lecturer in Sociology, University of Strathclyde; author of various articles on social stratification and sociological theory.

Michael Hughes, B.Tech., is a lecturer in Sociology, University of Strathclyde; author of articles on capital investment and on stratification.

Contents

1. Introduction: An Open Society?   1
   A.A. MacLaren

2. The Middle Class and Working-class Housing in the Nineteenth Century   12
   Enid Gauldie

3. Bourgeois Ideology and Victorian Philanthropy: The Contradictions of Cholera   36
   A.A. MacLaren

4. Aspects of Sexual Behaviour in Nineteenth Century Scotland   55
   T.C. Smout

5. North-East Agriculture and the Labour Force, 1790-1875   86
   Malcolm Gray

6. Class and Culture among Farm Servants in the North-East, 1840-1914   105
   Ian Carter

7. Thrift and Working-class Mobility in Victorian Edinburgh   128
   Robert Q. Gray

8. The Political Behaviour of the Working Class   143
   James G. Kellas and Peter Fotheringham

9. The Scottish Ruling Class: Problems of Analysis and Data   166
   John Scott and Michael Hughes

   Index   189

1. Introduction: An Open Society?

A.A.MacLaren

It was in 1961 that E.H. Carr made what is perhaps the most well-known plea for some form of rapprochement between the disciplines of History and Sociology: '..the more sociological history becomes, and the more historical sociology becomes, the better for both. Let the frontier between them be kept wide open for two-way traffic'. (1) In a sense it was somewhat ironical that Carr should choose to make such a plea within the context of lectures dedicated to the memory of G.M.Trevelyan — one of the greatest of the Whig narrative historians. Although such a proposal at the time was radical if long overdue, Carr's advocacy for such a rapprochement has long since been swallowed up by the ongoing debate concerning the relationships between history and sociology. (2) Whilst the debate itself has undoubtedly kept alive the need for interdisciplinary cooperation it is clear that Scotland has lagged behind England in producing the fruits of such cross-fertilisation. One of the reasons for this has been the strongly entrenched position in Scottish universities of historians subscribing to the 'narrative' tradition. The idea that history should take the form of a 'factual narrative' which 'should at the same time provide some interpretation' remains an important element in British, perhaps particularly Scottish, historiography. (3) It is an idea which has been defended quite recently in an eminent work on modern Scottish history. (4) The supposition that somehow the facts must be allowed to speak for themselves, and that the historian who sifts these facts, is in some undisclosed way divorced from them, is an ideological assumption with a lineage extending back into the mid-nineteenth century. It is an assumption which disallows any attempt to apply general theory or even a concept such as social class. Indeed it has been argued that for social scientists to attempt to do this is to pervert the evidence of history. (5)

The purpose of this volume is to attempt to achieve some sort of balance with the older historical traditions of scholarship and to look more closely than has been done before at certain aspects of social class in nineteenth and twentieth century Scotland. The aim is not to produce a text-book, nor is it an attempt to produce an overall class analysis of Scottish society. The aim is to probe selected aspects of social class and to assess its importance in determining attitudes, beliefs, and relationships within the total society. The approach is essentially of an interdisciplinary nature, drawing as it does upon the works of historians, political scientists, and sociologists. Consequently differences naturally occur both in the use and application of the concept of class. Nevertheless what is clear is the pressing need for structural analyses of Scottish society — both of a contemporary and historical character. As Kellas has pointed out Scots have a tendency to seek an escape in the historical past:

> Scotland has problems of housing, unemployment and religious bitterness which make it a society torn by class and racial tensions. Scots often prefer not to discuss these, and when they think of Scotland they conjure up a picture of the past. (6)

The problem presented by this type of 'historical escapism' is that it may well be based on a mythical representation of the past. This past although not a Golden Age is held to be more admirable in many respects than the present. The belief that Scotland was an open society whose fundamental egalitarianism was gradually eroded, in part by contact with its more powerful neighbour, is not just a piece of popular nationalism but has penetrated and been propounded by works of academic scholarship. (7) The ideological hero is undoubtedly the 'lad o' pairts' born into poverty but succeeding in the world despite formidable obstacles. His success, however, although related to his own and his parents' resolve that he should strive to rise in the world, was not simply the result of adhering to the teaching of Samuel Smiles (interestingly enough himself a Scot). Success came because the institutional means to mobility were there and every encouragement was given to the young man who sought a university education. The contrast with England was great:

> Hardy's *Jude the Obscure* presents us with a picture (corroborated by much other evidence) of conditions almost incredible to a Scot, and impossible alike in modern England and at any time in the history of Scotland. There Shon Campbell, who would be Jude's analogue, may sometimes have died of scant fare and overwork, but he much more generally warsled through by the proud and willing help of his family and one of the very many bursaries, which had been loyally kept to their proper function of helping the lad who joined parts with poverty. (8)

Two important elements are apparent within Scottish society as depicted by what one for want of a better term might call the 'Scottish Myth'. Firstly the egalitarianism so often portrayed is not that emerging from an economic, social, or even political equality; it is equality of *opportunity* which is exemplified. All men are not equal. What is implied is that all men are given an opportunity to be equal. Whatever the values attached to such a belief, if expressed today it would be termed elitist not egalitarian. The second important element in the 'Scottish Myth' is that the equality of educational opportunity is assumed to have existed – not on the basis of the Scottish situation – but on the Scottish situation relative to one which obviously was lacking in England. An assumption of universality built on a comparison of this sort and tested only by one or two case studies of successful careers of poor but gifted children is not methodologically acceptable. A study of elite recruitment in nineteenth century Scotland, and the role played by the parish school, is long overdue.

Nevertheless, whatever doubts one might cast on the effectiveness of the educational system, it is clear that education, as such, was held in much greater esteem in Scotland. It may well be that the educational system of the eighteenth century had been more effective in creaming off gifted children and that the advent of rapid industrialisation, urbanisation, and the emergence of an urban bourgeoisie, whose own mobility was not related to educational opportunity, led to a deterioration in educational provisions. Whilst industrial capitalism as it developed created a dynamic society which swept away many of the old tyrannies inherent in rural society by destroying the older paternalistic obligations, it left a vacuum which had to be filled. By the middle decades of the nineteenth century it is clear that the middle class were desperately attempting to make up the ground that had been lost and in one Scottish city at least a vast and varying array of educational provisions had been instituted for working-class children. Unfortunately very few of these schools came anywhere near the better eighteenth century parish school and most were concerned with maintaining social control in the community rather than advancing any form of egalitarianism based on educational opportunity. (9)

Despite the many problems confronting them however it is evident that many members of the middle class retained a belief that educational opportunity was a vital element in maintaining an 'open society'. Events such as the Disruption in the Church of Scotland (ironically many of those in the forefront of the debate to improve educational provisions were to secede) adversely affected the quality and quantity of graduate teachers available by drawing off many members of the teaching profession into the ministry. Thereafter denominationalism continually thwarted efforts to provide a national system of education although there was a fairly general recognition of the need. Neither was the matter resolved by the 1872 Education Act: the debate merely moved into the realm of providing universal secondary education. When 'senior' and 'junior' secondary schools were instituted, dividing communities along what approximated to class lines, the way was open for the continuing debate and controversy over elitist and comprehensive education. (10)

One is inevitably confronted by the problem of why Scotland, lagging as she did behind England in terms of material wealth and economic development, should place such a high premium on the need to provide adequate educational provisions. The traditional explanation is well-known and appears convincing enough to remain safe from any challenge. Although one would like to know more about the reasons why Presbyterianism was able to put down such deep roots in Scottish society, and survive the Episcopal challenge, it seems clear that concern for grass-roots education at the parish level was a product of the Reformation and John Knox, as well as subsequent reformers. The *First Book of Discipline* in 1560 set the ideal and this 'avowal of the Kirk's responsibility for education, popular as well as professional, and its resolve to establish one school in every parish, determined the course of events for some 300 years'. (11) The ideal was never fully realised in that many parishes, particularly in poorer, more remote areas, never received a school. However, the importance of the Church's control over education can scarcely be over-estimated. The Calvinist doctrine of predestination was an essential part of Scottish Presbyterianism and the necessary education to allow one to read and understand the scriptures was fundamental to such a belief. Evidence suggests that even in urban areas of utter 'spiritual destitution', where the majority rarely or never attended church, a tenuous 'connection' was retained with the working class largely through a form of education by which religious doctrines were 'instilled into the minds of the young'. (12) Religiosity and allegiance to the Presbyterian Church ran much deeper than any figures suggested by church attendance.

Presbyterianism, of course, is both a central feature of the 'Scottish Myth' and not unexpectedly a vital vehicle for its dissemination. In terms of constitution and government the Scottish Presbyterians were ostensibly much more 'democratic' than the Episcopal and Roman Catholic Churches which certainly by the nineteenth century came nowhere near to challenging the Presbyterians' hegemony. With lay members controlling the kirk sessions, and giving powerful voice in the presbyteries, synods, and general assembly, the Church had all the trappings of an institution based on liberal-democratic principles. Indeed one facet of the Disruption which was given a great deal of prominence in the long debate leading up to the secession was the need to protect these democratic principles of popular representation. Ultimately control over all the Presbyterian Churches lay in the hands of the kirk sessions. However constitutionally democratic, evidence suggests that these bodies for a variety of reasons found themselves perpetuating the social composition of the session by co-opting or carefully 'managing' the election of new members. (13) In the cities and smaller towns this meant middle-class control over the sessions but clearly the situation differed in the rural and highland areas and here again lies a fruitful field of research. Certainly by the middle decades of the nineteenth century bourgeois values and attitudes permeated the three numerically important Presbyterian Churches — Established, Free, and United Presbyterian; interestingly enough perhaps to a greater extent in the latter two Churches, which also had the more 'democratic' constitutions. Indeed it should be recognised that the 'Scottish Myth', based as it was on an educational equality of opportunity — not a social equality, was very much a product of the bourgeois mind, perhaps refined from inherited eighteenth century assumptions concerning the natural equality of Man.

The first three chapters of this volume deal with this dominance of bourgeois values in nineteenth century Scottish society and how the dynamic social and economic changes which were taking place created ideological tensions and even contradictions within the middle class itself. Although each author differs widely in choice of topic and treatment, all are to some extent concerned with the analysis of developing class awareness and how this recognition of class identity influenced middle-class attitudes and actions. Enid Gauldie looks at these attitudes with regard to the provision of working-class housing in the nineteenth century; Allan MacLaren probes the relationship between bourgeois self-interest and philanthropy and some of the effects of Calvinist beliefs on this relationship; and Christopher Smout ventures bravely into an important and neglected area of the importance of class and cultural differences in determining sexual behaviour.

A vital element in Gauldie's chapter is the failure of the middle class to distinguish effectively between *needs* and *demand.* Because newly constructed houses might remain empty for some time, it was claimed that there was a lack of demand for better accommodation when in reality higher rents and unsuitable sites were the determining factors. Speculators were allowed to infill what little space remained in certain areas with jerry-built houses lacking sanitary facilities other than those already in existence. Thus urban Scotland's heritage of overcrowded substandard housing was created. Failure to control such developments partly resulted from laissez-faire ideas and also simply because there was a pressing need for accommodation. Interestingly enough, Scotland had administrative advantages over England in that the Dean of Guild had the power to control and regulate new buildings. However, these powers were never effectively utilised. There was also a gradual decline in concern for housing the new working class as employers increasingly found it unnecessary to build houses for their labour force in order to tempt them into employment and to exert an element of social control over their behaviour. As industry became increasingly centred on the towns, and the labour force lost its former rural characteristics, so the old paternal employer disappeared. In line with these social structural changes the middle class increasingly moved out into new residential areas, leaving the older areas to the working class, and thus intensified social and cultural differentiation. The increasing middle-class awareness of this cultural dichotomy led to concern over the vast slum areas which were regarded as seed-beds for crime and social discontent. The result was that the first great slum clearance efforts in Scotland were concerned with demolition, not construction, and were motivated by a desire for crime prevention rather than improving housing.

MacLaren (chapter 3) is concerned with similar sorts of motivation in his study of bourgeois ideology and philanthropy. Stressing the importance in Victorian society of the expectation of individuals being motivated by rational self-interest, he goes on to probe the contribution of self-interest in producing a dynamic philanthropy. In an effort to demonstrate the importance of this relationship MacLaren takes middle-class responses and reactions to cholera epidemics as his main theme. Although cholera made only four rather brief visitations to Britain in the nineteenth century, the virulence of its attacks, its dramatic nature, and the terror that it invoked, all led to a scale of administrative intervention far greater than for any other epidemic disease. Cholera not only seriously disrupted trade and commercial activity; unlike typhus it had no respect for class divisions and once established in an area it indiscriminately attacked rich and poor, respectable and disreputable, and mansion and slum dweller alike. Consequently cholera provoked yet again a debate on the origin and nature of disease and its mode of communication among its victims. The triumph of the miasmatic explanation over contagion is seen as an effective fusing of humanitarianism and a dynamic self-interest. Belief in contagion was backward and medieval, and led to the desertion of families and friends; it also resulted in severe restrictions on trade. Unlike England however, no effective public health movement emerged and MacLaren sees this as resulting from Calvinist elements incorporated into the bourgeois ideology. Scottish Presbyterians had a clearer conception of the origin and nature of epidemics, and the belief in divine origin and the 'unknowability' of God's intentions inhibited secular intervention, effectively preventing a coalescence of self-interest and philanthropy which was a necessary prerequisite of a successful and sustained public health movement. However, perhaps because of these same Calvinist elements, the Scottish middle-class had less difficulty in accepting the doctrine of predisposing causes (certain behaviour made one liable to contract the disease) because this idea was in line with popular equations of economic with spiritual destitution.

In a lengthy chapter on sexual behaviour in nineteenth century Scotland, Smout interestingly enough finds similar explanations of the origins of syphilis in that it was held to be God's judgment on fornicators and adulterers. However, the core of this chapter is concerned with cross-cultural comparisons of attitudes and behaviour as determined by differences in class, sex, religion, and regional area. The author utilises well-known although often largely neglected source material as well as new materials derived from the work of oral historians. The increasing class polarisation and associated residential segregation created problems for middle-class males customarily denied access to girls of their own class outside marriage. The consequence was that they turned to working-class girls as temporary partners, and the two occupations providing such contacts were those of domestic servant and prostitute. Partly as a result, domestic servants had a very high rate of illegitimate births, and prostitution flourished in the cities. Such practices were condemned by middle-class moralists and no doubt those who indulged in them did so secretively, often with considerable pangs of conscience, and with a real fear of what discovery and exposure would mean to their career. The landed class on the other hand, according to Smout, suffered far less from conscience and dual standards of behaviour. Within the working class there appeared a wide range of differing patterns of behaviour — 'it would be impossible to talk of one code of proletarian morality for the urban population as a whole' — but the most significant would appear to be that of the 'labour aristocracy'. Smout suggests that they were likely to have followed the middle class regarding sexual behaviour and this does have some bearing on a later chapter in this volume by Robert Q. Gray. It would seem reasonable to assume that the diversity of working-class morals was related to behavioural norms inherited from a rural past, and it is in his comparisons between various highland and lowland areas that Smout draws out an equally diverse variety of sexual behaviour and attitudes. The most notable of these differences would appear to be the generally high level of premarital pregnancies and illegitimacy in the south-west and the north-east compared to the rest of the country. Smout explains these differences in terms of the local economic situation, variations in the authority relationship between parents and children, and what he calls the 'privatised vision' of the Victorian middle class.

Chapters 5 and 6 of this volume are both concerned with the rural north-east, but the approach of the two authors — Malcolm Gray and Ian Carter respectively — is very different methodologically, and in terms of the type of source material utilised. In a sense Carter is relating the cultural consequences of the socio-economic structure as described by Gray. Although a great deal of further comparative work remains to be done, to some extent at least it would appear that both authors are implicitly arguing that Scottish society, as far as agricultural labourers in the north-east were concerned, was more 'open' and certainly less deferential than its English counterpart. Certainly Gray, and Carter, provide new interpretations of the role of the agricultural labourer, his career pattern and life style, within the north-east rural social structure.

Gray criticises the assumption that improvements in agriculture led to a division of rural society into two conflicting camps — capitalist farmers and landless labourers — and argues that such a view is over-simplified. He demonstrates that the needs of capitalist farming was that labour should be efficiently exploited, but as demands for farm labour varied seasonally, so it was necessary to utilise labour occasionally rather than continuously. In order to be able to draw upon a skilled labour force when circumstances demanded, it was found convenient to allow the development of crofts on marginal land, or to limit size, thus making the small-holder dependent on outside earnings for his family subsistence. Because of the continued availability of such smallholdings, a distinctive career pattern emerged whereby a labourer might begin his working life as a farm servant, and as he grew older and married he would move on to a croft and provide the local farmer with his own labour on a daily basis. His sons and daughters would eventually be recruited as farm servants and thus the cycle would be completed. Gray confirms this hypothesis by studying the relationship between age and occupation of farm servants, day labourers, and crofters in ten widely differing Aberdeenshire parishes. He maintains that the consequence of this was that there was no effective ideological polarisation of landed and landless. The possibility of a small landholding at some time in the future produced a cultural identification with the farmer rather than with one's fellow labourers.

This might be seen as Carter's starting point in his analysis of class and culture amongst north-eastern farm servants. His concern, however, is not in any way to challenge Gray's findings but to probe an aspect of the ideological consequences of the career pattern as described by Gray in order to challenge the position of Harold Newby and others who maintain that agricultural labourers are deferential traditionalists. (14) Utilising source material hitherto largely neglected by historians and sociologists, Carter reinterprets institutions such as the feeing market and rituals such as 'The Horseman's Word' and the 'clean toun', to detect levels and types of solidarity which have not been fully appreciated. Although unionism could make little headway (both Gray and Carter agree that farm servants had the outlook of smallholders rather than labourers), this did not prevent a group co-operation in actions such as the 'clean toun' — all servants leaving at feeing time — nor did it prevent a fair degree of independence and wages and conditions bargaining at the feeing markets when contracts were renewed. Interestingly enough, these markets were much condemned at the time by middle-class writers. Carter's conclusion is that north-eastern farm servants showed few signs of 'deferential traditionalism' because of the heavy constraints of what was fundamentally a peasant culture. It is to be hoped that his plea for further regional studies along these lines does not go unheeded.

Chapters 7 and 8 indirectly raise some of the issues connected with deferential attitudes and behaviour, but in an urban context. Robert Q. Gray analyses 'Thrift and working-class mobility in Victorian Edinburgh'; and James G. Kellas and Peter Fotheringham look at the political behaviour of the Scottish working class. However, as these chapters deal with rather different problems, they will be dealt with separately.

Robert Q. Gray provides new insights into that segment of the working class which has been described as the 'labour aristocracy', and this chapter should be seen within the perspective of other work which he has produced on this subject. (15) His concern is to probe the prevalence among working class people in Victorian Edinburgh of those modes of behaviour broadly described as responding to the norms of 'respectability and independence'. The problem is whether these labour aristocrats were, as Smout earlier describes them, simply 'aping their betters' or whether their behaviour was explicable only in relation to their own social experience in that by behaving in this manner they foresaw a long-term possibility of improvement in their socio-economic situation. R.Q.Gray, after examining levels of participation in various 'thrift' institutions such as Co-operatives, Friendly Societies, and the Savings Bank, goes on to look at ages of marriage of skilled and unskilled workers. The differences which emerge are explained within the terms of the superior economic situation of certain groups and their expectation of continued improvement. R.Q. Gray then takes up the question of whether the Victorian usage of terms such as 'self-improvement' or 'social elevation' implied *embourgeoisement* of this stratum of the working class. His conclusion is that generally speaking this was not the case. The labour aristocrat did not uncritically adopt such ideas from the middle class but saw them as meaningful only in terms of his own class situation and after they had been filtered through the lens of a growing perception of class identity.

The approach of James G. Kellas and Peter Fotheringham (chapter 8) differs from earlier chapters in that the authors tackle the problems of working-class political behaviour through to the General Election of October 1974. It is interesting, and praiseworthy, that they attempt to fuse the methodology of the historian and the political psephologist. Kellas deals with the historical aspects and Fotheringham the contemporary electoral behaviour. The authors set out to examine the electoral behaviour of the Scottish working class within the context of the three main themes in the literature of British electoral politics since the early 1960s. The first of these themes is the pre-eminence of social class among the other various sources of voting behaviour — approximately four-fifths of the British middle class vote for the Conservatives while two-thirds of the working class vote Labour. (16) The second theme — working-class conservatism — follows from the first in the tendency for about one-third of the working class in England and Scotland, but not in Wales, to provide the Conservative Party with about half its electoral support. The third theme is concerned with the issue of the development of British political homogeneity which is held to result from a convergence of socio-economic and cultural conditions leading to similar patterns of political behaviour. It follows that national differences in Britain have been politically less important than apparent socio-economic distinctions within and between regions. Fundamentally the questions which emerge are: How distinctive are Scottish patterns of class structure, socio-economic conditions and voting behaviour compared to other national and regional patterns in Great Britain? And secondly, do Scottish working-class voting patterns differ significantly from working-class behaviour in comparable social environments in England and Wales? Certainly distinctive differences between Scotland and England do exist in terms of nationalism, religion, and simple geographical separation. It is maintained that there is increasing class polarisation in Scotland but that this polarisation has been constrained by what Kellas and Fotheringham describe as 'static clientele politics'. It is argued that 'the only challenge to this polarisation and clientelism so far has come from the Scottish National Party, which draws on an amorphous social base'. However the observable differences do not clearly emerge from the detailed analysis of contemporary voting behaviour and this leads the authors to stress in the conclusion to their chapter the necessity of giving full consideration to both electoral and non-electoral evidence — perhaps particularly in view of the recent rise in support for the SNP and consequent changes in traditional party allegiances.

Indirectly the final chapter in the volume may have some bearing on the apparent gathering support for the 'separatist' policies of the SNP. In an exploratory study of the formal structure of power in Scotland, John Scott's and Michael Hughes's aim is to provide some knowledge of what is a totally neglected subject and at the same time provide a basis for future research on the subject. After a preliminary discussion of the nature and types of elite formations, the authors set out to investigate the question of the existence of a specifically Scottish ruling class, given that London is both political centre and economic metropolis whilst Scotland is a peripheral satellite. Their method is to gather and analyse what they describe as 'economic notables' (i.e. 'all those individuals who are directors of the top manufacturing and retailing firms, banks, insurance companies, and investment trust companies') in terms of the numbers of interlocking directorships. In an attempt to get round the problem of the unavailability of data on 'political notables', Scott and Hughes analyse membership, in terms of what they see as *representations*, of the Edinburgh and Glasgow Chambers of Commerce, and the Scottish Council (Development and Industry). The authors find that Edinburgh is 'the focal point of the Scottish financial system', is senior partner to Glasgow in terms of interlocking directorships and in the very much greater amount of funds under its control. Although careful to stress the tentative nature of their conclusions Scott and Hughes find that Scotland has a ruling class largely centred on these Edinburgh financial firms, and that this ruling class has a relative autonomy with regard to the British ruling class.

As one would expect from a stimulating and pioneer work of this sort, a whole range of new and absorbing questions arise from Scott and Hughes's findings. One (of which both authors are very much aware) is the central problem as far as the 'Scottish Myth' is concerned. To what extent, in terms of membership, is there an historical continuity in this ruling class? Following from this, one might ask who were the 'newcomers' and how were they recruited? The answers to these questions await a definitive study of nineteenth and twentieth century social structure, but they would shed a great deal of light on the problem of just how 'open' was the open society portrayed in the 'Scottish Myth'.

It is important to remember that the belief in a specific Scottish egalitarianism never implied that Scotland was in any sense a classless society. It held that the social gap between classes was never important and through societal encouragement and institutional means the 'lad o' pairts' with ability and resolution could easily effect a crossing. Certainly the contributions to this volume clarify the importance and often decisive nature of social class in determining a whole range of values, beliefs, actions, attitudes, and behavioural patterns. There is some evidence to suggest that the 'Scottish Myth' is a product of a former rural paternalism, rather than an urban industrialism in which class identity and economic individualism overruled a declining concern for communal and parochial obligations. It is difficult to see how the sort of egalitarianism which flourished in the North-East — in the form of a smallholder ideology and a lack of deference — could easily survive the rigours of the urban industrial environment. Yet the idea of the 'lad o' pairts' survives in popular ideology if not in social reality. An explanation of its survival will require the combined efforts and co-operation of both historians and social scientists. After all 'the past is intelligible to us only in the light of the present; and we can fully understand the present only in the light of the past'. (17)

REFERENCES

1. E.H. Carr, *What is History?* (Penguin Books, Harmondsworth, 1964), p.66.
2. Clearly it is not possible to provide a review of the many works on this topic since Carr's publication. The following are merely a selection: Asa Briggs, 'Sociology and History' in A.T. Welford *et al., Society: Problems and Methods of Study* (Routledge & Kegan Paul, London, 1962); W.J. Cahnman and A. Boskoff (eds), *Sociology and History: Theory and Research* (Free Press, New York, 1964); T.C. Cochran, *The Inner Revolution: Essays on the Social Sciences in History* (Harper & Row, New York, 1964); P. Laslett, 'History and the Social Sciences', *International Encyclopedia of the Social Sciences,* VI,

(Free Press, New York, 1968), pp. 434-40; G. Leff, *History and Social Theory* (Merlin Press, London, 1969); D.C. Pitt, *Using Historical Sources in Anthropology and Sociology* (Holt, Rinehart & Winston, New York, 1972); W. Todd, *History as Applied Science: A Philosophical Study* (Wayne State University Press, Detroit, 1972); H. Trevor Roper, 'The past and the present: history and sociology', *Past and Present,* no. 42 (1969); B.R. Wilson, 'Sociological methods in the study of history', *Transactions of the Royal Historical Society,* 5th ser., No. 21 (1971), pp.101-18.

3. For a stimulating appraisal of this aspect, see Gareth Stedman Jones, 'History: The Poverty of Empiricism', in R. Blackburn (ed.) *Ideology in Social Science* (Fontana/Collins, 1972), pp.96-115.
4. William Ferguson, *Scotland, 1689 to the Present* (Oliver & Boyd, Edinburgh, 1968). In his preface to the volume the author declares his intention not to resort to 'sweeping sociological generalisations' but to work 'in the older historical tradition, not out of conservatism but simply because I believe it to be the best way of studying the past'. (p.v).
5. For a clearly stated and extremely readable defence of this position see G.R. Elton, *The Practice of History* (Methuen, London, 1967), *passim.*
6. James G. Kellas, *Modern Scotland, The Nation since 1870* (Pall Mall Press, London, 1968), p.17.
7. For example see G.E. Davie, *The Democratic Intellect. Scotland and her Universities in the Nineteenth Century* (Edinburgh, 1961); and L.J. Saunders, *Scottish Democracy, 1815-1840* (Oliver & Boyd, Edinburgh, 1950).
8. A.M. Mackenzie, *Scotland in Modern Times, 1720-1939* (W. and R. Chambers Ltd., Edinburgh, 1941), p.187.
9. A.A. MacLaren, *Religion and Social Class: The Disruption Years in Aberdeen* (Routledge and Kegan Paul, London, 1974), pp.145-57.
10. I am indebted to D.J. Withrington, of the University of Aberdeen, who kindly showed me a draft outline of an article in preparation containing some of the points raised in this paragraph. Needless to say he is in no way responsible for my interpretation.
11. R. Rait and G.S. Pryde, *Scotland* (Ernest Benn Ltd., London, second ed., 1954), p.288.
12. MacLaren, op. cit. p.148. This point is also developed by the same author in 'Presbyterianism and the working class in a mid-nineteenth century city', *Scottish Historical Review,* vol. 46, 2, no. 142, October 1967.
13. MacLaren, op. cit. pp.121-6.
14. See H. Newby, 'Agricultural workers in the class structure', *Sociological Review,* 1972, 20, pp. 413-39; C. Bell and H. Newby, 'The sources of variation in agricultural workers' images of society', *Sociological Review,* 1973, 21, p.233.
15. For example see 'Styles of life, the "labour aristocracy" and class relations in later nineteenth century Edinburgh', *International Review of Social History,* vol. XVIII (1973), pp.428-52; and 'The labour aristocracy in the Victorian class structure', in Frank Parkin (ed.), *The Social Analysis of Class Structure* (Tavistock Publications Limited, London, 1974), pp.19-38.
16. For a fuller discussion of these aspects see D. Butler and D. Stokes, *Political*

Change in Britain (MacMillan, London, 1969), chap. 5.
17. Carr, op. cit. p.55.

2. The Middle Class and Working-class Housing in the Nineteenth Century

Enid Gauldie

In Scotland the 'ferm toun', the cluster of hand-weavers' cottages, or the mill hamlet were more common forms than the feudal village. 'The rich man in his castle, the poor man at his gate' was not a good description of the way most Scottish people were living at the beginning of the 19th century. Because of this Scottish society might seem to have been more egalitarian than England's, (1) the difference between the Scottish farm house and the cottar house, the mill house and the spinners' row, being nothing like so marked as the difference between castle and cot, squire's mansion and hind's hut in England. There was nevertheless a clear gap in housing standards between those with some power and the powerless and it was a difference which widened rapidly with the growth of population and the spread of industrialisation in the first quarter of the 19th century.

The most potent factor in creating that difference was the inability of the working class to exercise choice in the location of their homes. Working people must live near the source of their employment, however scarce or inadequate housing in that area may be. Those immigrants from the countryside who flooded into the towns during the 19th century might seem to have been exercising choice over their dwelling place, to be voting with their feet against agricultural living and working conditions. In fact the choice had been removed from them by agricultural improvements which cut the need for farm labour, and the very common destruction of cottages by landowners who did not want unemployed labour as a burden on their parishes. For many town immigrants the choice was between homelessness in the country and crowded conditions in the towns.

Natural increase of population, combined with heavy immigration, caused town populations to grow with such unprecedented rapidity that town administrative systems could not cope with the extra strain. Because the immigrants had no economic power to create a market demand for housing, houses were not built quickly enough in the quarters where they were most needed. The strain on existing housing meant that the living standards of the poor deteriorated steadily while the more prosperous, able to move away from crowded areas, lived in increasing comfort.

The 19th century saw increasing middle-class awareness of the need to improve the housing of the workers, but attempts at improvement were bedevilled by confusion about both means and ends. What might seem to be general middle-class agreement that the desired end was a docile population in clean comfortable houses became less unanimous as discussion progressed. There was much confusion about whether the docility or the comfort of the population should have the first priority. If safe, clean towns, free from crime, disease and riot, were what the middle class most desired, their course of action was easy and clear. Peaceful cities could be most easily achieved by wholesale slum clearance, abolishing the streets where crime and disease lingered, without troubling about where the dispossessed tenants went, so long as they disappeare

Middle-class fear of the working class as ridden with epidemic disease, criminal and potentially riotous, was a strong motive towards slum clearance.

It was less potent as a rebuilder. That section of the middle class which would have preferred more house-building to wholesale demolition, which nurtured a genuine wish to see working people comfortably housed, was weakened by a confusion about the best means to achieve its end. The bourgeois conception of working-class needs was founded on misunderstanding and coloured by the wish to impose middle-class standards of behaviour. When new homes for working people were built in answer to middle-class campaigning for housing reform, they were too often of the wrong kind and in the wrong place. Because they excluded tenants who did not fulfil the requirements of respectability, they left unhoused sections of the working class in greatest need. And, because middle-class housing reformers had little conception of what was within the bounds of possibility for people with low and irregular wages, too much reliance was placed on schemes needing self-help and initiative from the working class themselves. Middle-class anxiety about the kind of trouble which might be growing in the festering slums blinded them to the fact of working-class apathy and hopelessness.

In spite, then, of their declared wish to provide housing for the very poor, the middle class, charitable model dwellings associations and private landlords alike, refused to house the disreputable, the undesirable, those who seemed both unrespectable and undeserving. (2) In 1885 the Glasgow Landlords' Association wrote to Sir Charles Dilke, as chairman of the Royal Commission on Housing: 'The housing of the well-doing poor would be greatly facilitated by an amendment of the law so as to enable landlords to remove expeditiously and inexpensively tenants who can prove to be a moral and physical nuisance to the neighbourhood.' (3) This rejected section of the population could not simply disappear. It found its way necessarily into the most crowded and dilapidated property, owned by the most indifferent landlords. On this consistent refusal to admit the need of even the least respectable to house their families the whole housing problem is based.

Housing reformers of the 19th century split again into two camps over the question of whether disease or poverty was the chief reason for the evil conditions of the poor, and agreement was never reached over which should be treated first. The public health campaigners believed poverty to be a result of disease, which by interrupting wage earning and causing high mortality in heads of families gravely reduced the money coming into workers' households. Their faith was that, by creating conditions in which disease could not flourish, they would not only improve existing housing by making it cleaner, but also improve the workers' chances of earning the kind of regular wage which would bring better homes within their means.

Others saw poverty as the base root of the housing problem and believed that disease was the result, not the cause, of the poor diet, damp houses and insanitary surroundings which poverty made unavoidable. An argument between the two schools of thought was published in the 1842 *Reports on the 'Sanitary condition of the Labouring population of Scotland'*. Dr Neil Arnott supported the theory that fever was borne by an 'aerial poison' and that the first step towards improving the living conditions of the people was the cleaning of the surroundings in which the poison was nurtured. Dr. W.P. Alison declared that the public was being misled by the theory that 'by removing all causes of vitiation of the atmosphere contagious fever may be arrested at its source'. It was destitution which caused the troubles of the poor. Fever could not be caught through filthy homes, but 'starvation and filth make the poor easy prey'. (4)

It is not difficult now to see that both parties had an incomplete understanding of the problem. In present day Scotland it is obvious that neither the removal of epidemic disease, the provision of social security benefits during unemployment, nor even enormous state expenditure on housing has managed to banish the slums. Housing reformers, local authorities and the architectural profession have begun only recently to listen to a demand for participation, for consultation, for consideration of the wishes of those people who are to be rehoused. In short, middle-class people, given power by their position in society over the disposal of public money for housing, have had to admit that one of the reasons all previous reformers have failed was their misconception of the real needs of the working class. Their work has entailed the imposition of their own conception of what is a right and proper way to live upon those less powerful people who were to be displaced or, less often, rehoused. Class has always been a central issue in the history of housing. It has only recently been acknowledged to be so.

On February 4, 1840, a debate was called for in the House of Commons on 'the causes of discontent among great bodies of the working classes in populous districts'. It was suggested that the most important ground of complaint was 'the want of legi-'slative provision for the preservation of their health and the comfort of their houses'. (5) Very real fear was expressed that the squalor in which townspeople were living would breed 'the germ of sedition' and that unless some improvement in housing conditions was achieved the people would become so rebellious as to be a danger to the structure of society.

Seventy years later, the Report of the Royal Commission on Housing in Scotland contained the words, 'There are other and serious causes of industrial unrest...but, so far as housing is concerned, we cannot but record our satisfaction that, after generations of apathy, the workers all over Scotland give abundant evidence of discontent with conditions that no modern community should be expected to tolerate'. (6)

These two statements betray the vast change that had taken place in seventy years in middle-class attitudes towards working-class discontent. In the 1830s and 40s the middle class was affected by real fear that discontent would lead to a breakdown of law and order: 'A population so extensively demoralised can neither be happy in themselves nor safe to the community of which they form a part'. (7)

By 1918 it was possible for a report to Parliament openly to encourage working class protest against poor living conditions because protest had been channelled into acceptable means of expression and there was no real fear that it could get out of control. There was certainly some uneasiness about the mood of returning troops, some scare-mongering cries about revolution, but the middle class still felt secure enough to channel working-class protest in the cause of housing reform. This almost complacent middle-class tolerance, of course, was bred in the 'generations of apathy' which had followed the suppression of working-class radical energy after 1848.

Whatever else may be read into the two statements, however, they both make clear that social class was an important issue in the long campaign for improved urban housing and that, in the context of the history of housing, as elsewhere, 'class' means something more than economic position in society. When members of parliament in the 1840s feared the consequences of 'the want of attachment of the people to the institutions of the country' (8), they feared something not quite the same as trouble from the lower income groups. They were considering, and fearing, the opposition of a class of people cohering in common cause against middle-class institutions inimical to them. M.Ps, very much for the moment spokesmen for their own kind, were displaying their consciousness of themselves as a class with common interests and they were showing some apprehension that the less fortunate in society, those herded together in the slum areas of towns, might have a similar awareness of themselves as a class with potential power.

Certainly there was in the middle class a fairly early realisation of their necessary separation from the rest of society. (9) However, it is not the purpose of this chapter to describe the origins and realities of class distinction in Scotland. It is, for the moment, enough to consider the extent to which entrenched class attitudes helped to produce the kind of housing we have inherited from the 19th century.

The 'housing problem' has always been a creator of social differences. At every level of society people have supposed that 'a good address' implied some degree of superiority over citizens from less desirable neighbourhoods. For the respectable poor, to have one's own entrance was considered enviable. This was one of the reasons why cellar dwelling seemed more attractive to slum dwellers than to those reformers who condemned all below-ground living. The cellar was entered by a separate doorway, while those living in parts of the building upstairs had to share a common entrance. (10)

In various ways, then, living in one house could confer distinction from those living in another. In most cases the distinguishing feature was something which made possible a degree of privacy, of separation from neighbours. A separate door, a window looking on to open space, a tap of one's own, walls thick enough to deaden sound, a privy with a key, all conferred distinction dearly bought and only reluctantly relinquished. For the middle class, not to be over-looked was important. For the most comfortably placed, high walls and railings, ample garden ground, separated house-owners from the lower orders. (11) In Dundee, in 1878, there was considerable demand for ground to feu for private building on the east of Constitution Road, but it was considered necessary to build a very high wall between the new feus and Rosebank because the new property owners wished to see as little as possible of the poor spinners and weavers who lived in that manufacturing district. (12)

To the extent that both classes sought, when they had some choice, to live in houses which could confer some degree of status upon their inhabitants, the basic differences of class were masked. But the middle class had usually some choice, could even, on occasion, wall off the working class from its precincts, while the workers had seldom any real choice of district or type of house.

It could be claimed that class differences created the housing problem. It was, in the first place, because land-owners, speculators and employers found it possible to think of the people being crowded into fast-growing industrial cities as a separate class of individual, having different and less pressing human needs, that they were able to condone the deterioration of inner urban areas into slums. In the next phase, it was again because the middle classes saw slum dwellers as of another kind from themselves that plans for housing reform were made with the chief idea of reforming and changing the working class into an image more congenial to their 'superiors'. Housing evils were 'degrading the character of their humbler fellow subjects...and counteracting the moral and religious impressions they might receive from education'. (13) 'Let but the working classes...rise to the improved, and, we trust, improving habits of the middle classes'. (14) The *Dwelling Houses (Scotland) Act, 1855* was supported in Parliament because there was 'nothing more likely to raise the moral character of the people of Scotland'. (15) The reality of housing need was put second to the supposed need for moral reform.

Finally, when eventually government did take action to build the low cost housing desperately needed to replace the homes destroyed by slum clearance schemes, the separation of the classes was completed by the creation of huge areas of one-class housing built on the edges of towns and distinguished by kind and by distance from other urban dwellers. This in spite of the fact that there was at least some official recognition of the undesirability of this kind of segregation. (16)

In fact in Scottish society this kind of separation of the classes had not been usual. Better off members of society might live in bigger, warmer, brighter houses than their poorer neighbours, but they were still neighbours. (17) Economic differences necessarily distinguished one person from another because in a developing capitalist society money can buy house room as easily as any other commodity. But there was not in the emergent industrial towns of the late 18th and early 19th centuries much sign of the relentless separation of one class from another which was to be achieved in the more advanced industrialised society of the later 19th century.

For Scotland the textile trades had been of sufficient importance during the 18th century for their needs to have affected the shape of growing towns and the structure of her society. The mill village, placed necessarily on a water course to give power, formed the nucleus from which the industrial town was to grow. The mill was as much the focus and protector of a limited society as had been the manor for English feudal villages. Within parts of Glasgow, Dundee, Aberdeen, Edinburgh, Paisley and, of course, more obviously in smaller towns where growth has made fewer changes, the original mill villages are submerged.

Around the mill, houses to serve the needs of its employees naturally clustered, and among these houses there was a clear differentiation between the types of occupant. The owner capitalist, the manager, foremen-overseers, skilled workers, casual labourers, all had their place in the mill society, and their own kind of housing. Very often the fluctuating needs of the textile trade produced a demand for temporary seasonal workers. The separation of this type of casual worker from the permanently resident employees was emphasized by the housing of the casuals in 'bothies', large dormitory buildings for single workers, while the residents lived in tied cottages.

The essentially hierarchical structure of capitalist industry was, therefore, reflected in housing from the beginning, and, because these mill and factory settlements were the nuclei for town growth, the pattern of growth was set by them. In this set-up there was differentiation but not physical separation between the classes. The owner, or at least the manager, lived in a better house than his workers, but he lived among them, their neighbour.

'House for sale' advertisements in the first quarter of the 19th century show the effective neighbourhood-patterning this kind of society had created. Houses for 'genteel families' plus rooms for workers would be advertised and sold as one lot. (18) The genteel families would buy for themselves more room and a better outlook. They had not yet begun to object to having their employees as neighbours. The classes were not much separated either by district or by method of ownership. There was much rented property among the well-to-do, some self-owned property among the working people. All could live in the same street, even in the same block of buildings, their children inevitably playing together, shopping in the same shops, their water collected from the same wells, and their 'night-soil' removed by the same scavengers.

There was, in fact, no threat to the middle class in its proximity to the lower orders. Differentiation might be insisted upon, but separation was not necessary. The removal of middle-class homes to parts of the towns away from the homes of working people was made necessary by the terrifying spread of epidemic disease and the breakdown of town administration brought about by the rapid growth of urban populations. (19)

Services which had been designed to maintain a decent and orderly life in a slow-growing small town were strained to collapse. The habit of leaving piles of human faeces on street edges for periodic collection by scavengers who operated for their own profit or, for a small wage, to the profit of the Town Council, became a serious danger. Wells ran dry and water became impure. Unpaved streets which had satisfactorily carried the comings and goings of small populations now disintegrated into morasses of mud and filth. (20) Houses built for occupation by single families were subdivided and extended until hundreds of people were accommodated in buildings designed to hold a dozen. In Glasgow population density reached more than 1,000 persons per acre. (21) The large numbers of people gathered together in small town areas presented problems of servicing and policing quite beyond the administrative abilities of councils and corporations constituted to deal with mediaeval communities. Town Councils of the period which saw such rapid expansion had neither the experience, the ability nor the powers to deal with the new situation.

Town decay, over-crowding and filth were known throughout Great Britain, but the long-term scale of the disaster was greater in Scotland than in England. 'There is evidence,' wrote Chadwick in his Report of 1842, 'to prove that the mortality from fever is greater in Glasgow, Edinburgh and Dundee than in the most crowded towns in England.' (22) The Report of the Select Committee on the Health of Towns recorded that 'penury, dirt, misery, drunkenness and crime culminate in Glasgow to a pitch unparalleled in Great Britain.' (23)

It might have been expected that, where there arose an obvious need for new houses, speculative builders would quickly respond by providing sufficient homes for the growing numbers of town dwellers. But while there was indeed a mushroom growth of house-building in many towns, it did not begin to fill the new need for houses. Those most in need were not those able to create a demand for houses. They needed homes, as the overcrowding of existing houses showed, but they did not have the steady incomes which could have brought about a market demand for houses. Thus in most towns, speculative building of houses satisfied the demand, which because of the poverty of those in most need was low, but it did not attempt to fill the need. The confusion between need and demand has delayed the solution of the housing problem from the beginning. Those in need created no demand. Builders could claim that there was no demand for new houses because newly built houses sometimes stood empty for long periods. They stood empty, however, not because there was no need for them but because the rents asked were too high or the houses built in inconvenient areas. (24)

Proof that the need for more low-cost housing was not being filled lies plain in the census figures showing numbers of persons per inhabited house. (25) This is not to discount the evidence of building activity during the period of rapid growth. There is every indication that very large numbers of houses were being run up, for the most part by small-time builders or small groups of building tradesmen. (26) Figures for numbers of houses built do not appear in the Census until after 1851. Inhabited house duty was imposed on houses over £20 annual value in 1851 but complete records for houses exempt from duty, those which now most concern us, do not begin until 1875. (27) Records of houses for whose building statutory approval was sought are available for Dundee from 1867 and for Glasgow from 1862. (28) But contemporary comment plus the visual evidence remaining in town centres makes plain that a considerable amount of building took place during the first half of the 19th century in the large centres of population. Glasgow's rental showed a thirty-fold increase between 1712 and 1815, a seven-fold increase between 1773 and 1815. (29) Dundee's evidence to the Select Committee on Building Regulations in 1842 remarks on a boom in speculative house building. (30) But the new immigrants to the towns and the poorer of the native inhabitants had only a poor chance of living in the new houses.

In the first place, landowners considering the feuing of their lands for building speculation were concerned to achieve and maintain a superior character for their new estates. C.W. Chalklin, discussing the planning of 18th century housing estates, found that 'Working class housing was not considered as desirable in itself while high quality dwellings redounded to the credit of the landowner.' (31) Especially where land was apportioned in smallish feus over a fairly long period of time it was felt necessary for landowners to impose safeguards to maintain the class of housing on the early estates so that those pieces of land feued last should still prove attractive to speculators. Landowners and the larger speculative builders, who maintained friendly contacts with each other and with the elected officials of the towns, found it fairly simple to maintain the value of their lands by excluding working-class housing. (32) Builders who had no connections with the landed families, the business circles or the Town Council sometimes found their housing estates threatened by the building on adjacent feus of an undesirable class of property. (33) For the most part, however, proprietors feuing land were successful in imposing minimum values on new house building which must necessarily exclude from the new estates all members of the working class.

Prices, then, were kept high so as deliberately to exclude the poor. But this was not only because the poor were unable to pay the necessary rental but also because they were considered socially undesirable: 'The poor are not always a *desirable* class of tenants; for they are troublesome, uncertain and changeable.' (34) It was pleasanter for the inhabitants of the new houses not to have working-class people as neighbours.

The new houses being built, then, were not available to the working class. That was one reason why it was necessary for poorer families to crowd into old subdivided properties, or shoddy buildings run up as lean-to additions to older houses, or as infilling to tenement courts and alleys. The warrens of slum housing were created, in the period before the enforcement of building regulations, by the closing off of already narrow streets with extra blocks of houses, which left the original blocks accessible only by narrow arches set in the new tenements; by the building over of back courts so that tenement squares once spaced by open greens now looked over a Chinese puzzle of blocks within blocks. This kind of building was highly profitable because it seldom involved any outlay on land, the sites used being already in the hands of the speculating landlord. It need not involve the introduction of services of any kind, the older occupants being forced to share privies and water supply with the new tenants. It resulted in the rapid deterioration of mixed-class urban areas into slum ghettoes from which anyone with income or enterprise enough removed himself as rapidly as possible.

So that, at one end of the scale, new building excluded the working class, at the other end new building, by its shoddiness or by its miserly use of land, excluded the middle class. The partition of towns into exclusively one-class areas was begun then chiefly because of the pressure of rapid population growth upon land resources. Land became so expensive that in some areas it attracted superior estate lay-out, while in others high cost encouraged infilling of marginal land to the detriment of the existing neighbourhood.

This effect of land shortage, however, had to be accompanied by lack of concern by one class for the conditions in which the other class lived. It could not otherwise have been so effective in achieving the almost complete segregation of classes in towns. In spite of considerable anxious talk, the middle class as a whole bore with some complacency the deterioration of working-class living standards.

For instance, overcrowding of existing houses came to be accepted as a natural consequence of variations in employment. It was an accepted matter of course that crowded living conditions would be the lot of workers in a fluctuating trade. (35) Because it seemed inevitable, there was little thought about how the overcrowding could be avoided.

This complacency has often been excused by the powerlessness of town officials to alter the situation. Scottish towns, however, were less badly served by the legal arrangements of their predecessors than most English towns. In the office of Dean of Guild, for instance, there were already vested powers to control and regulate new building, to demolish insanitary and dangerous existing buildings, and to prevent nuisance. (36) If he did not use these powers properly so as to maintain his town in the kind of decent order envisaged by the medieval drafters of the rules it was because he did not choose to or because he interpreted the needs of those whom he represented differently. He used his powers, in fact, in the short-term needs of the middle class instead of in the long-term interest of the community.

Scotland was ahead of England in achieving some measure of reform of local government, in her Burgh Police and Improvement Acts (37) which consolidated existing powers and gave new powers for the prevention of nuisance and the improvement of urban areas. In Dundee at least the Police Commissioners were chosen by an electorate paying rates of only £2 and over, a figure low enough to include many working men. Meetings affecting the duties of the Police Commission were enthusiastically attended by a section of the community called variously 'rabble and blackguards' or 'substantial looking citizens', depending on the viewpoint of the speaker but certainly including large numbers of working-class people. (38) In spite of these powers and an unusual degree of democracy, vested interests were too strong to prevent the decay of Scottish urban areas into disease-ridden slums.

The apparent complacency of the middle class in the face of high mortality rates, overcrowded crumbling tenements and the breakdown of sanitary arrangements was, in fact, a mask for very real uneasiness. The process of segregation begun by rising land costs was completed by fear. The middle class feared that disease, spreading from the slums, would eventually decimate their numbers as it was patently decimating the poor. They feared, too, that the desperation of the working class might lead them into protesting riots against those who were spared their miseries. There were prayers 'that the working class may not be tempted in blind despair to destroy that fabric of modern civilisation which they have helped to rear without as yet sharing its blessing'. (39) Those who could afford to do so began to move away from the overcrowded inner areas to higher, drier ground on the outskirts of cities. They left behind dirt, noise, germs, and a class of people they preferred to forget.

This separation of the classes in towns, a separation amounting to abandonment, was reflected in a relinquishing by very many employers of their paternal role as providers of housing for their employees. (40) Earlier employers had been forced to attract workers into mills and factories by the provision of houses. Particularly in those industries where the need for abundant water forced them to remain outside the main conurbations, it was necessary for employers to build houses if they wished to attract a permanent labour force. But the builders of company towns set out to do something more than provide houses for their employees. In their constantly expressed concern for the moral welfare of the inhabitants they implied their own ability to teach a better way of living. There can be no clearer way of demonstrating the separation of one class from another than this claim to show others how to live. There is more here than the suggestion that people who have lost the habit of cleanliness will have to relearn it when the means of cleanliness is given them. There is a definite hope in the employers' claims for the benefits of their new towns that a new set of behavioural patterns will percolate through to the inhabitants.

Employers may very well have been right to suppose that the more spacious layout of streets, the less crowded rooms, windows admitting light and air, would by themselves encourage a new kind of behaviour that would be different from the code prevailing in the slums. The habit of possessing worldly goods gives practice in their possession and grace in their use. Conversely those unaccustomed to owning things, even space, cannot know how to benefit from them, must be taught how to care for them: 'the natural relation between rich and poor is simply one of dependence'. (41) This kind of thinking was the fore-runner of the 'coals in the bath' myth. But whether the assumption that the middle class has something to teach the working class has justification or not, the fact that it was so widely and firmly held does underline the central importance of class to the history of housing.

This benevolent attitude of employers towards company towns should not be allowed to mask an equally paternal but perhaps less benevolent intention, to separate loyal employees from other less docile sections of the working class. The earlier settlements, like David Dale's, had gone through troublesome periods, but the isolation from the rest of their class of a community dependent upon their employer not only for their livelihood but for their homes ensured that trouble could not last. *The Old Statistical Account* reported the presence in New Lanark of 'individuals who, either from ignorance or from violence and temper, will not listen to the cool voice of reason, who chime in with the ravings of the "Friends of the People" as they call themselves'. (42) But by the time of the *New Statistical Account* the mill town was peopled by an industrious and respectful work force, 'compared with other establishments of the kind remarkably decent in behaviour'. (43)

As the industrial villages became absorbed within the creeping towns, other homes became available to the workers in them and other influences could be felt among them. Only in those industries which, sometimes because of a continuing dependence upon water-power, remained outside the large conurbations, was the employer able to maintain the separation of his employees from the main body of the working class.

By the middle of the 19th century most industrial employers in Scotland had ceased to provide homes for their workers. In 1868 Baxter Brothers of Dundee were finding 'the double relationship of master and landlord at times awkward' and declared, 'it is against our principle as employers to build houses'. (44) This is not to say that employers disposed in a wholesale way of house property they already owned. (45) Nor is it to claim that no employer in Scotland built cottage rows for his workers after 1850. It does seem, however, that house building for workers became less common and it is certain that there was no repetition on the scale of New Lanark. The reasons are not at all difficult to find. In the first place the need to attract labour had gone. People had accepted mill and factory routine and could be induced to enter the gates by their need for wages, without the added inducement of housing. The increased cost of building caused by rising prices of labour and materials and by restrictive building regulations acted as a disincentive to employers to build. There was also a conscious wish by the employers not to be more closely associated than was absolutely necessary with their employees, and above all not to feel any longer responsible for their workers.

This general abandonment by the middle class meant two things. The labouring classes were physically left to themselves in exclusively working-class areas. 'One of the great evils of St. Davids parish, in common with other manufacturing districts, is a want of a mixture of the different ranks of society ... Those who once lived in the neighbourhood of their workmen have removed with their families to more healthful and agreeable residences ... You will see in what a helpless state the social system is left ... bereft of that resident upper class ... I state the fact of that total disruption between rich and poor which characterises our town population and which is pregnant with so many evils for all classes.' (46)

In middle class areas small nuisances, which if neglected could accumulate to cause the deterioration of a neighbourhood, things like unemptied closets and ash-pits, blocked drains, broken pavements, were quickly reported and put right. The law of nuisance required the reporting of nuisance to the authorities by those persons affected by the nuisance. (47) In the slum areas those persons affected by the nuisance were too often in arrears with their rent and for that reason, as well as the diffidence of uneducated people dealing with officials, unwilling to report the neglect of their districts.

Secondly, as well as the physical separation and its effects, the tenants of decayed town housing were psychologically left alone. There were whole areas inhabited by people with no steady employment, or employed sporadically in industries of so large a scale that there was no contact at all between workers and managers. In these areas lived people who, for the most part, did not go to church, or, if they did, did not feel accepted by the church community, children who did not go to school (48), whole communities of people out of touch with the influence of bourgeois respectability. A.A. MacLaren found 'failure to communicate — both at the physical level of social contact, and at a more psychological one in attitude of mind' a 'dominant feature' of the relationship between middle and working class in Aberdeen. (49) There is no evidence to suggest that the same situation did not prevail in other large Scottish towns.

James Hole, the nineteenth century writer on workers' housing, wrote of 'the isolation of class from class and the antagonism of employer and employed which has unhappily become a feature of late years. The evil and suffering that a man sees affect him more powerfully than those which reach him at second hand'. (50)

The abandonment of one class by another was encouraged by the attitude of the church leaders. Chalmers' speeches 'On the Christian and economic polity ... of large towns, on the moral state and prospects of society, on the right management of the poor' served to increase social distances. His intention was to encourage a charitable frame of mind in the middle class and a healthy independence in the poor. But his way of using words dramatised the fear of the wretched which already characterised the thought of his listeners: the offering of financial help to the poor was to be blamed for 'luring more into existence than it can meet with the right and requisite supplies, and, after having conducted them towards manhood, leaving them in an unsated appetency and withal in leisure for the exercise of their ingenuities ... the higher feats of villainy, the midnight enterprise, the rapine sealed, if necessary, with blood, the house assault, highway depredation'. (51)

There were, fortunately, other forces at work, countering imaginative harangues with collections of facts. The dissemination of the work of the new statistical societies, of the parliamentary committees on health and housing, of the public health reformers Edwin Chadwick and John Simon, eventually had some effect. By abandoning the closely built streets the middle class was allowing a forcing house for the development of working-class ideology. Realisation of the possible consequences helped to induce an interest in *moral and sanitary reform.* Not only the streets but the minds must be cleaned. The houses must be aired and alien ideas shaken out of the window. All the images of cleansing, fumigating, disinfecting, were aimed at dispelling the threatening clouds of disaffection, the 'physical as well as moral miasma, at once pestilential and fatal' (52), at abolishing the germ of sedition along with the germ of disease. This is why the emphasis was on moral as well as sanitary reform. It was necessary, although Chartism seemed to have been soundly squashed and radicalism effectively suppressed, to ensure that middle-class ideas were more thoroughly impressed on the minds of those great masses of the people who had been allowed for a period to escape their influence. 'The wealthy and educated gradually withdraw themselves from these closed and crowded communities which thus stand more and more in need of some superintending paternal care.' (53) It had been recommended to 'the operative population' during the cholera epidemic of 1831-2 that 'an inflexible adherence to the canons of morality' (54) would defy even cholera. The campaign to improve the housing of the working class was steadily dogged by the confusion in the public mind about whether the improvement was desirable for reasons of health and justice or chiefly as a means of improving the moral condition of the working class. For instance, in spite of the public health reformers' pressure for the sanitary inspection of houses, Parliament would not, in 1857, pass a Bill allowing entry into private houses by sanitary inspectors. (55) The need for improved public health was not pressing enough to be allowed to interfere with the Englishman's private property. But a clause in the Dwelling Houses (Scotland) Act, 1855, which provided for the compulsory purchase of houses 'which have become a receptacle or place of harbourage for persons of dissolute and vicious character' (56) was passed without protest. Law and order came before public health.

The surface calm and shuttered respectability of mid-19th century Britain was maintained by police whose first task was to keep the distance between the middle class and the potentially criminal class. Professor Best makes the suggestion that the first improvement schemes were deliberately driven through not the most insanitary but the most unruly neighbourhoods, the first motive being not the improvement of housing but the dispersal and suppression of petty crime. (57) London found that neighbourhoods once 'frequented by such a desperate and verminous class of inmates that police seldom dare to visit' became, after a little judicious demolition, 'peaceful and orderly, sweet and clean'. (58) The first large and comprehensive clearance scheme in Britain was driven in Glasgow through 'a moral sewer of a most loathsome description, crowded with population, showing by its physique the extent to which the human form divine could be degraded by drunkenness and every attendant form of vice and profligacy'. (59)

The Burgh Police and Improvement Act, 1851 was an attempt to create a general town improvement act for Scotland in place of a diversity of local acts. It answered pressure for more effective machinery to suppress 'nuisance', speed slum clearance and improve urban districts. But it contained among its sanitary provisions an extension of the powers of the police and it restored whipping as a punishment for civil disorder. In spite of a great deal of talk about the need to improve working-class housing, the only action taken during the 19th century in Scotland was the destruction of houses and the opening up of streets. (60)

An important impetus towards housing reform was middle-class fear of social unrest among the working class from whom they now felt separated by more than income. It was the debate raised in the House of Commons by Richard Slaney on what was felt to be the alarming discontent of the working people which caused Parliament to appoint the Select Committee on the Health of Towns in 1840. That report was the first to reveal the appalling conditions in which the working class of Britain was living. From its shocking revelations arose the evangelical reaction in favour of 'moral and sanitary reform'.

There was a great deal of confusion about the best means of producing the much wanted improvement in the ways of the working class. Some reformers believed that the homes of the people must be improved and poverty relieved before moral improvement could be expected. Others felt that independence and self-help, encouraged by precept and example, were the only road to the elevation of the working class. (61) All the schemes proposed for the improvement of housing conditions relied heavily upon the exertions of working class people themselves. A large proportion of middle-class energy was expended on the encouragement of working-class self-help.

The patronage of model lodging houses and the buying of shares in building societies were perhaps the most useful expressions of this kind of goodwill. The model dwellings associations so active in London did extend their activities to Scotland but on a scale too small to affect the problem of homelessness and bad living conditions. Model Lodgings, excessively paternal in their care of their inhabitants and dealing almost exclusively with single men and women, could not help the working class family. (62) And Scots workers, in spite of meetings and pamphlets aimed at them by their employers, were not quickly enticed into becoming building society members. (63) The Royal Commission on Friendly and Benefit Societies found that there were very few building societies in Scotland. When Samuel Smiles preached the virtues of building societies to the National Association for Social Science in 1864 he expressed very clearly the reasons why the middle class wanted working men to join building societies: 'The accumulation of property has the effect which it always has upon thrifty men — it makes them steady, sober and diligent. It weans them from revolutionary notions and makes them conservative.' (65)

Dundee's experience was not untypical of the way in which middle-class interests combined to encourage working men towards better homes. In 1864 the 'Dundee Working Men's Houses Association Ltd.' was formed, its purpose 'the providing of dwelling houses within the town of Dundee suited for the occupation of the working classes'. 1,043 shares of £1 each were subscribed for by 113 shareholders, 53 of these were reported to be working men who between them took 113 shares. The other 930 shares were taken by 'merchants and others'. Lord Kinnaird, along with some important manufacturers in Dundee, gave donations amounting to £130.18s. The scheme was not a success, some of the houses remaining unoccupied for years despite an acute housing shortage. To dispose of the houses it was necessary to lower prices until the association was running at a loss. (66) The purchase of a share in a building society required many weeks' saving for workers in a town where wages were low and alternative employment rare. The finding of a regular weekly or monthly payment was perhaps even harder. (67) But it was not only the finding of the money which militated against working-class participation in such schemes. Building societies were middle-class institutions run by middle-class administrators. Working-class distrust of such people must have been confirmed by the experiences of one Dundee artisan who achieved ownership of a house through the Association only to find he had no right of access to his house, his way being blocked by the activities of a speculative builder. (68) Three other building societies founded in the seventies were equally unsuccessful. (69)

The much greater financial success of similar schemes in Edinburgh was, of course, partly explained by the different industrial pattern of the two towns. Certainly there would appear to be a background of success for such ventures, perhaps because they were worker-organised. (70) The Edinburgh Working Men's Building Association and the Edinburgh Co-operative Building Company Ltd. seem to have been commercially viable and to some extent successful in housing working people. However, the fact that the Co-operative was formed by operative masons during the lock-out of 1861 as a means of support for working people in their struggle against their employers suggests that its first aim was the increase of workers' savings by investment rather than the housing of members. (71) By 1894 it had 'assumed the character of an ordinary trading concern and lost the higher aspirations of its youth'. (72)

Another, more conventional Edinburgh Building Society, the Property Investment Association, found that those few workers who used its resources usually sold their property on completion of payments and bought inferior houses to live in themselves. They were using the building society as a means of saving, not as a step towards better housing. (73)

In some smaller towns there were instances of co-operative societies which, if they did not act as building societies, played a role in aiding their members towards better housing. In Forfar, for instance, members of the Equitable Co-operative Society prospered so well that they could count on their dividends to pay their rents. At least 1500 families were said to 'sit rent-free' in Forfar in 1872. Entry money for this society was one shilling and the subscription 3d. (74)

It was, however, in those industrial quarters most in need of help that least could be done. Building societies rely upon regular employment for steady payment. In Glasgow and Dundee there was little enough certainty of regular employment. Even when the weekly wage rose high enough to allow the putting aside of a small sum towards house owning, savings were liable to be eaten into in times when the wage earner was laid off. Dr. Begg, the chief proponent of freehold land societies as the best means of improving the condition of the working class, saw little chance of the Scottish working man reaching a vote by this means 'except by a huge struggle'. (75)

If, then, the means conventionally recommended by the middle class, thrift, saving, hard work and patience, produced for only a small minority of working people the homes they needed, what other means were open to them, what other means did they take? However bad conditions in large towns became, they seem never to have been the direct cause of riot or political disturbance. Parliament found, in 1840, that 'The growth of a disposition to turbulence by no means kept pace with the growth of population'. (76) Professional people, used to visiting among the most oppressed part of the slum population, found little evidence of open discontent and reported widespread apathy. (77) But if there is little evidence of town disturbance directly attributable to discontent with living conditions, there were plenty of indications of unorganised protest, spontaneous outbursts of anger which made parts of the large towns unsafe to enter, ungovernable and unvisited by any officials. (78) 'You can tell when you open the door what sort of people live in the house — you can tell they are not a safe sort of people.' (79)

The lack of organised protest specifically directed against living conditions was due largely to the long-term nature of the housing problem. During famine a 'meal mob' could be roused to attacks on farmers and shop-keepers, could be fed and appeased by stolen bread and grain, and could be quickly dispersed. Quick, sudden action of this kind could give the mob food, but not housing, for housing is a matter of long-term planning. A latent respect for property, even in those most lacking in it, and a fear of the consequences prevented the open seizure of houses, although squatting without payment of rents in property condemned as insanitary was common enough practice. (80)

During the first half of the century, however, if there was little open working-class protest against bad housing there was not complete acquiescence either. The Health of Towns Association, striving during the 1840s to enlist working-class support for town improvement, found that there was 'not everywhere docile acceptance of middle-class tutorship'. (81)

Edwin Chadwick declared himself anxious that working people should be encouraged to press for housing reform on their own behalf and he had helped to organise the collection of petitions in factories. But Chadwick wanted protest organised on middle-class, orderly lines, not rabble-rousing. He was not happy to hear from Glasgow that 'some noisy, brawling turbulent Chartists had got mixed up with the agitation' and 'their way of doing business had disgusted the more discreet'. (82) There was to be no middle-class support for street protest which could get out of hand. Similarly, Parliament might emphasize the 'common interest' (83) of the working people in securing better living conditions, but had no wish to see that common interest directed into worker-organised protest.

After 1848 not only the middle class but many of the workers' own leaders advocated concentration of their resources on orderly pressure for a wider suffrage and better conditions of employment. The ready if quiescent support accorded them seemed to prove 'that sanitary reform could not easily become a political catch phrase even among enlightened working men whom it was designed to benefit most'. (84)

If noisy political protest became unlikely in the second half of the century the economic position of a large proportion of workers made industrial action in the cause of housing even more unlikely. By the 1860s landlords and employers could count on the knowledge that 'neither obscenest lodging nor foulest drinking water will be appreciable inducements towards a strike'. (85)

This was, in fact, the first of the 'generations of apathy' (86) deplored by the Royal Commission in 1918, an apathy induced by shortage of employment, food, education, housing. Just as the number of unemployed waiting to step into any job made protest against working conditions difficult, so the number waiting for a house made protests to landlords about conditions in available houses quite impossible. House factors were in such a strong position, because of their ability to let empty houses in the needy areas over and over again, that no pressure could be put on them to execute repairs or carry out improvements. (87) When Parliament eventually forced local authorities to insist upon the improvement of their insanitary areas, factors raised rents to cover the cost of improvements, increasing for most working people the difficulty of finding the housing they could afford. (88)

The peak of house-building activity was reached in 1876. (89) From then on a steady decline in the rate of house-building, especially of low-cost houses, accompanied by campaigns of slum clearance in most towns, increased overcrowding (90) and weakened the chance of any organised protest against housing conditions. In 1884 *The Builder* carried the report that 'the poor cannot afford to pay more than a rental of from 1s to 2s per week for their dwellings of whatever size and construction and wheresoever situate' and 'no practical plan has yet been devised by which dwellings can be built... which can let at these low rentals and prove remunerative to builders'. (91)

In other words, the poor were in no position to argue. The proved existence of many empty houses in some cities made then no real difference to the position of those in need of cheap houses near their work. Empty houses were either too dear or in the wrong part of the city. (92) The so called transport revolution did not make the marked difference to the working people of Scotland, where even the biggest towns were still relatively small, that it is reported to have made in English cities. (93) Trams and cheap trains helped the lower middle class to reach small terraced houses in outlying districts. They were of little use to the labouring class who had to live within reach of the 'bummer' or the 'knocker-up'.

Pressure for better housing, therefore, had to come from the middle class. It came with increased force, if without much clearer direction, as successive reports to Parliament made the steady deterioration of urban areas harder to ignore. (94) Scotland was well represented by her M.Ps in this instance and on at least one occasion a Scottish housing Act preceded the English version and set the tone for it. (95) Acts purporting to bring about change for the better in housing went regularly through Parliament in the second half of the century. (96) But for two reasons none of them did anything at all to make better houses available to the working class.

First, all the housing Acts of the nineteenth century up to 1890 were demolition-oriented. Their intention and their result was the destruction of insanitary areas, and this they achieved at the cost of increased overcrowding. Secondly, while some of the Acts (97) contained clauses allowing the actual building of houses, they were adoptive, not mandatory, and as such easily ignored. No houses were built with public money for the working class in Scotland during the 19th century. (98)

The Royal Commission on the Housing of the Working Classes in 1885 made an inquiry into rural and urban housing conditions which, although it was very far from exhaustive in its Scottish report, (99) had the effect of shocking Parliament into a new series of Acts. Local authorities were given new powers not only to demolish insanitary houses, which many of them did with new enthusiasm, but also to rebuild from public funds, which few of them chose to do. (99)

They were partly able to justify their inactivity by pointing to the increase in speculative building of low-cost houses. The 1890s saw in most towns a distinct upturn in private house-building. Because land costs were cheaper away from the chief centres of employment, most of these cheap new houses were in areas not suitable for working-class tenants who needed to be near their work. (100) Town Councils could point to empty, unlet houses as an excuse for not using their powers to levy rates for house building. They could and did ignore the fact that overcrowding actually increased instead of decreasing in the period 1890 to 1911.

Nevertheless, the classic theory that some easing of the worst miseries of the oppressed must precede the open expression of discontent seems to hold good for housing. The upturn in house-building activity towards the end of the century accompanied an improvement in the economic position of the working man, and the organisation of labour had become effective in many trades. National Housing Conferences in 1901, 1902, 1905 and 1907 sought to enlist the energies of the Trade Unions in the cause of housing reform. Through these housing conferences, through their trade unions, and through the now cheaper daily papers, working people could become informed about the new powers held by local authorities for re-housing. In Dundee a new Town Council was elected on the housing issue after a well attended 'citizens' meeting 'had heard the Social Union's report on housing conditions'. (101)

The most effective action by working people for better housing was taken by the Scottish miners. Conditions in mining towns were exceptionally bad. In some miners' rows there was no sanitation at all and no paving, and the primitive construction of the oldest houses and the general lack of amenity in the colliery villages compared unfavourably even with the worst urban areas. Because one-roomed houses were common and houses of more than two rooms had only rarely been built in mining areas, over-crowding was persistent and increasing. (102)

The Scottish Miners' Federation organised protest in the form of a deputation to the Secretary of State for Scotland in 1909. As a result the Local Government Board for Scotland called for reports from medical officers in the mining counties on housing conditions in their districts. The matter was left in the hands of the local authorities without noticeable result. Miners continued to press for a proper inquiry and, although they did not achieve any quick improvement in their own housing conditions, their protests led directly to the appointment of the Royal Commission on the Housing of the Industrial Population of Scotland in 1912. The report of the Commissioners was delayed by the First World War and did not appear until 1918, by which time the whole climate of opinion about subsidised housing had changed.

Meanwhile other workers in Scotland had begun to make more troublesome protests. The direction of skilled workers in armaments to new districts had faced some families with living conditions worse than they had been accustomed to. Torpedo workmen sent from Woolwich to work on the Clyde in 1914 refused to live in the tenements available to them in Glasgow and came out on strike against the conditions in which they were expected to settle. (103) War workers, because they were temporarily of national importance, were in a strong position to protest, and the torpedo workmen succeeded in improving their conditions and eventually in achieving the planning of a new garden village for workers. (104)

The riots and protests in Glasgow against rising rents and housing shortage, which led to the passing of the Increase of Rent and Mortgage Interest (War Restrictions) Act, 1915, were more widely effective and had more lasting results. (105) But if indeed they do prove an increased awareness of power to act together to achieve better housing, it was a short-lived power, dissipated entirely by the economic depression which was to follow the War.

In the circumstances of the 19th century, improvement in working-class housing had to be inspired and worked for by the middle class. But the sincere Christian anxiety of the 19th century middle class about the need for better housing was nullified by confusion about the best means of achieving it. Condemnation of unscrupulous landlords was always accompanied, and weakened, by reluctance to interfere in the private contract between owner and tenant. But 19th century thought generally abhorred such interference with the liberty of the individual. Steeply rising land values caused commercial building in central areas cleared of slum housing and left the previous inhabitants homeless. It was not profitable to build low-cost housing where high rents could be raised for commercial development. Consternation about homelessness was weakened by strong belief in the inalienable right of businessmen to profit by their business activities. The obvious difficulty experienced by the working class in paying regular rents for good housing led to the discussion of Government aid towards workers' housing. But the idea of subsidy was rejected because of the firmly held belief that to grant direct aid was to discourage self-help, to abet shiftlessness and to interfere with the working man's independence and self-reliance.

The undoubted humanitarian concern of much of the Victorian middle class left them nevertheless horrified at any tendency to regard housing as 'a legitimate channel for that eleemosynary aid which the most advanced socialist would still hesitate to offer in the more direct, though only equally objectionable form of food and clothing'. They could not, in the light of their own education, help but deplore 'interference in social affairs incompatible with the accepted theory of personal freedom'. (106)

So every move towards greater understanding of working-class needs and towards more help for the overcrowded and homeless was counteracted by the weight attached to dearly held middle-class beliefs. Every clause in the housing bills of the 19th century which could have brought about change for the better was balanced by a limiting clause or else lost in the passage of the bill through Parliament. (107)

The weakness and confusion of middle-class ideas left the way open to those with clear direction, no confusion about their motives, no doubts about the right way to behave. Those who speculated in land, those who drew rents from overcrowded insanitary property, those who put up jerry-built workers' rows, could benefit from the reformers' confusion.

REFERENCES

1. Cf. Donald MacRae, *Ideology and Society, papers in sociology and politics,* 1961 p.69.
2. *Royal Commission on Housing,* 1885 Parliamentary Papers, vol.xxx, Minutes of Evidence, 4740, 4835-8, 11,540-11 et seq.
3. *Royal Commission on Housing,* 1885, Appendix C, p.135.
4. W.P. Alison, M.D., 'Observations on the generation of fever' in *Reports on the Sanitary Condition of the Labouring Population of Scotland,* 1842, p.13.
5. Hansard, 3rd series, 4 February 1840.
6. *Royal Commission on the Housing of the Industrial Population of Scotland,* Report, 1918, Cd 8731, p.346.

7. *Select Committee on the Health of Towns,* Minutes of Evidence, PP 1840, vol.xi, 1328.
8. Hansard, 3rd series, 4 February 1840.
9. Asa Briggs, 'Middle class consciousness in English politics, 1780-1840'. *Past and Present,* no.9, pp.65-72.
10. *Select Committee on the Health of Towns,* Minutes of Evidence, 1830. *Select Committee on Buildings Regulations,* PP 1842, vol.x, Minutes of Evidence 1106-37.
11. Geoffrey Best, *Shaftesbury* (London, 1964), p.108-9.
12. John Gray, 'Old Dundee, the town and its folk, change and progress over 70 years', *Dundee Advertiser,* 26 December 1905.
13. Report of the Select Committee on the Health of Towns, p.xiv.
14. Rev. George Lewis, *The pauper bill of Dundee (*Dundee, 1841*),* p.12.
15. Hansard, 3rd series, vol. cxxxvi, 1649, Feb. 1855.
16. 'It is obviously inexpedient to segregate the classes in any such scheme', Report of Royal Commission on Housing, 1918, p.290.
17. 'It was unusual even for the better class of employers to dwell in houses much superior to the rank and file of everyday workers.' Alexander Elliot, *Lochee as it was* Dundee, (1911), p.27.
18. Fairly clear examples of this can be seen in *Dundee Advertiser* columns, 17 February, 1809 and even as late as 26 March 1841, but the most typical and most commonly recurring advertisements pointing to mixed class areas are in the first three decades of the century: 'Two houses suited to genteel families, also a range of houses' is typical.
19. Glasgow's population grew from 77,000 in 1801 to 275,000 in 1841 and by 37% between 1831 and 1841. Dundee grew from 26,000 in 1801 to 63,000 in 1841, Aberdeen from 27,000 in 1801 to 63,000 in 1841 and Edinburgh from 83,000 in 1801 to 166,000 in 1841, Paisley from 25,000 to 48,000, Greenock from 17,000 to 36,000. B. Mitchell and Phyllis Deane, *British Historical Statistics,* pp.24-5.
20. Dock St. in Dundee was ankle deep in mud, Blackness and the Seagate 'very dirty and disagreeable', *Dundee Advertiser,* 7 Jan. 1851.
21. Charles M. Allan 'The genesis of British urban redevelopment with special reference to Glasgow', *Economic History Review,* 2nd series vol.18, 1965, p.603.
22. *Reports on the Sanitary condition.....* op.cit. p.78.
23. *Report of the Select Committee on the Health of Towns,* p.xiii. Giving evidence, Jelinger Symons said 'I did not believe, until I visited the wynds of Glasgow, that so large an amount of filth, crime, misery and disease existed in one spot in any civilised country.' Minutes of Evidence, 1074.
24. *Unlet houses in Dundee,* Lamb Collection, Dundee Public Library, 227 (2).
25. Already noticeably higher than England's in 1801, Scotland's figure grew from 5.46 persons per house in 1801 to 7.8 persons per house in 1851. The average number of persons per family in Scotland was 4.41 in 1801, 4.81 in 1851, so that the average house is shown to have held more than one family. There is, of course, difficulty about the census definition of the word 'house' but correction would tend to strengthen rather than weaken the implication of overcrowding.

26. There were exceptions: see John R. Kellett 'Property speculators and the building of Glasgow', *Scottish Journal of Political Economy,* vol.8, 1961, pp.173-232.
27. Marion Bowley, *Housing Statistics of Great Britain* (London), 1950.
28. B.P. Lenman *et al. Dundee and its textile industry* (Abertay History Society Publication), 1969, Appendix 1; John Butt, 'Working class housing in Glasgow, 1851-1914' in *The history of working class housing,* ed. S.D. Chapman (Newton Abbott, 1971), p.71.
29. Kellett, op.cit. p.211, *n.*2.
30. *Select Committee on Building Regulations,* Minutes of Evidence, 1091-2.
31. C.W.Chalklin, 'Housing estates in the 18th century', *Urban Studies,* vol.5, 1965, p.79.
32. The Police Commissioners in Dundee, 'supported most cordially by the enlightened ideas of Mr. Harry Scott, the son of the proprietor, were delighted in 1868 to have 'settled forever all the nonsense about proprietors being allowed, for the sake of the working classes, to build houses on any plan they chose, to become in a short time, as building progressed, dens of darkness and of filth.' *Dundee Advertiser,* 3 January 1868.
33. Kellett, op.cit. p.230. David Laurie, for instance, who planned the lay-out of the Gorbals in Glasgow as a superior housing estate, found neighbouring feus let to industrial enterprises. Their nuisance value lowered the character of his property to such an extent that the Gorbals, although planned for the middle class, was already in 1822 holding 'an uncommon proportion of the working class', 'inundations of poor', and a large number of Irish immigrants.
34. James Hole, *The homes of the working classes* (1866), pp.2-3.
35. Asked if it would not be better if the working population could be housed in new cottages instead of being crammed into existing tenements, William Scott, master of works, answered: 'In a town like Dundee, where trade fluctuates so much, we, of course, have a rush of people into it, and, of course, a number of families go into one house and live in it.' *Select Committee on Building Regulations,* Minutes of Evidence, 1190.
36. John Hill Burton, 'On the state of the law as regards the abatement of nuisances...' *Reports on the sanitary condition....* pp.49-50; and *Select Committee on Building Regulations,* Minutes of Evidence, 1070-3; and Charles Baird, 'Law on nuisance in Scotland', in *Reports on the sanitary condition...,* p.71, *n.*
37. Dundee's passed in 1837, Glasgow's in 1843.
38. *Dundee Advertiser,* 23 March 1832; 18 February 1851. In Aberdeen and Edinburgh £10 and upwards gave the vote.
39. Rev. George Lewis, *The Church in the Fire* (Dundee, 1841), p.19.
40. 'We do think that the employers of large numbers of work people who have brought to the town for the carrying on of their mills and establishments thousands of Irish and others of a class lower than ever lived in it before owe it to the whole community to provide or see provided shelter for those whom they employ. The owners of large mills who have amassed fortunes and live in princely houses cannot permit their work people to live in wretchedness without having a heavy reckoning to pay.' *Dundee Advertiser,* 17 January 1854.

41. John Honeyman, F.R.I.B.A. 'The dwellings of the poor', *Scottish Church* (1885), p.29.
42. *O.S.A.* vol. 15, p.42.
43. *N.S.A.* vol. 6, pp.22-23.
44. Enid Gauldie, *The Dundee Textile Industry*... (Scottish History Society, 1969), pp.189-90.
45. They did offload property as the occasion arose. The Cox family sold off housing in small lots between 1850 and 1870. *Dundee Valuation Rolls.*
46. Rev. George Lewis, *The pauper bill of Dundee* (Dundee, 1841), p.12.
47. Burton, 'on the state of the law...' op.cit. pp.42-47; John Simon, *Public Health Reports,* vol.2 (London, 1887), p.215.
48. *Reports of the Committee of Council on Education in Scotland,* 1876-6, 1900-1.
49. A. Allan Maclaren, 'Presbyterianism and the working class in a mid-19th century city', *Scottish Historical Review,* vol.46, 1967, p.127. See also *Religion and Social Class: the Disruption Years in Aberdeen* (Routledge & Kegan Paul, London, 1974).
50. James Hole, *Homes of the working classes,* op.cit. p.4.
51. Dr. Thomas Chalmers, *On the Christian and economic polity of a nation, more especially with reference to its large towns,* vol.2 (Glasgow,n.d.), p.281.
52. *N.S.A.,* vol.11, p.504.
53. *Report of the Select Committee on the Health of Towns,* p.iv.
54. *Dundee Advertiser,* 22 March 1832.
55. *Hansard,* 3rd series, 20 August 1857, Crowded Dwellings Prevention Bill.
56. Dwelling Houses (Scotland) Act, 1855, PP. vol. 11, p.101.
57. Geoffrey Best, *Shaftesbury,* op.cit. pp.108-125.
58. *Hansard,* 3rd series, 18 August 1857.
59. Charles Allan, op.cit. p.603, quoting J. Morrison, *Sanitary Journal,* vol.1, 1877, p.268.
60. John Nelson Tarn, 'Housing in Liverpool and Glasgow, the growth of civic responsibility, *Town Planning Review,* vol.39, no.4, 1969, p.330.
61. The Roman Catholic Church in Scotland advocated very much the same course for housing reform as the Presbyterians, recommending patience, forbearance, cleanliness, etc. as the prime aids to social improvement. Rev. Bishop Gillis, ed. *Report of the 1st annual festival of the Hay Gild* ... (Edinburgh, 1843). Prizes were awarded for best kept houses.
62. Most lodging houses were planned to be, not so much homes as 'a refuge for the unfortunate and a model of ideal house-keeping for the neighbouring inhabitants', *Dundee Advertiser,* 2 February 1855.
63. James Cox of Camperdown Works, Dundee, purchased 30 copies of Rev. Dr. Begg's *Happy Homes* for distribution to the Working Men's Club 'to try to get the workmen interested in the scheme'. Lord Kinnaird published *Working Men's Houses* in 1874. Dr. Begg addresses a large meeting in Dundee on 'Workmen's Houses and the advantages of building societies' in November 1864. Cox Letter Book, 21 May 1874.
64. *Royal Commission on Friendly and Benefit Societies,* Minutes of Evidence, PP 1871, vol.25.

65. Quoted, Seymour J. Price, *Building Societies, their origin and history* (London, 1958), p.137.
66. *People's Journal,* 16 May 1874.
67. A weaver's wage in the 1860s was 12/6d, a spinner's 8/6 to 10/-. Even as late as 1905 only mechanics and overseers earned over £1. See Lenman et al. op. cit. Appendix 3.
68. Henry, 9th Lord Kinnaird, *Working Men's Houses* (Dundee, 1874).
69. Dundee Public Library, Lamb Collection, 227/21.
70. Ian MacDougall, *The Minutes of Edinburgh Trades Council* (Scottish History Society, 1968), pp.29-32, 52n., 54, 277, 303-5. The Edinburgh and Leith Joiners Building Company Ltd., formed in 1868, was managed by Peter M'Neill, who was also secretary of the local branch of the Reform League. He was paid as a full-time employee of the Company and was proposed as a working man's candidate at the 1870 municipal election.
71. MacDougall, op.cit. Its directors were working masons. It had a nominal capital of £10,000 in shares of £1 each with 200 founder members. *The Builder*, vol.19, 1861, p.758. It would appear to have become well known in the labour movement. In 1869 the operative stone masons of Vienna wrote to Edinburgh asking for information about the structure of the society. Mac Dougall, p.277.
72. John Nelson Tarn, *Working class housing in 19th century Britain,* Architectural Association paper n. 7, London, 1971, p.40, quoting Sir Hugh Gilzean Reid.
73. The *Builder,* vol. 19, p.899. However, an earlier workers' housing venture in Canning Place remained worker-occupied, perhaps because costs were kept low. Six separate blocks of eight flats were built in 1826, each house containing a room and kitchen with 'a light bed-closet and two dark bed-closets, with water supply, soil-pipe, sink and water closet'. The cost of each house was £80 and in 1862 they were reported as being 'a fair example of what workmen's houses ought to be'. At least some of the original co-operators were then still in occupation. *The Builder*, vol.20, p.484.
74. Robert Chalmers, *Autobiography of the old political and social reformer,* (Dundee, 1874), p.63.
75. *Dundee Advertiser,* 20 January 1858.
76. *Hansard,* 3rd series, 4 February, 1840. The debate on 'Discontent among the working classes' was introduced by Richard Slaney and seconded by W. Smith O'Brien. The vote of the House was the earliest, as John Simon pointed out in *English Sanitary Institution,* p.189 n., to be made on the subject of health and housing.
77. When one witness was asked, 'Do you observe a great deal of discontent among the poor people?' he answered, 'The great proportion of those people I should say are of the lowest class of Irish and I hardly ever see a discontented Irishman; he seems quite contented in whatever condition he may be.' A builder, when questioned whether the poor felt the evils of their living conditions, replied: 'I am not quite sure whether they feel them so as to be fully aware of them'. A doctor believed: 'amidst the greatest destitution and want of domestic comfort I have never heard, during the course of 12 years' practice, a complaint of

inconvenient accommodation.' *Select Committee on the Health of Towns, Minutes of Evidence,* 2518, 204. *Sanitary Condition of the Labouring Population,* ed. Michael Flinn (London, 1967), p.93.
78. E.N. Williams, *A documentary history of England,* vol. 2, p.238.
79. *Select Committee on Artisans and Labourers' Dwellings Improvement Final Report, Minutes of Evidence,* 1237, PP 1882, vol. vii, p.249.
80. *Select Committee on the Health of Towns, Minutes of Evidence,* 1079.
81. R.A. Lewis, *Edwin Chadwick and the public health movement, 1832-54* (London, 1952).
82. Lewis, op.cit. p.109. 3,000 signatures were collected in Edinburgh.
83. *Report of Select Committee on the Health of Towns,* p.l.
84. Report of meeting of the Health of Towns Association, Sheffield, *Times,* 5 February 1848, quoted S. Pollard, *A history of labour in Sheffield* (London, 1958), p.11; see also MacDougall, op.cit. pp.288-289 et seq.
85. Simon, *Public Health Reports,* op.cit. vol.2, p.194.
86. *Report of the Royal Commission on Housing,* 1918, p.346.
87. *People's Journal,* 13 April, 1874.
88. *Dundee Council Minute Book,* vol.40, p.512; vol.42, p.53.
89. B. Weber, 'A new index of residential construction'. *Scottish Journal of Political Economy,* vol.12, pp.104-32; Lenman et al. op.cit. Appendix 1; Butt, op.cit. p.71.
90. *Dundee Council Minute Book,* vol.40, p.512; Dundee Lamb Collection, 196 E; Butt, op.cit. p.61.
91. *The Builder,* 1884, vol.47, p.746.
92. *Dundee Advertiser,* 27 February 1877.
93. H.J. Dyos, 'Railways and housing in Victorian London' *Journal of Transport History* vol.2, pp.11-21 and 90-100; John Kellett, *The impact of railways on Victorian cities* (London 1959); Tarn, 'Housing in Liverpool and Glasgow', op.cit. p.330.
94. Enthusiastic application of existing Acts only aggravated the situation. Under the Lodging Houses Acts, for instance, Dundee had caused in 1855 the eviction of 489 people from over-small houses, 256 from cellars, and 2,408 from overcrowded lodgings. 'But as no provision has been made for them it has only increased the pressure of need for accommodation in town.' *Dundee Advertiser,* 2 February 1855.
95. The *Dwelling Houses (Scotland) Act, 1855,* 18 and 19 Vict. c.88 preceded the *Labourers' Dwellings Act,* 1855, 18 and 19 Vict. c.132. It was presented by Alexander Dunlop, M.P. for Greenock.
96. Those applying to Scotland were: Dwelling Houses (Scotland) Act, 1855; Nuisances Removal (Scotland) Act, 1856, 19 and 20 Vict. c.103; Burgh Police and Improvement (Scotland) Act, 1862, 25 and 26 Vict. c.101; Public Health (Scotland) Act, 1867, 30 and 31 Vict. c.101; Labouring Classes Dwellings Act, 1867, 30 and 31 Vict. c.28 (this extended the provisions of the Labouring Classes Dwelling Houses Act, 1866, 29 and 30 Vict. c.28 to Scotland); Police and Improvement (Scotland) Act, 1868, 31 and 32 Vict. c.102; Artizans and Labourers Dwellings Act, 1868, 31 and 32 Vict. c.130 (Torrens); Artizans and Labourers' Dwellings Improvements (Scotland) Act, 1875, 38 and 39 Vict.

c.49; Artisans and Labourers' Dwellings Improvement (Scotland) Act, 1875, 38 and 39 Vict. c.49; Artisans and Labourers' Dwellings Improvement (Scotland) Act, 1880, 43 and 44 Vict. c.8; Public Health (Scotland) Act, 45 and 46 Vict. c.11; Local Government (Scotland) Act; 52 and 53 Vict. c.59. The housing acts from 1882 applied equally to England and Scotland.
97. Shaftesbury's Act, 1851 allowed the erection or purchase and repair of buildings by local authorities; the Dwelling Houses (Scotland) Act, 1855 was introduced as a 'Bill to facilitate the erection of dwelling houses for the working classes in Scotland'; Torrens (1868) provided for 'the building and maintenance of better dwellings'.
98. Glasgow had begun building workmen's houses by 1889 but they were few in number and let to well-to-do artisans. Allan, op.cit. p.608; Tarn, Liverpool and Glasgow, op.cit. p.329. In Greenock new houses for working people were built on land cleared by the Town Council with a Public Works Commission Loan but the houses were not built by the Council. *Returns of the number of representations made,* PP 1883, vol.58, p.14.
99. *The Third Report,* PP. vol.31, pp.1-331, deals with Scotland.
100. *Dundee Town Council Minute Book,* vol.32, 5 May 1881, Tarn, Liverpool and Glasgow, op.cit. p.330.
101. Rev. Walter Walsh, minister of Gilfillan Church and editor of *For the Right,* was elected housing convener after the people had voted for 'civic advance, better houses, better surroundings, better health.' *For the Right,* November 1908.
102. Report on Housing, 1918, pp.124-161.
103. Sir Patrick Geddes, *Cities in evolution* (London, 1915), pp.140-141.
104. Geddes, op.cit. p.141.
105. Bentley Gilbert, *British social policy (1914-1939,* London, 1970), pp.137-158.
106. John Honeyman, op.cit. p.16.
107. Enid Gauldie, *Cruel habitations, a history of working class housing in Britain* (Allen and Unwin, London, 1974), pp.268-272.

3. Bourgeois Ideology and Victorian Philanthropy: The Contradictions of Cholera

A.A.MacLaren

In a nation constructed on the twin institutions of private property and free enterprise it is important to recall just how cherished and all-pervasive was the principle of the rational pursuit of self-interest in nineteenth century society. A Victorian businessman with little concern for philosophy could respond warmly to Bentham's dictum that 'generally speaking there is no one who knows what is for your interest so well, as yourself — no one who is disposed with so much ardour and constancy to pursue it'. (1) Likewise the truth of Adam Smith's advice must have been self-evident to the business mind: 'Man has almost constant occasion for the help of his brethren and it is vain for him to expect it from their benevolence only. He will be more likely to prevail if he can interest their self-love in his favour, and show them that it is for their own advantage to do for him what he requires of them.' (2) So deeply imbued was the appeal to self-love or self-interest that advocates of humanitarian reforms or philanthropic endeavours openly advanced their claims within such a framework. Industrialists such as David Dale and Robert Owen were active in demonstrating how philanthropy could be made to be profitable. Despite much high-flown oratory the debate on the Scottish Poor Law was also marked by such appeals. Thomas Chalmers maintained that humanitarianism was misconceived unless based on the self-interest of both donor and recipient. (3) W.P. Alison, on the other hand, pleading for an improvement in 'feelings of humanity', believed that if his proposals for reform in the system of poor relief were adopted 'our duty to our poor brethren would be most efficiently, and (what is, no doubt, with many the chief recommendation of the system) most cheaply performed'. (4)

This same sort of appeal was made by philanthropic organisations. Whether secular, religious, or a combination of both, such bodies were eager to claim that their activities were easing the pressure on the poor rates. One can only assume that by making these claims it was expected that financial support would be more easily obtained. However, the important point to note is that debates (such as that over the Poor Law) or the activities of industrial schools, city missions, temperance societies, and so on, were all concerned with a variety of means rather than different ends. Certainly a marginal change in the distribution of income may have been involved in the question of the scale of poor relief, or contributions to humanitarian concerns, but the end remained a more efficient capitalist society. The appeals to economic self-interest were meant to maintain and facilitate the growth of private property and free enterprise; and the union of philanthropy and self-interest was regarded as being natural and mutually beneficial. Indeed this belief has survived and remains an important aspect in contemporary capitalist society. (5)

The purpose of this chapter is to probe more deeply the relationship between bourgeois ideology and philanthropy, particularly with regard to the dynamic element which self-interest lent to humanitarianism. Certain differences will also be drawn out concerning the Scottish and English middle class. Specifically the chapter will examine the ideological response to, and the humanitarianism engendered by, the socially and economically disruptive cholera epidemics. Cholera during its visitations provided perhaps the most serious, and certainly the most dramatic, epidemic threat to the working of economy and society. These epidemics began in 1832 and visited Britain on four occasions down to 1867. They therefore encompass a period which saw the emergence and final stabilisation of what could be termed the truly urban bourgeoisie. (6) Moreover cholera provides a useful case study of such responses as it was an externally imposed problem (7) unlike poverty, crime, drunkenness, unemployment, prostitution, and perhaps even irreligion, which were conditions either generated from within the socio-economic structure, or were related to the system's overall economic performance. However, before examining the response to cholera, one must look at the situation prior to its arrival.

In the cities the main medical welfare provisions were centred on the infirmaries. These institutions, which were erected towards the end of the eighteenth and extended during the nineteenth century, provide examples *par excellence* of the fusion of humanitarian ideals with the widely prevailing ideas of free enterprise, the sanctity of property, and the pursuit of economic self-interest. The infirmaries were set up to provide suitable medical and surgical attention for the working class. It was claimed that

> The infirmary is universally acknowledged to be the most liberal and useful of all our charitable institutions. It embraces at once several objects of charity: To the indigent sick, who are confined to cold, damp, loathsome, miserable hovels, it affords a warm, clean, comfortable habitation: To those who are pining for want, it offers wholesome substantial fare: To the diseased, it affords the best medical assistance: To the ignorant, it administers useful religious and moral instruction. (8)

The city infirmaries were financed by a system of voluntary contributions. The fact of giving an annual contribution, however, vested the contributor with certain 'property' rights over the institution; a strict quota being observed between the level of contribution and the number of patients the contributor could recommend at any given time. Thus parish councils, kirk sessions, or individuals subscribing one guinea a year, had the right to recommend 'two out-patients constantly, and one inpatient — and one lying-in patient in the year'. (9) Those recommended for admission were required to be 'proper objects' for treatment and sponsors (generally a magistrate, employer, or church elder) were expected to ascertain the patient's moral condition. (10) Care was taken by the infirmaries to protect the property 'rights and privileges of the Subscribers' and it was only under severe pressure of circumstances that these rights were violated. (11)

Furthermore, although the infirmaries were set up to provide medical provisions for the working class, they also served the needs and conveniences of their middle-class sponsors. In appealing for financial support the infirmaries continually pointed out the usefulness of their function in the treatment of industrial accidents, and in the removal and treatment of domestic servants who otherwise might have proved a trouble to the family or even a danger as possible sources of infection. (12) The role of the infirmary as 'an effectual barrier against the spread of contagion' (13) was regarded as vital — not only because typhus fever (the main killer) by its propensity to take parents as its victims and spare the children — could place a substantial long-term burden on the poor rates, (14) but also because of its occasional outbursts beyond the normal areas in the poorer areas of the city where it was endemic. Typhus was widely recognised by the medical profession as a disease which responded to the vagaries of the trade cycle and reached its height in times of high unemployment and destitution, but because of its continual presence in areas of ungodliness and irreligion it remained in many middle-class eyes as the disease of spiritual as well as economic destitution. However, because medical practitioners were unaware of the fundamental differences between typhus and typhoid the disease at times seemed to act in an unpredictable manner. In 1828 'a remarkable outbreak of fever' occurred among the 'richer classes' of Edinburgh and prevailed chiefly 'not in the districts where typhus is invariably to be met with, but in the most fashionable parts of the New Town'. (15) Godliness was not seen in itself as a sufficient protection against typhus. In the periods in which the disease reached serious epidemic proportions in the poorer areas of the cities the property rights and privileges of subscribers, and the system of recommendation, were abandoned, and all working-class victims were admitted to the infirmaries, albeit with regret on the part of the hospital authorities. (16)

The infirmaries, therefore, were charitable institutions in the best traditions of middle-class philanthropy. They were supported by private enterprise and operated on a subscription-related quota system. Whilst a product of genuine humanitarian concern they were also to some extent founded on the interests of the middle class in the sense that they acted as barriers against contagious diseases, thus helping to ease economic and social dislocation and lighten possible long-term demands on the poor rates. Finally, as we shall see in more detail later, although epidemic disease such as typhus was widely held to be divine punishment of the ungodly, there were sufficient exceptions to this rule to warrant practical measures against contagion. Cholera was to provide even more exceptions. However, to understand the terror which cholera invoked and the crises which it precipitated, it is necessary to describe the dramatic nature of the disease itself. (17)

First reports of the disease reached Britain in 1818 when an outbreak in India decimated the British army serving in the Central Provinces. Thereafter newspapers recorded its march into Europe via the Persian Gulf. Reports told of how in one outbreak in Teheran and Basra 15,000 people died in 18 days. Following the trade routes, it had entered Russia by 1822 and Moscow by 1830. The following year it had entered central Europe and in three months 100,000 people were reported to have died in Hungary alone. Despite all efforts to stop its progress, by the summer of 1831 every European capital had suffered at least one outbreak and the Middle East was suffering a second major epidemic — 30,000 dying, it was claimed, in Cairo and Alexandria within 24 hours. Attempts to set up cordons by Russian, Prussian, Austrian, and Spanish generals were of no avail and riots and rebellion followed its path. Probably proceeding through the Baltic ports it arrived in England in the autumn of 1831 — the first death being reported in Sunderland in October. It next made its appearance in Scotland and by 1832 the disease was raging throughout Britain.

The dramatic approach of the disease across Europe, although in itself a frightening phenomenon, was more than matched by its often spectacular outbursts in a neighbourhood, and the horrific symptoms of its manifestation in its victims. Cholera struck suddenly and without warning — often giving notice of its presence by seizing its victims where they stood. Although accustomed to epidemic disease, medical practitioners were alarmed by the course that cholera took in the patient. The onset of the disease was marked by severe diarrhoea and acute spasmodic vomiting accompanied by painful cramps. The consequent dehydration of the patient gave him a shrunken, dark appearance, and the 'blueness' of his features became one of the well-known characteristics of the disease. Death often came within a day, and sometimes within a few hours of its first appearance. The death rate from cholera was high — more than 60 per cent of reported cases — and even today if left untreated it reaches similar proportions. Cholera thrives on insanitary conditions and the condition of nineteenth century towns is too well-known to require description. (18) Although this was not known at the time, cholera is transmitted from person to person either through contact or more usually through water or food contaminated by the excrement of cholera victims. The disease is also transmitted through fish or shellfish from infected rivers or marine zones, and the bacillus survives in sugar and salt for more than a day and for seven or eight days in bread and meat. It is not difficult to understand, therefore, the ferocity of the four epidemics which occurred in 1832, 1848, 1853 and 1866, nor to appreciate the terror these epidemics induced.

Of the four epidemics, the first two were the most severe — certainly in terms of the numbers who died. The first 'caused nearly ten thousand deaths, of which Glasgow and its suburbs had about one-third, Edinburgh, Leith, Dundee, Greenock, Paisley and Dumfries, another third, while a large part of the remainder occurred among the mining and fishing populations'. (19) However, these figures conceal much of the horror itself. The disease had a tendency to search out 'weak spots' and, having established itself, to explode with devastating suddenness over a wide area. Thus, in both Glasgow and Edinburgh, in both of the first two epidemics the disease began in poor areas and eventually spread itself out over the entire city. The deaths 'included many among the wealthier class'. (20) Outbreaks occurred throughout Scotland, few areas escaping its ravages. In some small villages half the population died in a few days. (21) Unlike endemic typhus, cholera was not a disease which could be disregarded — posing as it did a threat to the entire community.

The response to the threat of cholera, therefore, was predictable. As had occurred earlier when typhus reached epidemic proportions, there was an immediate abandonment of the rights of subscribers to the infirmaries, and these institutions were utilised as isolation hospitals in an attempt to contain the spread of the disease. Local Boards of Health were instituted or revived and these took over the raising of voluntary contributions for the provision of temporary hospital accommodation, and the payment of additional doctors and medical supplies. (22) There was a general outburst of humanitarian feeling which, feeding on a new-found generosity derived from fear, urged greater concern for the living conditions of the poor. All persons 'having influence with the poorer Classes' were asked to press the need upon them to seek 'the advice of the Medical Men within their reach' (23) at the first sign of illness. Free parcels of 'Medicines for the Poor' were also provided. (24) House-to-house visitation of the working-class districts was urged and even the inhabitants of remote areas in the highlands and islands found themselves the centre of interest in correspondence between factors and proprietors concerning the need for improvements in their dwellings, and the providing of medical practitioners, as precautionary measures. (25) Cholera was the great catalyst — fusing as it did humanitarian endeavour with elements of economic self-interest to create a renewed concern for all members of the community. 'No subject has ever arisen that has demanded more general attention or involved the interests of mankind and humanity more than the *Indian Cholera*', declared a Brechin surgeon. (26) And it was a claim confirmed in neighbouring Dundee where cholera induced 'a sense of the wants of the town' and raised 'something like a general cry for a new burying ground, a new jail, a larger supply of water, better watched streets and better lit suburbs'. (27)

The fusion of humanitarianism and economic self-interest, however, was essentially a *mariage de convenance*. The passing of a cholera crisis led to a strained relationship, although with each recurrent crisis the union was renewed in all its former vigour. Nevertheless there is general recognition of the importance of the relationship as far as the dynamics of the public health movement is concerned. The view of Creighton 'that the greatest of all the lessons taught by cholera was the need of sanitary reform' has subsequently been reflected by historians with only slight variation. (28) Nevertheless, however much the cholera epidemics stimulated social and administrative action, it is clear that cholera created a great deal of ideological confusion among the administrators and the middle class generally. Certain differences are also apparent between the Scottish and English experience.

In 1848, when the second cholera epidemic broke out in England, it was confidently believed that the nation was better equipped to fight the outbreak than it had been in 1832. The volunteer bodies which had struggled with the first epidemic had been superseded by the Poor Law Unions, with their surgeons and fever wards, and finance from the local rates. The Poor Law Guardians had the means at their disposal to fight the epidemic — what stood in their way was not lack of means, or finance, but a total inability to redefine their function in the face of changed circumstances. Having been 'set up as a breakwater to protect property against the rising tide of pauperism' (29), their master principle of administration had been 'to do nothing except on application and then only upon proof given of the urgency of the case'. (30) The Guardians were expected now to break completely from this hallowed principle; not only were they expected to forget their function as protectors of the local ratepayers, they were actually required to seek out actively those in need of relief. Preoccupied with their existing functions, the Guardians were slow to adapt to the role of defending the community as opposed to their narrow class interests. Generally their response to the recommendations, pleas, and threats of the General Board of Health was to undertake half-hearted measures or to delay in the hope that cholera would pass the area by. (31)

But if the attitude of the Guardians was a narrowly defined class view of their function, as well as a dislike of central interference in what they regarded as a local or regional matter, it was also a near enough reflection of the economic interests of middle-class traders and shop-keepers. Cholera cost money — not only in terms of rising rates — but also in the often severe economic dislocation that it caused. News of the impending arrival of cholera led to a flight from the cities and towns to the supposed safety of the countryside, (32) business and production was disrupted, and perhaps worst of all — quarantines were occasionally imposed. Thus every effort had to be made to avoid giving rise to unnecessary alarm to the population (as we shall see later, fear itself was described as a predisposing cause of the disease). The measures which were advocated by the General Board, such as whitewashing of dwellings and cesspool cleansing, were likely to cause a panic in the community. Even when cholera made its unmistakable appearance, attempts were made to disclaim its presence and strong economic interests pressed doctors to withhold information or to retract their diagnoses. (33) Likewise strong pressure was applied to have areas declared safe before the epidemic had actually ended. (34)

Although severely hit by cholera and undergoing the same sort of economic dislocation, there is no real evidence to suggest that serious tensions of this sort developed in Scotland between the medical profession and local businessmen. Some of the reasons for the absence of conflict were administrative. When Scotland underwent the first and worst onslaught of the second epidemic she had neither effective Boards of Guardians nor a General Board of Health. When attempts were made by London to establish a central Board of Health in Edinburgh the resistance from other areas in Scotland was such that the idea was dropped. (35) However, regionalism represented the strength of the business sections of the community and it seems much more likely that the absence of such conflict resulted from the general weakness or inability of the medical practitioners to act as a pressure group. By contrast with the pattern in England, the Public Health Movement failed to develop effectively and Scotland lagged behind her neighbour by more than a generation in tackling the problems of sanitation and epidemic disease. (36) Various explanations have been offered for the relative failure of sanitary (and other) reform movements to develop effectively in Scotland despite the threat of cholera. The main elements of these explanations will now be outlined and an attempt will be made to show that the main constraint was ideological.

Whilst it is clear that the main impetus to sanitary reform came, as in England, with the outbreak of serious epidemics such as cholera, the difference lies in the fact that activity lapsed in Scotland between epidemics, whereas in England some element of continuity was successfully maintained. The reasons advanced for this slowness in the development of sanitary reform as an issue in Scotland can broadly be described as *diversionary* explanations. The energies of middle-class reformers were diverted into other channels which, although obviously not opposed to sanitary reform, were regarded as more urgent and pressing. The more specific of these is argued by Brotherston, who maintains that middle class attention was entirely 'devoted to the problem of destitution as the chief cause of increasing misery and ill-health'. (37) The more general explanation has been offered by historians, such as Kellas, who have argued that the Disruption of the Church of Scotland in 1843 was the great diversion out of which grew the bitterness which absorbed middle-class energies and 'pervaded Scottish life for two generations, affecting politics, education, social welfare and family ties'. (38)

The first of these two explanations – that bourgeois energies were absorbed by the attempt to alleviate destitution and improve the standard of living of the poor – is the more easily dealt with. Brotherston's case rests on the demands for a new poor law which was finally realised in 1845. His evidence is largely based on the work of W.P. Alison, whose plea for reform in poor relief has already been remarked upon (see p.36). Alison's humanitarianism, however liberal in its time, was strongly laced with appeals to middle-class self interest. Brotherston's interpretation is really a non-explanation – 'Some good came from the Act, but after its passage the will to reform seemed temporarily to have spent itself. Perhaps the reformers had concentrated too exclusively on the remedying of destitution ...' (39) This is not an explanation but an apology for middle-class inaction. The extent by which the Act remedied destitution is certainly debatable. In any case the disappearance of the 'will to reform' would require further analysis.

The second more general explanation — that inaction was the result of middle-class energies being consumed by the Disruption and the events that followed — has a long pedigree which goes back to the time of the Disruption itself. Moderate clergymen lamented the rash action of the seceders of whom 'a considerable number ... were incapable of appreciating the principles at stake. They had followed the more prominent leaders; perhaps in a moment of excitement they had made rash pledges, which they felt in honour bound to fulfil'. (40) The Disruption was a regrettable incident which could have been prevented by the action of sensible, moderate men on both sides. Such a theme has been developed by later historians in the category of what Carr might describe as 'the "might-have-been" school of thought — or rather of emotion'. (41) How different things would have been if the Disruption had been avoided and energy expended in other fields! Such an interpretation sees the Disruption as an *event* and not a *symptom* of a deeper structural and ideological schism within Scottish society, of which the actions of 1843 were only an outward manifestation. Whilst it is perfectly true to say that the Disruption, and the events preceding and following it, did absorb middle-class energies, such a statement leaves unexplained *why* the middle class were driven to expend their energies in such a manner. The social structural aspects, although fundamental in understanding the Disruption, are not the concern of this chapter and have been analysed to some extent elsewhere. (42) What must be examined, however, are the severe ideological constraints that Scottish Calvinism laid on the emergence and development of a widespread support for sanitary reform. It is important to remember that Calvin's *doctrine of predestination* was not confined to the Scottish Presbyterians, who were of course the overwhelming majority, but was shared to varying degrees by the Congregationalists, Baptists, Methodists, and certain smaller bodies. (43)

Before the first appearance of cholera in Britain in 1832, the general explanations of the origin, and mode of communication, of epidemic disease could broadly be described as fatalistic. At one level it was argued that 'if the death rate from one disease decreased, the death rate from some other disease must automatically increase, on the principle that nature abhors a vacuum'. (44) At a higher spiritual level epidemics were seen as the work of God, or a withdrawal of His protection from the evils perpetrated by the Devil because of the unregeneracy and unfaithfulness of the nation. Epidemics were akin to floods, earthquakes and other natural disasters — a temporal means by which God achieved the spiritual purification of human society and also rid it of unregenerate sinners.

To the strict Calvinist, however, such interpretations of divine intervention bordered on the heretical. In Scotland clergymen such as Thomas Chalmers denounced the belief that any natural law or process of selection was at work and maintained that whilst temporal happenings might appear to follow certain laws, it was God alone who understood their operation and His influence on such laws was forever hidden from human understanding. (45) When cholera made its appearance, few doubted that its presence was anything other than yet another demonstration of God's omnipotence, and both lay and medical opinion were to a large extent in line with the clergy. At Edinburgh, the professor of surgery, who also acted as medical officer at the cholera hospital, agreed that cholera 'has been cast upon us by the inscrutable workings of divine Providence, which human power cannot avert'; the 'Christian people' ought to bow 'with reverence and humility to the inscrutable decrees of HIM, whose *fiat* they have vainly tried to avert'. (46) Nevertheless, even hardened mission visitors could be stunned by the 'awful calamity' and pleaded 'that it may lead many to consider their ways before they stumble on the dark mountains'. (47) Away from the spiritual and economic destitution of the cities, however, it was believed on Lewis that it was not God's will that plague should visit the island, but even if it was the 'Will of Providence' that the malady should come, the poor would not suffer from its ravages as did the 'dissipated' urban dwellers. (48)

The problem for anyone seeking to advocate sanitary reform was that the plea had to be made in a way which did not suggest that secular intervention was being advanced as a means of averting divine providence. Although by the time of the third epidemic in 1853 this had been got round by the view that the cholera visitations were 'God's judgment against filth', such a rationalisation would not have been accepted earlier, and was not generally accepted even then. (49) Likewise the close association in the middle-class Calvinist mind between spiritual and economic destitution made the humanitarian efforts of men like Alison and Lewis extremely difficult. Both sought to link economic interests with the needs of humanity whilst taking account of the fact that epidemics were 'undoubtedly to be regarded as the visitation of God'. (50) Calvinism stood between humanitarianism and economic self-interest, and only in times of crisis was anything like a dynamic fusion accomplished. Cholera, and to a lesser extent typhus, induced the whitewashing of houses, the cleansing of cess-pits, and the increase in numbers of infirmary beds but, although 'the needs were appreciated by a minority at least as early,' no effective sanitary reform movement developed. (51)

But if the medical profession in Scotland failed to act as a spearhead of sanitary reform, as did their English colleagues, they were important in advancing the theories by which the mode of communication of disease was explained. Their successful attack on the idea that cholera was contagious, and their alternative explanation that the disease was transmitted through the medium of a vapour which they termed a miasma, had important social and economic consequences. In denying contagion and advancing the miasmatic explanation, they were following, of course, the doctrine of the sanitary reformers of the Chadwick school. It was believed that miasma occurred under certain atmospheric and climatic conditions and could be observed in low-lying areas suffering from inadequate drainage. The concept of a miasma was not a new one. In the first half of the eighteenth century, Richard Mead — an English physician — had developed the idea of a miasma transmitting disease because he recognised that 'something more than contagion alone was essential for an explanation' of bubonic plague. (52) Mead had never advanced the view that the miasmatic explanation was an alternative to contagion, he had merely sought to explain how contagion could be transmitted without direct contact.

He had in fact argued strongly that to avoid the importation of plague 'lazarettos should be built at every port for the reception of both men and goods'. The 'very Quintessence of Contagion' was harboured in the clothes of infected persons, 'But the greatest Danger is from such Goods, as are apt to retain Infection, such as Cotton, Hemp and Flax, Paper or Books, Silk of all sorts, Linen, Wool, Feathers, Hair, and all kinds of Skins'. As a consequence Mead advised a quarantine of seamen and goods from incoming ships for forty days, and a further quarantine of twenty days in internal travel between towns but no goods or materials whatsoever which might be retentive of infection were to be transported. (53)

In the 1830s, however, the debate concerning the transmission of epidemic disease ceased effectively to be one concerned with explaining how the contagious infection was spread, and moved into using the miasmatic theory to disprove contagion. Despite the fact that the medical profession was prepared to admit the importa of contagion in epidemic diseases such as plague, smallpox, syphilis, and fevers broadly described as typhus, those who tried to maintain that cholera was also contagious were ridiculed. The difficulty for the contagionists was how to explain the spasmodic nature of cholera which might occur simultaneously at any number of places where individuals obviously had had no direct contact whatsoever. Mead's 'quintessence of contagion' became simplified into a miasma related to atmospheric and climatic changes. Once the premise that cholera was an atmospheric disease was accepted, one can see how easy it was to demonstrate the difference between it and smallpox, which was unaffected by atmospheric changes. Moreover, smallpox could be contracted only once and anyone exposed to the disease was liable to fall victim, whilst in the case of cholera the disease often acted in an extremely capricious manner, devastating an entire area and then throwing up isolated cases here and there. It would seem that the very capriciousness of the disease made the miasmatic explanation more logical to the Calvinist mind. The same Edinburgh surgeon who believed that cholera was the result of the 'inscrutable workings of divine Providence' nevertheless also believed that 'Cholera is not a mysterious, but an explicable disease, and it is as free of contagion as a cut finger or an amputated thumb'. (54)

Whilst not all medical practitioners would have shared that view in 1832 (55), it is clear that by the middle of the century the profession had accepted the miasmatic explanation. Indeed the miasmatists had so consolidated their position that no place at all was allowed for contagion and it was maintained that it was nothing more than coincidence that 'the first case of cholera in a given community is often definitely traceable to an individual who has come from a previously infected area'. (56) Moreover, the miasmatists had extended their argument beyond that of cholera itself and now regarded other diseases such as typhus and influenza in the same light. These were regarded as transmutable, in that one could develop out of the other — 'in the absence of Asiatic cholera, diarrhoea like typhus is a distinct species of disease, it is very readily converted into cholera on account of its close resemblance to that malady'. (57) It was claimed retrospectively that six months before the outbreak of cholera in 1832, cases of typhus were taking on the characteristics of cholera. Likewise 'as every case of diarrhoeia ... was potentially a case of cholera' it followed that the successful treatment of the former was regarded as a victory for medical science. (58) So strong was the concept that there was little room for deviation. Those who argued that cholera under certain circumstances might become contagious went unheard. Even when Snow clearly demonstrated the relationship between polluted water supplies and cholera, the real significance of his work — that the disease was transmitted through the alimentary tract and not the atmosphere — was overlooked. (59) As late as 1894, when Creighton published his *History of Epidemics,* the entire work is permeated with the miasmatic explanation.

Some attempt has been made to explain the miasmatists' remarkable success in the nineteenth century in terms of its being yet another example of the human mind having 'an incurable tendency to what we may call "the fallacy of the single cause" '. (60) More recently it has been suggested that the nineteenth century mind was incapable of undertaking the complexities of multivariate analysis. (61) Although such views deserve some attention, they explain very little as they do not distinguish why any *one* cause should be favoured in relation to another. Moreover it should be noted that they are attempts to explain a monocausal explanation by means of a single cause! As we shall see, the forces which ensured the success of the miasmatic explanation were diverse and varied and drew their strength from middle-class humanitarianism and the same class's perception of economic self-interest.

The main propagandist of the miasmatic explanation was Edwin Chadwick — a layman whose energy, arrogance, sincerity, and singlemindedness, forced on local authorities an explanation which they did not always want to hear, that filth was the unique cause of epidemic disease. His biographer has claimed that 'more than any other individual he had been responsible for civilising the life of the great towns'. (62) The truth of this statement, however, need not concern us, although clearly he was far less successful in stimulating sanitary reform in Scotland than he was in convincing the Scottish middle class of the truth, and expediency, of the miasmatic explanation. Although the personal dynamism of Chadwick was no doubt important, his success is less impressive than one might at first suppose. The miasmatic explanation appealed to various sympathies and sections of the middle class. As an explanation it appeared to be far more scientifically based than that of contagion, which was depicted as superstitious and backward, a hangover from the darkness of medieval society. The idea of miasma was more humanitarian and progressive, denying as it did that cholera was spread principally, if not entirely, by contact with infected persons and therefore seeking to avoid the panic the disease provoked 'and the neglect, and often abandonment of the sick even by relations and friends'. (63)

Nevertheless, although at a theoretical level it is clear that the atmospheric explanation appealed to a fundamental middle-class humanitarianism, it was also the case that at a more practical level the middle class were less than convinced. Cholera accelerated a movement already apparent, by which middle-class families were abandoning the older residential areas of the cities for new housing developments in the city suburbs. Low-lying neighbourhoods subject to atmospheric mists fell into disfavour. In Glasgow, Gorbals had developed as a residential suburb in the first decades of the nineteenth century but from the 1830s declined in fashion, and merchants turned to the Blythswood and Woodside districts which were removed from the river mists and possessed superior drainage. In Dundee epidemics heightened middle-class suburban developments in the eastern outskirts and in Broughty Ferry, and in Aberdeen extensive suburban developments took place on the higher land overlooking the Denburn, which acted as a city sewer. (64) Whilst cholera was only one cause among many for increasing popularity of these residential developments, their existence made it all the easier for the middle class to be *objective* about the threat of contagion. Indeed Boards of Health set up during the cholera epidemics took it upon themselves to reassure the middle class on this very point. The Dundee Board assured the 'upper ranks' that

> there is very little chance of the disease prevailing among persons in easy circumstances ... they ought to keep their servants as much as possible at home, or, at all

events, prohibit them from visiting their friends in infected districts of the town, or admitting visitors from these quarters ... They ought to withhold all encouragement from beggars ... and ... should insist on their servants keeping their outer doors shut ... These precautions being observed, they may dismiss from their minds all over anxiety and fear of infection; which in their instance is uncalled for ... (65)

Although in the event *self-isolation* was to prove less than effective, it seems reasonable to assume that the ability of the middle class to undertake such a measure must have stiffened their resolve to resist or ignore the contagionists' demands for strict quarantine. If God's actions could never be fully understood, it seemed likely that His intention was to punish unregenerate sinners and frighten others into observance of the Holy Writ; certainly it was not His plan to interfere with the progress of trade and commerce. Quarantine was not only a vain attempt to avert divine providence, it was also a gross violation of individual liberty. After all, when 'all the powers of despotic governments' had enforced such drastic measures, what had been the result?

In Europe, with all the apparatus of lazarettos, and cordons, and plague-boards ... the disease has spread as widely, while the mortality has been proportionately greater than in India, where no such precautions are thought of ... this extraordinary mortality is to be attributed, in no inconsiderable degree, to rigorous sanitary regulations; which, while they have in no respect arrested the progress of the disease, have increased its evils, both by their direct operation and by the causeless and enervating panic which they have been so powerful a means of promoting. (66)

The atmospheric explanation therefore justified an irresolution regarding quarantines and such measures. Responses varied from outright resistance to simple inaction and the result was general ineffectiveness. It followed that considerable attempts were made to restrict the movement of those thought particularly susceptible to the disease − seamen, pedlars, vagrants, and others − and little or no effort was made to limit the travels of respectable citizens or to hinder trade. Quarantine stations were set up to which ships were diverted by naval frigates, and merchantmen were required to fly a yellow flag if coming from a cholera-infected port, or a black flag if cholera cases were on board. These restrictions would appear to have applied to the ship and the seamen rather than the cargo. At Dundee cargoes were unloaded and 'sheds were erected on the ground, the bales and bundles of flax were placed in rows so that the wind might freely pass through', it being presumed that this would dissipate and blow away the infection. (67) Some of the smaller towns and villages erected their own cordons, but exceptions were generally made. Similarly, when outbreaks of cholera occurred at Kirkintilloch and Coatbridge, the Glasgow Board of Health felt it necessary to close the Forth and Clyde, and Monkland, canals to passenger traffic but allowed goods to proceed as usual. (68)

It would be wrong, however, to interpret the success of the miasmatic explanation in the simple terms of crude economic determinism. Nevertheless, as far as the business sections of the middle class were concerned, here was a theory much preferable to that of contagion, with all its impediments to the progress of trade and commerce. In advancing such an explanation, the medical profession also appealed to a fundamental middle-class humanitarianism. Whilst one might explain the presence of economic self-interest as coincidence, when one looks at the remaining facet of the miasmatic explanation, the class origins and orientations of the overall explanations become clearer. Built into the miasmatic explanation were certain refinements known as predisposing causes. These broadly confirmed all the class prejudices of the bourgeoisie. Because cholera acted in a capricious manner, striking here and there, occasionally devastating an entire district and at other times casting up isolated cases, it was necessary to explain why the miasma which was obviously present did not affect all those with whom it came into contact. The doctrine of predisposing causes was a subtle and socially significant means of affording just such an explanation.

The idea of predisposing causes was not new. It had been used with considerable success to explain the pattern of earlier typhus epidemics and it now emerged in reinvigorated form. Whilst Calvinism had stood in the way of sanitary reform movements as examples of secular intervention, such difficulties did not arise regarding the predisposing causes doctrine which in many ways confirmed in middle-class minds the association between spiritual and economic destitution. It was confidently believed that certain life styles or behavioural patterns predisposed one to contract epidemic disease and these predispositions were rooted in an irreligious proletarian culture. For example it was believed that typhus fever would strike when any behaviour took place which tended 'to debilitate the nervous system'. This was particularly the case with 'excesses of any kind' — all manner of which laid the individual open to attack. It was essential to eat regular and proper meals, and to avoid going out after dark and keeping untimely hours. Despite the seriously debilitating effects of 'extreme passion', it seemed that getting to bed early was to be recommended — 'one hour's sleep before midnight restoring the exhausted powers of the body and mind more effectually than two hours after it'. (69) There must also be 'a strict attention to personal cleanliness', but above all perhaps the danger lay in alcohol — 'nothing can so much tend to promote the increase of the Disease as *an improper indulgence in the use of Ardent Spirits*'. The 'poorer Classes' had to be warned 'against the fatal consequences of Intoxication'. (70)

> Experience has shown, that the most essential precaution for escaping the Disease is Sobriety, — that Intoxication, during the prevalence of the Epidemic, is almost sure to be followed by an attack, — and that those addicted to Drinking, are the most subject to take Cholera, and the most likely to sink under it. (71)

Apart from cautioning the poorer classes concerning the danger of such behaviour, the duty of the middle class was clear. They had by their example 'to exert themselves in allaying panic and alarm', as fear itself was held to be an important predisposing cause. However, there seems little doubt that the demands of civic duty and the requirements of personal safety were irreconcilable. Never fully convinced by the non-contagionists' arguments, and in some doubt over the predisposing causes doctrine, the middle class recognised that 'safety may occasionally be found in deserting the quarter of the town or district in which the disease particularly manifests itself'. (72)

In the event the predisposing causes doctrine was less successful than it had been with regard to typhus fever. Although generally substantiated, in that the working class provided the greater number of victims, cholera proved far less socially discriminating than had been expected. The fact that the disease was not entirely socially delineated, and was not yet another 'poor man's disease' as some had hoped or predicted, certainly led in the first epidemic to some awkward moments. When eminently respectable citizens died of cholera, problems arose and no doubt there were murmurings of unmentionable secret vices or concealed excesses. Indeed there would seem to be some general truth in Rosenberg's claim regarding the New York middle class that in 1832 they believed that 'to die of cholera was to die in suspicious circumstances'. (73)

The need to explain such exceptions does reveal an increasing awareness of the middle class as a separate class within society. It was precisely because cholera (unlike typhus) was community-located rather than located in a specific class that class perceptions were intensified. Whilst, as we have seen, the middle class could attempt to isolate themselves, the working class were expected to make use of the infirmaries converted for the use of cholera victims. However, there was a marked reluctance on the part of the working class to enter *any* hospital and during cholera epidemics this unwillingness emerged as an outright resistance. It was believed that the cholera hospital was more than halfway to the graveyard, and figures collected by medical practitioners to some extent substantiate this belief. (74) Informed opinion during the epidemics recognised that the death rate was much higher than was actually reported — the working class concealing cases and if possible falsifying the cause of death. There were a number of reasons why working-class people should do this — most of these being determined by their class situation. Although many doctors laboured unremittingly on behalf of cholera victims, there was a deep distrust of the medical profession, and throughout Europe riots occurred when it was reported that doctors were poisoning their patients. Medical knowledge was such that there was clearly some truth in these reports. (75) Moreover the line between life and death in cholera was not always clear and cases did occur of premature burial. The need to dispose of the corpses as soon as possible led to a Haddington man being pushed into his coffin while his arms were flailing and his 'chest undulated with spasms'. (76) Such reports were not helped by doctors who debated the matter openly. One medical practitioner who claimed considerable experience of the disease advocated the 'tying of the limbs of the newly deceased ... to prevent such distressing occurrences'. (77) Obviously a thousand rumours could spring from a single case. However, those who could be expected to be particularly afraid of such rumours were those reliant on the poor rates for medical provisions.

There were other reasons for concealment of the disease. Boards of Health confiscated and destroyed the clothing and bedding of cholera victims, and whilst this may have been justifiable it nevertheless was a much greater economic blow to the poor than it was to the better off members of society. Discrimination also took place with regard to the burial of cholera victims. The great majority were buried in 'cholera ground'; or, worse, they were simply tipped into the 'cholera hole'. (78) The speed at which those who died of the disease were buried was well-known. Although a majority of the working class attended church at best only intermittently, they still retained a belief in church 'connection' and certainly sought a 'full and proper' Christian burial. There was a genuine fear, perhaps not without substance, that this would not be forthcoming if the true cause of death was known. (79)

Such problems did not arise to anything like the same extent with regard to typhus which, although occasionally breaking out of its class confines, was essentially a disease of destitution. Cholera, however, unfailingly began in working-class areas but speedily spread to neighbourhoods normally safe from fever. It was a disease which threatened the entire community and, because of its dramatic nature and lethal quality, could not be ignored. Social attitudes towards, and response to the disease, were predictably different. The working class could not isolate themselves in the residential suburbs, and had little hope of escaping to the supposed safety of the countryside. Whilst the middle-class response was to seek to contain the disease by isolating its victims in the infirmaries, there were many pressures acting on the working class leading to concealment. If, as was claimed, 'the working classes were well aware of the connection between their insanitary dwellings and the disease which afflicted them' (80), it seems probable that the sudden concern for their living conditions which cholera provoked, was regarded with some cynicism, distrust, and heightened class awareness.

Nevertheless cholera, more than any other disease, could effectively fuse bourgeois humanitarianism with the dynamics of self-interest. The triumph of the miasmatic explanation demonstrates the success and importance of this fusion. On the one hand contagion was seen as a backward, unscientific, medieval conception, which led to the desertion of family and friends through fear of infection; on the other hand the miasmatists offered an explanation which served the needs of industry and commerce — rejecting as it did any measures such as quarantines as useless restraints on trade. In the event the least successful aspect of the explanation was the doctrine of predisposing causes which, substantiated to some degree by the course of typhus, left too many loopholes and social exceptions to be effective in understanding the vagaries of cholera. However, as a doctrine it perhaps had a particular appeal to a Calvinist middle class in whose eyes spiritual and economic destitution were inextricably related. Likewise, whilst the failure of any effective sanitary reform movement to develop in Scotland was related to the economics of public health — 'epidemics were brief, memories short, and municipal purses tight' (81) — it was also deeply rooted in Calvinist ideas concerning the 'unknowability' of God, and the uselessness of any secular attempt to avert the workings of divine providence. Thus Calvinist precepts incorporated into a bourgeois ideology inhibited the fusion of philanthropy and self-interest with regard to sanitary reform and yet in no way hindered support for the miasmatic explanation or the doctrine of predisposing causes. Although by the 1850s one can detect doubts creeping into bourgeois thought regarding the precise relationship of epidemic disease to Divine Providence (82), the importance of Calvinist precepts remains strong and should not be underestimated. Indeed the incorporation of these precepts into middle-class ideology might be seen as one essential distinguishing feature between the Scottish and English bourgeoisie of the nineteenth century.

REFERENCES

1. Jeremy Bentham, *Manual of Political Economy,* vol. 3, p.33; cited by L.Robbins, *The Theory of Economic Policy in English Classical Political Economy* (Macmillan, London, 1952), p.13.
2. Adam Smith, *Wealth of Nations,* vol. 1, p.16; cited by Robbins, op.cit. p.14.
3. *On Political Economy in connection with the Moral State and Moral Prospects*

of Society (2nd Ed. Glasgow, 1832), *passim.*

4. *Observations on the Management of the Poor in Scotland and its Effects on the Health of the great Towns* (Edinburgh, 1840), pp.iii, v.

5. Oxfam provide an interesting example in their recent (1974) promotion of their Lifeline Assurance Plan: 'You can help fight — Poverty Disease Ignorance Unemployment Exploitation Malnutrition Over-population Hunger — and collect £1,000 for yourself at the same time'.

6. For a study of this social phenomenon see A.A. MacLaren, *Religion and Social Class: The Disruption Years in Aberdeen* (Routledge & Kegan Paul, London, 1974).

7. It is true one might argue that cholera was a disease which followed the trade routes and therefore was not external to the system. However the disease had long been present in India and trade had been in progress for two hundred years or more with that country. It was not until 1817 that the disease (for reasons unknown) 'acquired a new dynamism' and between 1826 and 1838 'it spread to practically the whole of the world between latitude 41°S and 65°N'. For a short account see A.H. Gale, *Epidemic Diseases* (Penguin Books, Harmondsworth, 1959), chap. 5.

8. *Report of the state of Dundee Royal Infirmary* (Dundee, 1832), p.3. Religious and moral instruction were seen as part of the medical treatment. Chaplains were appointed 'whose weekly instructions refresh the convalescents, and prepare their minds for returning to the duties of life'. (Ibid. 1827). At the Glasgow Royal Infirmary it was felt that insufficient effort was being expended in this sphere by the chaplain as many 'could not read, and seldom cared about religious instruction'. See *Annual Report of Glasgow Royal Infirmary, 1832*; cited by M.S. Buchanan, *History of the Glasgow Royal Infirmary* (Glasgow, 1832), p.34.

9. *By-laws of Dundee Royal Infirmary* (Dundee, 1824), p.11. Similar schemes were operated in other cities. For example see *Regulations of the Royal Infirmary of Aberdeen* (Aberdeen, 1838).

10. For a discussion of this, and other forms of social control, see A.A. MacLaren, op.cit. p.150ff.

11. Buchanan, op.cit. p.12. At Dundee Royal Infirmary regulations required that 'patients pay three shillings and sixpence a week until they succeed a gratis patient'. *Report* (1827), p.4.

12. For example see *An Account of Dundee Royal Infirmary* (Dundee 1815), p.6.

13. Buchanan, op.cit. p.12.

14. *Report of Dundee Royal Infirmary* (1841). It was claimed that 'higher motives, however, than those of self-interest — the feelings of benevolence, and the Christian duty of charity — alike enforce the duty of supporting this, the only asylum for the sick and suffering poor'. (p.5).

15. C. Creighton, *History of Epidemics in Britain* (1894), vol.2, p.788.

16. This was certainly the case in Glasgow Royal Infirmary. See Buchanan, op.cit. pp.12, 25.

17. For a readable and easily accessible account of the march of the disease, see N. Longmate, *King Cholera — The Biography of a Disease* (Hamish Hamilton,

London, 1966). See also G.M. Howe, 'Passage of a disease through 25 countries' in *The Geographical Magazine,* Oct. 1970, pp.57-8.
18. For a recent study of these conditions see E. Gauldie, *Cruel Habitations: A History of Working-Class Housing* (Allen & Unwin, London, 1974).
19. Creighton, op. cit. p.815.
20. Ibid. pp.809, 811, 812, 837.
21. Ibid. p.814.
22. For example in Glasgow £200 was voted from council funds by city magistrates in order to 'set the example to the more wealthy inhabitants'. R. Renwick (ed.), *Extracts from the Records of the Burgh of Glasgow,* vol. XI (Glasgow 1916), 16 Dec. 1831. According to Creighton £8,000 was raised. (op.cit. p.808).
23. Justices of the Peace for the County of Edinburgh, Cholera Handbill, 13 July 1832.
24. Ibid. Cholera Wall-poster 30 Nov. 1831.
25. See Bught Papers: Letters [GD23:6; 463/17]; Clanranald Papers [GD201 10/98]; Seaforth Papers [GD46 13/215]. These may be consulted at the Scottish Record Office, Edinburgh.
26. E.B. Sheriffs, *Remarks on Cholera Morbus* (Brechin, 1832).
27. E. Gauldie (Ed.), *The Dundee Textile Industry 1790-1885, from the Papers of Peter Carmichael of Arthurstone* (Scottish History Society, Edinburgh, 1969), p.55.
28. Op. cit. p.883. For example see C.F. Brockington, *Public Health in the Nineteenth Century* (Livingstone, Edinburgh, 1965), p.66; J.H.F. Brotherston, *Observations on the early Public Health Movement in Scotland* (London, 1952), p.42; T. Ferguson, *The Dawn of Scottish Social Welfare* (Glasgow, 1948), p.2; M.W. Flinn's introduction to *Report on the Sanitary Condition of the Labouring Population of Great Britain by Edwin Chadwick, 1842* (Edinburgh University Press, 1965), p.10.
29. R.A. Lewis, *Edwin Chadwick and the Public Health Movement 1832-54* (Longmans Green, London 1952), p.197.
30. *Report of the Epidemic Cholera of 1848 and 1849,* p.138; cited by Lewis, op. cit. p.197.
31. Ibid.
32. The desertion of the city for the countryside had always been a feature of epidemics and this pattern was repeated with regard to cholera. Throughout western Europe and the United States the middle class took fright and fled. New York provides a startling example: 'By the end of the first week ... almost everyone who could afford to had left the city. Farm houses and country homes within a thirty-mile radius were completely filled ... A merchant living in one of the principal residential streets recalled that his and one other family were the only ones in the street to remain ... Visitors to the city were struck by the deathly silence of the streets ... One young woman recalled seeing tufts of grass growing in the little-used thoroughfares – C.E. Rosenberg, *The Cholera Years: The United States in 1832, 1849, and 1866* (The University of Chicago Press, Chicago, 1962), p.28.
33. In Sunderland a gathering of eminent citizens declared that 'the alarm was

false' and called upon the medical profession to withdraw the 'wicked and malicious falsehood' which they were spreading. Demands were also made to lift the quarantine on the River Wear. The doctors complied and altered their diagnosis. — Creighton, op.cit., p.798. Similar complaints were made by a group of private citizens regarding the Medical Society in New York — Rosenberg, op.cit., p.27.

34. During the second epidemic London magistrates demanded that the city be declared safe. It was argued that all the talk about cholera had led to thousands of families fleeing in panic and as a result shop-keepers were 'paying hundreds a year for their premises, and only earning 6d *per diem* by their trade'. *The Times,* 8 Oct. 1849, cited by Lewis, op.cit., p.207.
35. Ibid. p.199.
36. J.H.F. Brotherston, *Observations on the early Public Health Movement in Scotland* (London, 1952), p.43; J. Ferguson, *The Dawn of Scottish Social Welfare* (Glasgow, 1948), p.4. Gauldie has recently stressed once more the importance of the medical profession as a spearhead in the campaign for public health (*Cruel Habitations,* p.112). This would appear to be less true in Scotland.
37. Op.cit., p.42.
38. J.G. Kellas, *Modern Scotland: The Nation since 1870* (Pall Mall Press, London, 1968), p.54.
39. Op.cit., p.43.
40. R.H. Story (ed.), *The Church of Scotland, Past and Present,* vol. 3, p.828. A more recent view sees the Disruption as a 'tragedy' which 'was preventable'. — R. Tait and G.S. Pryde, *Scotland,* 2nd Ed. (Benn, London, 1954), p.267.
41. E.H. Carr, *What is History?* (Penguin Books, Harmondsworth, 1964), p.96.
42. MacLaren, op.cit.
43. See James Ross, *A History of Congregational Independency in Scotland* (Glasgow, 1900); George Yuille (ed.), *History of the Baptists in Scotland* (Glasgow, 1926); D. Wilson, *Methodism in Scotland* (Aberdeen, 1850). The Scottish Episcopalians at that time also differed considerably from their Anglican counterparts. See MacLaren, op.cit., p.34.
44. C.A. Winslow, *The Conquest of Epidemic Disease: A Chapter in the History of Ideas* (Hafner Publishing Company, New York, 1967), p.242-3.
45. Thomas Chalmers, *The Efficacy of Prayer* (Edinburgh, 1832).
46. John Lizars, *Investigations regarding Cholera Asphyxia ... with Observations on the Disease in Edinburgh and Neighbouring Districts* (Edinburgh, 1832), p.60-1.
47. *Fourth Annual Report of the Dundee City Mission Association* (Dundee, 1834), p.4.
48. Seaforth Papers [GD 46 13/215], 11 Feb. 1832.
49. The words of Peter Carmichael, a Dundee industrialist. — Gauldie, *Dundee Textile Industry,* p.147.
50. W.P. Alison, op.cit.; G. Lewis, *The Filth and Fever Bills of Dundee and what might be made of them.* (Dundee, 1841), p.9.
51. J.M. Mackintosh's introduction, in Brotherston, op.cit., p.vii.

52. Winslow, op.cit., p.187.
53. R. Mead, *A Short Discourse concerning Pestilential Contagion, and the Methods to be used to prevent it* (Dublin, 1721), cited by Winslow, op.cit., p.189.
54. Lizars, op.cit., (preface).
55. For example at Glasgow Royal Infirmary one assistant 'being so much of a contagionist' stipulated 'that it would never be required of him ... to attend fever cases'. — Buchanan, op.cit., p.23.
56. Winslow, op.cit., p.254.
57. Ibid., p.255.
58. Lewis, op.cit., p.190.
59. J. Snow, *On the Mode of Communication of Cholera* (London, 1849). In the Report of the General Board of Health in 1850, unwholesome water was listed as seventh in importance and was regarded as a predisposing agent rather than the vehicle of infection. See Lewis, op.cit., p.191; Winslow, op.cit., p.247.
60. Winslow, op.cit., p.250.
61. A comment on the problem made by Dr. Michael Anderson on an earlier version of this chapter which was read to a postgraduate seminar held at the Department of Sociology, University of Edinburgh in January 1973.
62. Lewis, op.cit., p.375.
63. George Hamilton Bell, *Letter to Sir Henry Halford ... on the tendency of the proposed regulations for cholera* (Edinburgh, 1831), p.2.
64. J.R. Kellett, 'Property speculators and the building of Glasgow', in *Scottish Journal of Political Economy,* vol. 8, pp.211-32, Gauldie, *Dundee Textile Industry,* MacLaren, op.cit., pp.4f, 91, 93, 123f.
65. *Report of the Dundee Board of Health* (Dundee, 1832), pp.5-6.
66. Bell, op.cit., pp.6-7.
67. Reminiscenses of a Dundonian; Dundee Public Library, Lamb Collection [260(33)].
68. Creighton, op.cit., pp.814-5; 808.
69. William Dick, surgeon, *Remarks on Epidemic Fever commonly called Typhus* (Dundee, 1820), pp.27-8, 41.
70. Cholera Handbill, op.cit.
71. Cholera Wall-Poster, op.cit.
72. Bell, op.cit. p.13.
73. Op.cit., p.42.
74. For example the monthly percentages of deaths of those admitted to the Albion Street Cholera Hospital in Glasgow in the first six months were 82.5, 71.1, 66.3, 71.4, 74.5, 59.5. However, the figures are somewhat misleading, as it seems likely that many admitted were in the terminal stage of the disease. The falling-off in the rate may be explained by the spread of the disease to better areas where the residents had stronger constitutions. See Creighton, op. cit., pp.810-12.
75. Victims were liberally dosed with laudanum, opium, sulphuric ether, and calomel (suppurating gums — indicative of mercury poisoning — were regarded as a hopeful sign); were given tobacco, salt, and cayenne pepper emetics; were

bled by lancet and leeches ('the danger is, that too small rather than too large a quantity of blood is removed' — Bell, op.cit., p.11); were subjected to mustard poultices; and were inserted in a wooden box described as a 'hot air bath'.

76. Longmate, op.cit., p.54.
77. Ibid.
78. Manuscript notes, Dundee Public Library, Lamb Collection [260(33)]. See also Longmate, op.cit., p.53.
79. For example in Aberdeen the presbyterian clergy achieved a certain notoriety over their failure to visit those suffering from 'contagious diseases'. When the first city missionary was appointed in 1846 he refused to undertake the task. See MacLaren, op.cit., pp.38; 170-1.
80. Lewis, op.cit. p.182.
81. M.W. Flinn in his introduction to *Edwin Chadwick's Report on the Sanitary Condition of the Labouring Population of Great Britain* (Edinburgh University Press, 1965), p.8.
82. Perhaps the clearest and best-known example of the increasingly secular attitude towards epidemic disease is Palmerston's letter replying to the Scottish Presbyterians' demand for a day of national fasting: 'When man has done his utmost for his own safety then it is time to invoke the blessing of Heaven to to give effect to his exertions'. (19 October 1853). Such an impolitic statement would not have been possible 20 years earlier. The text of the letter is printed in Longmate, op.cit., pp.185-6. A grass-roots example of the changing attitude can be seen in Peter Carmichael, a Dundee industrialist. The family had earlier moved to 'a more healthful' habitation but were plagued by ill-health. Writing at the time of the 1853 epidemic, Carmichael declared: 'The Free Church have had a fast today, which would be very well after all the means in our power had been used, but no one will allow his pocket to be touched...'. — Gauldie, *Dundee Textile Industry,* pp.134; 147. In Aberdeen the South Parish missionary, essentially a practical man, prayed for those smitten by a typhus epidemic and at the same time declared that 'As a preventive against such epidemics, it is the duty of all those who are in the habit of coming into contact with the lower classes, to impress upon them the necessity of cleanliness, and of regularly airing their apartments.' — *Annual Report of South Parish Mission,* 2 May 1849, p.22.

4. Aspects of Sexual Behaviour in Nineteenth Century Scotland

T.C.Smout

The main purpose of this chapter is to establish what differences there appear to have been between social groups in patterns of sexual behaviour outside marriage in nineteenth-century Scotland. It is not, quite honestly, a task which a historian can expect to do well without a great more work on detailed primary sources than I have undertaken: careful study of such demographic sources as the census enumeration returns and the original registrar's books of births and marriages could, for instance, greatly extend our understanding of the social context of illegitimacy and bridal pregnancy. In other directions — for instance for work on the details of courtship — sufficiently detailed information for the nineteenth century can probably never be found to carry the description much beyond the unsatisfactory outline presented here. But even a partial investigation can make us aware of the complexities of the patterns of human behaviour involved, and perhaps form a starting point for discussion and future research. It is sad (but currently inevitable) that research into sexual history should generally appear to be either prurient or trivial: if social history aims to reflect what is important in people's lives, sexual history deserves much more serious and central attention from social historians than it has had so far. (1)

The sexual ideal to which the acknowledged spokesmen of Victorian Scotland paid lip-service was the traditional teaching of the Christian churches: all sexual intercourse before marriage was wrong, and all sexual intercourse after marriage except with the spouse was worse. Everyone knew that contemporary practice fell short of this ideal: the towns were full of prostitutes and illegitimacy, from 1855 when the figures were first collected, did not fall below eight or nine per cent of live births until the 1890s. The Church of Scotland had in the pre-industrial past made considerable efforts to compel society to conform to its teaching. In its post-Reformation enthusiasm, and especially in the seventeenth century, the local kirk-sessions had regularly punished fornicators and adulterers by public appearances on the cutty-stool, culprits being made to stand sabbath after sabbath in the face of the congregation until their sin was purged. If kirk discipline usually fell upon the weak, it did not altogether spare the powerful: there were several cases of landowners obliged to submit along with the peasant. In the eighteenth century, despite the experience of Robert Burns and his friends, the efforts of the church to secure public humiliation increasingly gave way to commutation, and sinners paid according to a more-or-less fixed tariff for their misdemeanours. (2) By the nineteenth-century public punishment was rare but not unknown: it survived, for instance, in Lewis at mid-century. (3) Private rebuke by the session, however, was still common enough in cases where a couple asked for marriage or baptism and subsequent inquiry revealed 'antenuptial fornication'. (4) We do not know if the church in the past had been more successful in imposing its standards than it was in Victorian times. But by then there were several different norms tacitly accepted in different social strata, all at variance with the church's ideal, though probably not totally influenced by it. It is these we must examine.

The Middle and Upper Classes: chastity and prostitution

It was the middle and upper classes who in some ways showed the greatest degree of ambivalence towards Christian teaching, owing to their frank espousal of the double standard. It does not, however, seem possible to make any very clear distinction between the moral norms of the upper classes (i.e. the landed families) and the bourgeois (i.e. professional, commercial and business families) in their expectations of the sexual behaviour of women of their own rank. For women, the Christian model appears to have been fully and elaborately followed. Cases of illegitimacy among upper class and middle class women were extremely rare. Of course, they had better opportunities for concealment, though until the coming of the great orphanage societies at the end of the century these were limited by the problem of disposing of the bastard: the evidence of the medical profession is, however, unequivocal that middle class women were almost never the mothers of illegitimate children, and, equally, were almost never pregnant before their marriage. (5) Indeed, the whole institution of Victorian bourgeois courtship, with its elaborate rules of chaperone and its romantic image of the undefiled and innocent maid, must have made it extremely difficult even for engaged couples to get to bed before they got to church. Once married, the bourgeois girl was expected to be unquestioningly faithful: the sanctions against the adulteress, the difficulty of divorce and the gross unfairness of the law in respect of divorced women are well known.

Hand in hand with this went a complete lack of even the most elementary knowledge of biology: absence of sex education, even in vestigial form, was common throughout society, but middle-class girls had even less chance than working-class girls of discovering the facts of life either by experiment or by observing their parents in overcrowded houses. For instance, one woman (born in 1889, the daughter of an engineering manager, and married as late as 1917) had this to say to an Essex University oral history interviewer:

> I know this, that when I was expecting my first baby I didn't know whether it was going to come out of my tummy or where it was going to come out of. And this is perfectly true, and I was 27½.

Total ignorance of sex followed by total commitment to marriage were what was required.

For the male, however, lip service paid to the Christian ideal was certainly not matched universally by the same real expectations of perpetual antenuptial chastity, and possibly not of postmarital faithfulness either. As one moralist put it: 'it appears to be almost taken for granted, as a matter of course, that young men should be found in a greater or lesser degree, giving way'. (7) For all that the teaching of religion demanded equal standards, the disapproval of the male peer group was evidently lacking. Doctors in Victorian times still occasionally recommended fornication on medicinal grounds for those of their own sex: to do so for women would have been unthinkable. (8)

Since the unmarried bourgeois male was thus disbarred from any sexual contact with girls of his own class, he had to seek it from girls in the class below him. Again, there was nothing new or specifically Victorian in this. Edinburgh, not without prostitutes even in the seventeenth century, took a turn for the worse between the 1760s and the 1780s: William Creech reported that whereas in 1763 there had been only five or six brothels and few whores, twenty years later there were 'twenty times' more brothels and 'every quarter of the city and suburbs was infested' with whores. (9) In the countryside the landowners or tacksmen might take mistresses from the daughters of their tenantry. In eighteenth-century Lewis it was even said that the peasant girls reckoned it an honour to have a daughter by a gentleman as it made them more sought in marriage by their own class afterwards. (10) In the Lowlands comfortable arrangements could also be made:

> Lord Crawfurd had a highland lass or mistress, a bonnie nymph, from Arran. Auld Auchinhane reported my Lord bairned her and (being tired of her) he garred Willie Orr, his servant to kipple with her, and take the wyte of his lordship's wane. Therefore Lord Crawfurd set Willie up as a farmer ... and tochered Jean, the issue of his amour. (11)

What was perhaps new in the nineteenth century was not the fact of inter-class sexual contact, but the degree of anxiety, guilt and furtiveness that now accompanied it. (12) It would be interesting to know exactly why. Perhaps it was a reflexion of the separation of classes themselves: if society moved to a polarity in which there was less and less day-to-day contact between the classes, the crossing of class barriers for sexual purposes might itself set up neuroses which would perhaps not have troubled Lord Crawfurd and his nymph. Again, the cult of respectability and the attendant spread of evangelical religious sentiments in Scotland, with their concomitant insistence on the importance of a 'lively sense of sin' in an individual's relationship with God, might have created extreme personal tensions in young men; they might be ground between religious prohibitions and the kind of peer group tolerance which amounted to equally lively expectations of extramarital sexual behaviour.

There certainly appears to have been a greater fear of venereal disease, signified partly by the opening of Magdalene hospitals (in Edinburgh in 1797, in Glasgow about 1815), (13) partly by the amount of medical literature on the subject, and partly by the debate on the Contagious Diseases Act. This anxiety might have been based on a real increase in the danger to public health: prostitutes who formed the pool of infection were almost exclusively urban, and as urbanisation developed, prostitution and V.D. could be expected to grow in proportion. On the other hand the exacerbated fear of sexually transmitted disease might not have been so rationally grounded, but may have derived only from the growing psychological anxiety about extra-marital sex. Moralists liked to observe that syphilis was God's judgement on the fornicator and the adulterer. (14)

There is some indication that even in the nineteenth century the aristocracy and landed classes were less smitten by shame than the middle classes. The whores who flocked to Musselburgh races were openly welcomed by the young blades of the turf, and Dr. Tait of Edinburgh reported:

> As an encouragement to brothel-keepers, some noblemen of the highest rank and title prefer taking up their quarters in a house of ill-fame rather than in a respectable hotel, and unblushingly visit all the 'lions' in company with the keeper

and one or more of her ladies. Only last year, it was currently reported that a minister in the west of Scotland let his manse, during the entertainments at Eglinton Castle, to a certain nobleman for the purpose of lodging his concubines. (15)

In economic terms at least such men had nothing to lose if they chose not to behave in a 'respectable' way; and their peer group did not condemn them as it would have done if (for example) they had been caught cheating at cards. On the other hand a young or insecure professional man might have to behave much more circumspectly, not necessarily because his peer group would disapprove of the action in itself but because to flaunt his fornication openly would be to challenge the canons of religion, and that challenge would not be approved by the peer group. A man discovered to be living with a mistress could not be thought respectable, and would be vulnerable to economic sanctions in his trade or profession. Thus a middle-class man might suffer from the social anxiety of being found out by his seniors or betters, as well as the personal anxiety created by any private moral tensions. 'Victorian hypocrisy' was created by all these contradictions; it must have been a miserable thing for the unfortunate hypocrite to live with.

Middle-class men could only get their extramarital sex from a working-class girl by persuasion or payment: in moral terms, the former was seduction, the latter prostitution. By the middle of the nineteenth century, they were unlikely to come into contact with many working-class girls on whom they could exercise their powers of persuasion except domestic servants living in the household. Servants, indeed, were vulnerable to sexual exploitation. On the one hand, they were regarded by their middle-class mistresses as frail beings, in great danger of being seduced from outside by working-class males from pimps to postmen. In many Edinburgh villas in the suburbs of Morningside and Newington the only barred window is on the maid's room. Furthermore, it was held that if they were kept from men their minds would be more concentrated upon their work. One critical observer of these views put it like this:

> The cry everywhere is "No followers!" as if the young serving girl had no title to love or to be loved, as if all her cares were to be concentrated in sweeping carpets, making beds, cleaning, ironing and responding to a thousand daily tugs at the bell, as if it were her sole duty to waste existence in ministering to the wants and comfort of others, and be but a bank herself.

But even he could go on:

> Before you retire to rest lock the doors with your own hand, and deposit the keys upon your toilet table, otherwise, while enjoying the blessings of respose above you may not know what junketings are going on below. Precaution is all the more necessary when the maid's sleeping-room is remote from yours. Satan is never busier than at night; under its dark shadow he leads thousands to destruction. (16)

Young girls thus systematically deprived as far as possible of all contact with men of their own age and class were in a situation of misery in which they might easily fall for the blandishments of any male in the house. On the other hand they were totally dependent on the goodwill of the mistress of the house: if a servant became pregnant, or even if she made allegations about any man in the family, she was virtually certain to be dismissed without a reference and become unemployable. This was why so many prostitutes were former domestic servants: for example four-fifths of the applications to the Edinburgh Magdalene Institute between 1855 and 1860 had once been domesti servants. (17)

Prostitutes, however, were an extremely small percentage of the total number of domestic servants, and servants were a very large percentage of total females in employment. It is easy to be misled. We cannot tell how large a proportion of servants were seduced by their employers' families, or how many middle-class men got their extramarital experience in this way. An investigation by the Registrar General in 1883 showed that almost half Scottish illegitimate births were to 'domestic servants' — but this includes very large numbers in rural areas sleeping in farm kitchens and elsewhere under no supervision at all (see p. 66), so one certainly cannot assume the majority of fathers were middle-class. Recent research on domestic servants in Edinburgh around 1870 suggests that while the 'general' servants of Newington in artisan or petty bourgeois households had at least as many bastards as women in other occupational groups, the 'higher' servants of the commercial or professional middle-class families living in St. Andrew's Parish in the New Town had appreciably fewer: the case is not quite conclusive, because in the middle-class parish there might have been more pressure on the respectable servant to leave the area and have her illegitimate child elsewhere. Perhaps, in any case, conditions changed over time. The oral history evidence available at Essex University from interviews with Scots brought up before 1918 suggests that by the early twentieth-century domestic servants were no longer cooped up in the way they had been, that they then had plenty of opportunities to meet young men of their own class, and that risk of seduction by the middle-class males of the household was not a prominent feature of their lives. (18) There was also, we must remember, an element of danger to the middle-class man if his adventure was discovered, in the sense that familial relations between the sexes in a respectable household would be unbearably strained if a brother or a son (let alone a husband) was known to be a fornicator. The evidence is inconclusive, but on the principle that it is a foolish bird that fouls its own nest, we may perhaps assume that the majority of middle-class sexual adventures were paid for, and took place outside the home.

Prostitutes were of many kinds, and commentators ranged them on a scale that varied roughly with the health, youth and beauty of the girls. At the one extreme was the kept mistress of the rich man maintained on private premises: at the other was the poor creature raddled with disease in a low-class brothel visited by soldiers. Virgins were the monopoly of the rich, a fact probably better explained by fetishism than by the much higher probability of their freedom from disease. (19) Child prostitution existed: Dr. Tait knew of patients admitted to the Lock Hospital suffering from venereal disease at the age of nine and ten. The majority of prostitutes were in the later teens. Tait examined the records of 1000 cases admitted to the Lock Hospital from 1835 to about 1840. The age breakdown of the prostitutes was as follows:

Under 15	4.2%
15 - 20	66.2
20 - 25	19.9
25 - 30	6.9
30 - 35	1.6
35 - 40	0.6
Over 40	0.6

But he qualified these figures with the comment that 'the above gives a very inadequate representation of the extent to which juvenile prostitution prevails, as the venereal disease amongst girls from ten to fifteen is much more common than the records of the Lock Hospital would indicate'. (20)

The background from which the girls came was mixed. Former domestic servants were a very large category: so, too, were ill-paid or sweated female workers (seamstresses, milliners, tambourers, Dundee mill-workers and the like). Shetland and Highland servants were said by Tait to be more prone to take to prostitution than others: perhaps they were vulnerable to seduction because they had least experience of the irresponsible urban male who could not be held accountable for his actions by social pressure, as a man would have been in the communities from which they came (see below pp. 76-78). The squalor in which prostitutes lived was often terrible, as, frequently, was the speed of their descent from the best paid type of prostitution to the lowest categories and the grave. Tait believed that 'perhaps not less than a fifth or a sixth part of all who have embraced a life of prostitution die annually'. (22)

Of the descriptions of Edinburgh brothels that survive few are as telling as that of Isabella Bird, a noted explorer who came to the High Street in the same spirit as she had visited Arctic Canada. After describing a room about twelve feet square, divided by rotten partitions, the floor heaped with ashes from the grate and the only furniture a bedstead with a straw mattress, a table and a stool, she continued:

> A girl about eighteen, very poorly dressed, was sitting on the stool; two others, older and very much undressed, were sitting on the floor, and the three were eating, in a most swinish fashion, out of a large black pot containing fish. I have shared a similar meal in a similar primitive fashion in an Indian wigwam in Hudson's Bay Territory but there the women who worshipped the Great Spirit were modest in their dress and manner and looked *human* which these 'Christian' young women did not. (23)

One fundamental distinction which commentators made was between the 'sly prostitute', or part-timer, and the professional. It was the latter whose numbers were more susceptible to economic pressure, and increased whenever the trade cycle threw numbers of millhands out of work or when the price for sweated labour sank desperately below subsistence. The numbers of prostitutes were in any case extremely hard to calculate. Tait in 1842 believed that in Edinburgh there were about 800 whole-time prostitutes, of whom a quarter were living privately and the remainder in about 200 public brothels (mainly in the Old Town): in addition, he thought there were almost 1200 sly prostitutes many of whom operated from 'houses of assignation' where a room could be hired and no questions asked. In Glasgow, which he knew only from report, 'the total number of females ascertained by the police to frequent houses of bad fame within the Royalty is 1475': others put the figure of prostitutes in Glasgow in the same year at 1600 'harlots' or at 1800 harlots plus 450 'mistresses', in 450 brothels: yet another estimate speaks of 1500 in brothels in 1842, together with another 2000 sly prostitutes in the city. (24) Surveying the two cities in 1870, William Logan thought that changes in the law had reduced the numbers to about 85 known brothels in Edinburgh, with a similar fall in Glasgow: 'the business is conducted with less ostentation and attractiveness to the outside world'. In Dundee, he believed there were two dozen brothels and at least 274 prostitutes. (25) Most of these latter figures seem to relate to professionals.

Who were the customers of the prostitutes? Certainly they were all sorts and conditions of men, not just the middle class. The comparatively shameless behaviour of the aristocracy at one end of the social spectrum and the association of soldiers and seamen with harlots at the other we have already noted. Some observers classified brothels into first, second and third class, like railway carriages. William Logan, whose experience of the problem lay mainly in Glasgow, was one of these. First-class brothels, he said, were supported by 'noblemen, wealthy merchants, military officers, sea captains and *gentlemen* who move in the higher circles of society.' Second-class brothels 'are chiefly supported by men in business, clerks, warehousemen, shopmen, etc.', and by many medical students and some theological students. Third-class houses 'are chiefly frequented by persons from the country, mechanics, apprentices, soldiers and sailors ...'. (26) Dr. Tait in Edinburgh gave a rather similar picture; on the one hand he stressed the upper and middle class importance in the market:

In summer, for example, there are a third part fewer (prostitutes) than in winter; and in autumn the number is still further diminished. During these seasons, the decrease may be proportioned to the decrease of the wealthier portion of the community who then seek a residence in the country, and to the diminished number of students at the University. (27)

On the other hand he drew attention to dancing schools and dancing parties 'of a particularly base description' which ended in the couples going to a house of assignation: 'the individuals who frequent them ... consist of sewing-girls, sly prostitutes, and shop and trades' lads'. (28) John Dunlop, too, drew attention to the working-class brothel goers, and described the High Street prostitutes as 'the chief relievers of the pockets of the operatives on pay night'. (29) In Stranraer, one of the few country towns with a problem of prostitution, the customers were Irish navvies. (30)

Nevertheless, it is evident that middle-class observers were worried by the numbers of their own kind who were tempted inside. No-one, of course, knows how many: Tait spoke of 'a crime which ... ruins and depraves the character of perhaps a fourth part of the rising population', but it can only have been a guess. He isolated as particularly at risk, 'lads who come from the country to learn businesses in town, or to receive a College education', young men with too much wealth for their discretion, and those who 'pursue the paths of literature and science':

In order to relieve the dull hours of study, they resort for recreation to the tavern and the brothel, till the habit becomes inveterate and irresistable. The young lawyer, physician, and general student, view this kind of relaxation as indispensable for their health ... It is painful to say it, yet a desire for the truth urges to the declaration that the pulpit is not even exempted from the inroads and consequences of these habits.' (31)

The reference to ministers echoes a modern Edinburgh tradition that the brothels of Rose Street were never so busy as in the week of the General Assembly. It was doubtless a calumny in recent times, but it can be traced back in documentary form at least to 1814 when a magistrate in the capital wrote to his business partners that 'I have the Police Court at present, and I will be needed very much to keep the whores and Ministers in order during the sitting of the Assemblies'. (32)

It was only too likely that the clergy were not immune from the frailties of the flesh which afflicted their other middle-class colleagues. The habit of depending on prostitution was formed among students living outwith parental control who were obliged both to delay marriage until their training was complete and to eschew all overtly sexual contacts (however partial) with girls of their own class. It put them in a situation from which not all would have the strength of character to escape unscathed.

The Working Class: the Pattern of Bastardy

The possibility that at least some sections of the working class might in important respects have different habits of sexual behaviour from those of the middle-class which we have attempted to describe first became a matter of public debate following the coming of civil registration in 1855, and the subsequent publication of the illegitimacy ratio (i.e. the proportion of illegitimate births to total births: the illegitimacy fertility *rate,* the number of illegitimate births per 1000 unmarried women of childbearing age, was not calculated by the early Scottish Registrar Generals). Most commentators before then, while being aware of 'improvident marriages' and even 'illicit unions' among the working class, seemed to associate them with industrialisation, and contrasted them with older peasant virtues of 'virtuous attachment' and long thrifty patience before the wedding. (33)

To understand the evidence of the sexual *mores* of the working class it is first necessary to follow the debate on illegitimacy. The first publication of the Registrar General to deal with illegitimacy appeared in 1858 and contradicted such early and complacent preconceptions: not only did Scotland appear to have an exceptionally high percentage of her children born before marriage, but the worst areas were the counties of the north-east and the south-west Lowlands where rural virtues might be expected to be deeply ingrained. The reaction in some quarters bordered on the hysterical: 'the inhabitants of Banffshire may clothe themselves in sackcloth, for there is no spot on the broad expanse of Europe so steeped in impurity', exclaimed one local moralist. (34) Even sober men close to the Registrar General's office gave themselves over to beating of the breast:

> let us freely but sorrowfully acknowledge that for drunkenness and illegitimacy (our native land) maintains an unenviable notoriety among the kingdoms of Europe. If Scotland is still to be regarded as entitled to the boasted character of being 'the most religious country in the world' it is to be feared that her *head* and *heart* do not go harmoniously together, and that the *doctrines* of the national faith are not generally illustrated by *practice* .... During the two years 1858-59 the average number of illegitimate births registered in Scotland amounted, as nearly as possible to 9 per cent (8.9), or one illegitimate child in every eleven births .... It appears that in England, Belgium, Norway and Sweden, the illegitimate births constitute only about 6.6 per cent; in France and Prussia 7.1 per cent; in Denmark 9.3 per cent; in Hanover 9.8 per cent; and in Austria 11.3 per cent. In other words, in six of these nine kingdoms, the percentage is very considerably lower than in Scotland, in two of them it is nearly the same, while only in one — and that Austria — does it decidedly exceed the Scottish ratio. (35)

Much of this alarm about Scotland's position in the international league table was groundless: countries with a lower bastardy rate, including England, turned out to have been substantially under-registering their births, and when adjustments were made to their figures Scotland appeared in a more favourable light. By 1889, out of 17 countries in Europe, Austria still had the highest illegitimacy ratio: Scotland was tenth and England fourteenth. (36) By 1900, using the alternative measurement of the illegitimate fertility rate, a map demonstrating variations of this rate in 700 European regions of county or province size shows all of England and most of Scotland in the bottom third of this scale; while the north-east and the south-west of the Lowlands are still the worst, and alone of the British regions fall into the middle third of the scale, they pale into insignificance before the practices of northern France, much of Germany, Scandinavia, Central and Eastern Europe. (37)

Nevertheless, Scottish illegitimacy statistics did show two striking features. One was that the proportion of illegitimate births to total births was higher in the countryside than in the towns, instead of being very much lower as it was in many European countries. The other was the wide variety of regional experience, especially of rural areas. In the 1860s and 1870s, with the national average running at 9.3 per cent of total births illegitimate, it was rare for Ross and Cromarty, for example, to touch 5 per cent, and for Orkney and Shetland to reach 6 per cent: but Banff, Aberdeenshire, Moray and Kincardine in one corner of Scotland, and Wigtown, Kirkcudbright and Dumfriesshire in the other, seldom had less than 14 to 18 per cent of their total births illegitimate.

The table below demonstrates some of these points, and also the convergence of most areas towards the Scottish national average in the years after the First World War. (38) Wigtownshire is the main exception to this rule:

	1861/5	1871/5	1881/5	1891/5	1901/5	1911/5	1921/5
Banff	16.62	16.53	13.62	13.70	12.61	13.44	12.55
Berwick	10.75	10.60	10.57	10.33	9.89	10.28	8.39
E. Lothian	9.60	8.71	7.76	6.99	6.00	7.08	6.30
Inverness	7.96	8.40	7.59	7.42	7.26	8.74	7.89
Orkney	5.56	5.90	6.50	6.85	5.24	6.82	6.79
Perth	10.87	10.18	9.65	9.12	6.67	9.61	8.85
Ross & Cromarty	4.24	4.57	4.78	4.79	4.30	7.10	5.79
Wigtown	15.65	15.79	16.25	15.49	13.18	15.71	15.62
Zetland	4.36	4.57	5.16	4.33	4.02	5.78	6.48
Scotland (total)	9.79	9.09	8.27	7.41	6.50	7.21	6.78

It was these self-evident contrasts, combined with the feeling of national disgrace which was not easily dissipated, that gave rise to a lengthy discussion of the causes of illegitimacy, and ultimately, of the sexual *mores* of the Scottish working class — or, rather, mainly of its rural component. It began as an early example of a fruitful dialogue between moralists, mainly represented by the churches, and statistical experts in the Registrar General's Office.

Some of the alleged causes were easy to refute. Those who believed bastardy was correlated with illiteracy and could be cured by education were confounded by the Registrar General's demonstration that the least literate Highland counties (like Ross and Cromarty) had the lowest proportion of illegitimate births, while in Banff, Aberdeenshire and Dumfriesshire over 95 per cent of the men and between 85 and

95 per cent of the women were able to sign their names. (39) Those who attributed it all to drink were confounded to be told that in Banffshire almost all the illegitimacy occurred in the agricultural community and virtually none among the fishermen, although 'our country labourers and small farmers are as free from intemperance as our fishermen are from abstinence or even moderation'. (40) The justice of this observation is suggested by a glance at the illegitimacy statistics of Banffshire, 1861-65: in the deeply rural inland parishes of Inveravon with Auchbrek, Tomintoul and Kirkmichael, out of 553 births, 107 were illegitimate (19 per cent), while in the fishing and rural parishes of Cullen and Seafield, out of 639 births only 69 were illegitimate (11 per cent). (41) Other observers attributed the black record of the north-east to orgies between farm servants at the annual hiring-markets, and with some reason as it was possible to prove that the peaks of illegitimate births in Banffshire came nine months after the fairs: but hiring-markets no less demonstrably Bacchanalian occurred throughout the rural lowlands, even in counties with half the bastardy rate of Banff. (42) In the south-east of Scotland some attributed it to the bondager system, whereby a hind, or ploughman, was obliged to provide an able-bodied female to work alongside him at his job, and if he did not have a wife or daughter might hire any strong girl and share his working life, at least, with her: but the bondager system did not exist in the north-east. (43) Some attributed it just to a local excess of females in the population, but in ostensibly virtuous Orkney and Sutherland the surplus was far greater than it was in Banff, Kincardine and Aberdeenshire. (44) Some again attributed it to the evident absence of prostitution in rural areas, but the Registrar-General was able to show that in the rural parts of Midlothian and Lanarkshire, with no prostitutes, the illegitimacy rate was for once actually lower than in Edinburgh and Glasgow where they swarmed. And one county that did seem to have a great deal of prostitution for a rural area, Wigtownshire, shared a record in high illegitimacy with Banffshire, where prostitution was almost unknown. (45)

Others invoked race, past religious traditions and even climate, but these were even harder to sustain. How could rainfall be a factor, when Wigtown and Ross shared two of the wettest climates in Scotland and Banff had one of the driest? (46) It was argued that perhaps the north-east had not experienced the Reformation in a sufficiently presbyterian form and so was lacking in moral fibre: but the south-west was just as bad for bastardy, and had held the very hearth-stones of the Covenanters. (4' Some, believing that the Irish and the Highlanders shared a justifiable reputation for chastity, attributed this to a lack of natural forces among the Celts. But others objected on the grounds of the Welsh: 'the laxity of morals among the female peasantry of Wales is unhappily notorious'. (48) And what about Irish navvies, never distinguished in the local traditions of the railway age for their continence or lack of natural forces in the parishes through which they passed? And how could this theory account for the Vikings of Orkney and Shetland, with almost as few bastards as the Celts of Ross and Cromarty? It was not easy for Victorians to account for such anomalies: it is not very easy for us.

More sophisticated and interesting were the arguments that hinged on the character of rural housing and the traditions of agricultural work. The simplest of these was the notion that the one-roomed house, so common in Scotland, made it impossible to observe the decencies: a family sleeping in the same room with or withou lodgers from other people's families, could not stay in ignorance for long of the facts of one another's lives. This, as the Society for the Promotion of Social Morality said, was 'a state of things very much fitted to destroy delicacy of feeling'. (49) Equally seriously, it destroyed the possibility of a personal religious life. As James Begg, the Free Kirk leader who drove his church into an interest in housing reform, put it in 1864:

> Jesus says to his people 'When thou prayest, enter into thy closet and shut thy door'. This evidently supposes a state of things to exist in regard to the dwellings of the people which in many districts of Scotland is not at present realized. (50)

Unfortunately for the argument that this led to moral depravity, the Registrar General and others were able to show that the counties with the greatest proportion of one-roomed houses were by no means those with the highest rates of illegitimacy. Industrial areas with much the worst record of bad and overcrowded housing were not worst in respect of illegitimacy rates. (51)

An object of still stronger attack from the churches was the bothy system. Bothies were communal sleeping quarters for unmarried farm servants, often (though certainly not invariably) mere comfortless sheds rigged out with a row of beds, some straw, and the most meagre cooking and sanitary facilities. Most bothies were for males only; some (especially in the Lothians) were for females only; a few (notably in Caithness) were mixed. The objections to the last class were voiced by the Rev. Charles Thomson of Wick:

> Deeds of shame are shamelessly committed in those dens of darkness ... he could not tell the Presbytery certain facts he knew regarding these barns, but he might indicate by stating that it was not only women that congregated there, and that it was a 'shame even to speak of those things that are done of them in secret'. (52)

But even in more ordinary circumstances the church found much to object to in bothies. There was the total absence of family life: 'this divine basis of social morality has been swept away'. (53) There was the presence of quite young boys of thirteen, fourteen and fifteen under no supervision except from older farm hands. There was the almost complete absence of paternal interest in the life of the bothymen by the farmer, in contrast to the good old days when the gudeman had them all under his eye as they ate together round the farm table. This led to the 'inveterate habit' among farm workers of 'wandering about at night, visiting either distant acquaintances, or it may be relations, or what, it is to be feared is of still worse tendency, fulfilling assignations made with women'. All this made them exhausted next day 'when so fatigued they become listless at work, and when they think they are unobserved, will throw themselves down on the ground to sleep whilst their horses are made to hang upon their legs at the risk of catching cold'. (54) In short, the bothy system let young men loose 'at the very age when the impetuosity of youth abounds', and the consequences were both morally and economically disastrous. (56).

Unfortunately the Registrar General once again expressed scepticism about cause and effect. Though the bothy system might well help to explain why Caithness had a higher illegitimacy rate than Sutherland to the south and Orkney to the north (where the system did not exist), it could not account for the situation in the main bulk of the eastern Lowlands. Bothies went with large farms that had a big labour-force, and were especially characteristic of Perth, Angus and Fife, in all of which the illegitimacy rates tended below the national average, although above the level of the Highland zone. Banff, on the other hand, was a county of small farms (an average of 64 acres, compared to 110 acres in Fife and 219 acres in East Lothian): therefore it had comparatively few bothies. (56) How could the bothy system be to blame?

James Begg, in an incensed reply to this criticism, began to shift the emphasis of the argument from the buildings themselves to the whole problem of the social context of the worker living away from home under circumstances where there was no alternative paternal care from the farmer. It may be, he said, that bothies as such are relatively scarce in the north-east, but the same iniquitous consequences can arise even in small and medium-sized farms where young farm servants of both sexes leave their own family circle and are housed in kitchens and attics of the farmhouse and where the employer remains totally uninterested in and alienated from his men. Then the servants would indulge in licentious conversation, wander around like beasts at night into the girls' bedrooms, and indulge in all manner of excesses. The only remedy must be a return to the old paternalism, and the construction of multi-roomed cottages where bachelor farm hands could be boarded out if necessary in a decently accommodated family of labourers. (57) This was a line with which many found themselves in agreement. Those who knew Banffshire and the other north-eastern counties most intimately began to claim that the root of its peculiarly high illegitimacy rate lay here in the scarcity of accommodation for married farm servants. (58) There were hardly any cottages attached to the farms. Even married horsemen often had to lodge in a room in the farm or in an outhouse, while their wives and children lived in the nearest town or village some miles away: bachelors and unmarried farm girls almost always did so, and there was abundant employment for the latter in and around the farm. This was the 'chaumer' system: the main difference in social terms between it and the bothy was that the farmhand ate and relaxed in the kitchen with the women instead of with other men in the bothy: there was no more social control in other directions but there was more occasion for social intercourse between the sexes. According to the commentators a tradition of incontinence and illegitimacy grew up because marriages were delayed in this environment. Dr. Gerrard of Banff reported how he had discussed the matter with many fathers of illegitimate children in the rural community.

> The great regret of these men had been that, when the first offence occurred they had not the means of making the proper amends by marrying and sheltering the mother and child in a dwelling of their own: nay more they needed no hint to assure me that, if houses could have been readily had, they would in every probability have married early and their children would have been 'born in wedlock'. (59)

Such housing shortages, they said, did not occur among the rural workers in other Lowland east-coast counties to anything like the same degree. An area like the Merse of Berwickshire employed more farm servants per farm, but there were plenty of cottages to which a worker could move when he got married, and, indeed, the bondager system of the Borders might positively encourage marriage by the necessity for a ploughman to find a helpmeet at work. (60)

It was an attractive theory, and it was evidently not directly contradicted by the Registrar General. Nevertheless, it was quite wrong to assume that the social conditions of the 'chaumer' system led to late marriage. The table below shows how, in the late nineteenth century, some of the rural counties married. In the first three, Orkney, Shetland, Ross and Cromarty, marriage for both sexes was distinctly later than for the remainder — but these had very low illegitimacy ratios. In Banff, men married just a little later than in East Lothian or Berwickshire — but women tended to marry just a little earlier. In Wigtownshire, with illegitimacy rates like those of Banff, the mean age of marriage for men was much like Banff, for women much like Berwickshire.

Mean Age of Marriage in Selected Scottish Counties, 1861-1901. (61)

		1861	1871	1881	1891	1901
Orkney	M	30.17	30.27	30.59	31.28	30.91
	F	27.08	26.68	26.94	26.98	27.96
Shetland	M	29.30	30.18	29.76	31.29	31.51
	F	27.05	27.64	27.30	27.97	29.00
Ross & Cromarty	M	30.85	31.38	31.44	31.46	32.11
	F	26.21	27.00	26.58	27.31	27.71
Banff	M	29.08	29.44	29.05	29.41	29.48
	F	25.89	25.77	25.99	26.30	26.53
E. Lothian	M	28.55	27.97	28.22	28.26	28.33
	F	26.26	26.09	25.76	26.07	26.42
Berwickshire	M	28.79	28.58	28.99	28.24	29.06
	F	26.21	26.18	26.40	26.25	26.90
Wigtownshire	M	20.08	29.51	28.62	29.38	29.25
	F	25.85	26.42	26.06	26.51	26.03

It was probably perfectly correct to associate the high illegitimacy figures of the north-east with the absence of familial control, the 'chaumer' system, and the availability of jobs for unmarried female labour whether with children or not — but the association with late marriage was not borne out by the facts.

The Working Class: Dr. Strachan and the pattern of courtship

Up to a point, then, the foregoing was accepted at the time as a satisfactory explanation of the pattern of bastardy in different regions, yet even without raising the reality of the late age of marriage, it begged one very large question. It seemed to explain why there were more illegitimate children in Banff than in Berwickshire, but why could not the men and women of Banff contain their lusts until they had a house? The middle-classes, too, often had to delay marriage until they could buy a house and keep their wives 'in the manner to which they had been accustomed', and condemnation of the early and 'improvident' marriage was a cliché of popular moralists. But in the middle-class society, although many men were unchaste, delayed marriages manifestly did not issue in a great crop of bastards borne by their girlfriends. Was it possible that the working class as a whole had completely different sexual conventions with respect to their women? The matter was hinted at more than once in the debate on illegitimacy, but the most careful investigations and the most explicit statements were made by Dr. J.M. Strachan of Dollar in a series of articles in *The Scotsman* for 1870. (62) He based his investigation on a search of the marriage and birth registers, on his own experience as a G.P. and on consultation with his medical friends. Within limits, his findings are confirmed by what other commentators wrote, before and afterwards, in less systematic terms.

Strachan began from a suspicion that ante-nuptial pregnancies were the rule rather than the exception in certain sectors of society. He examined 1569 marriages in thirteen rural parishes in different parts of Scotland over the years 1855-1869. Of these 1310 could be traced by the continuing residence of the parties, and in 493 cases, 'or rather more than a third', a child was born and registered within six months of the wedding. In all but seven cases the parents were working class. He also looked at 1206 illegitimate births in the thirteen parishes: again, in all but nineteen cases, the mother was working class. Most of the exceptions were daughters of small farmers 'who in their manners and customs resemble the working class'.

Perhaps the middle and upper classes were merely better at concealment? He thought not: 'I have conversed on this subject with a great many medical men of large experience and have only heard of three or four cases of illegitimate births, and none of a child being born within six months after marriage where the mother belonged to the middle or upper classes'. Perhaps the immorality of working-class women was caused by upper-class men? The evidence did not bear it out. In the statistics of Edinburgh maternity hospital, out of 337 cases of illegitimacy, only in seven were the fathers middle-class: in his own thirteen rural parishes out of 813 cases of illegitimacy (where the father was known) in 780 the fathers were working men, in 28 they were farmers, and only in five did they belong to any other class.

Evidence from other sources bears out the contention that illegitimacy was overwhelmingly restricted to working-class girls. James Valentine, in a paper on illegitimacy in Aberdeen covering the years 1855 to 1859, found that well over half the mothers were domestic servants or factory operatives and that almost all the rest were also working class: 'scarcely a case occurs where the mother moves in the middle or upper ranks of society'. (63) In 1883 the Registrar General for Scotland tabulated the occupations of 10,000 mothers of illegitimate children known from the records of civil registration and drawn from all parts of the country. 47 per cent were domestic servants, 24 per cent were factory girls, 10 per cent were farm girls (the line between them and domestic servants in rural areas must be very arbitrary), 6 per cent were seamstresses, 8 per cent were described as 'no occupation, chiefly daughters of working men', 4 per cent were described as 'no information, chiefly widows', and 0.5 per cent were the daughters of professional men. (64)

It is always more difficult to get evidence on paternity, but the Historical Demography Unit at Edinburgh looked at 679 illegitimate births in selected areas of Scotland for 1861: in nearly a quarter the father was known and his occupation given — the proportion of known fathers varied from 38 per cent in Orkney, 36 per cent in Lewis and Harris, and 34 per cent in Banff, to 22 per cent in Shetland, 15 per cent in East Lothian and only 10 per cent in Wigtown. The occupation of these fathers was overwhelmingly working class. One landed proprietor was mentioned, two farm managers and a few farmers and their sons. Six out of nine known fathers in Shetland were fishermen, but in Orkney the fathers were more diverse. In Wigtownshire, Banff and East Lothian farm servants accounted for between half and three-quarters of known fathers. (65) No doubt middle-class men had an advantage when it came to concealing paternity, and they may be better represented in the three-quarters of the cases where the father was not disclosed.

Dr. Strachan then proceeded in his articles to ask why there was more illegitimacy in the country than in the towns. He suggested it was because there was a higher proportion of middle-class in urban than in rural areas, and also because 'in towns and manufacturing districts a large proportion of the working men consists of skilled artisans whose position and whose feelings and manners approximate to the class above them'. This observation, if true, is of interest in relation to the concept of a labour aristocracy — i.e. that there existed a distinct stratum of respectable and highly paid workers who accepted the values and aped the outlook of those above them in society. In this case they would be motivated to keep their daughters more closely than other working men, but not necessarily to impose the same sanctions on their sons if they visited brothels. Plainly there were many working-class visitors in the 'third-class brothels', and from the frequency with which Tait, for example, refers to apprentices or shop workers, these customers included many in the categories of artisan and white collared workers which are associated with middle-class aspirations. (66) Whether such groups were dominant it is impossible to say. There may also be some confusion between the kind of brothel where you purchased a prostitute's services and one which was a 'house of assignment' where you simply paid for a room and, perhaps, brought your own girl. In an urban environment without barns and haystacks the latter may have had a function that had nothing to do with prostitution. Much courtship in town and country alike took place out of doors in any case — on the traditional walk where men and girls became better acquainted — but if you wanted to carry things further town life must have presented some problems.

There are, however, various other considerations in the urban situation. Firstly, there were apparently wide differences between one town and another. James Valentine illustrated this for the eight principal towns in 1858, showing that the percentage of illegitimate births in total births in Aberdeen was three times as high as it was in Greenock, with Dundee, Perth, Paisley, Edinburgh, Glasgow and Leith (in that order) coming between. He was inclined to link high urban illegitimacy with a low rate of marriage and a large excess of females together with the influence of the morals of the surrounding countryside. (67) The substance of his argument largely disappears, however, if one corrects the figures to take account of the number of women at risk: cities with a large proportion of unmarried female workers aged 15-49 had more bastards mainly because there were more girls to have them, not because the girls were more 'immoral'. More real were the differences between towns (as a group), and the countryside, demonstrating appreciably lower illegitimacy rates in the urban population. There were no doubt many reasons for this. Towns often had large Irish communities, whose morals (at least those of the girls) were often very different from those of the Scots (see below p. 73). Again, in addition to the higher proportion of middle-class people, and of workers voluntarily imitating the middle-class in a 'labour aristocrat' sense, there was a higher proportion of girls controlled by the middle classes as domestic servants in their households than would be the case in rural areas: assuming that this control was more often successful than otherwise, it could be said to enforce 'respectable' behaviour. Thus in towns the sexual *mores* of working-class groups were probably very various, and it would be impossible to talk of one code of proletarian morality for the urban population as a whole.

Dr. Strachan, having disposed of the towns to his satisfaction, then asked why there were substantial differences between the Highlands and the Lowlands. He examined in depth the records of four Ross-shire parishes and four parishes in Aberdeenshire and Banff and found that in the Highland ones only five per cent of working class births were illegitimate, and in only fifteen per cent of working class marriages did a child come within six months, whereas in the Lowland ones twenty-four per cent of working-class births were illegitimate and in sixty-five per cent of working-class marriages a child came within six months. He attributed this to the superior moral tone of the Highlanders who simply did not permit their daughters to misbehave in the same way as the Lowlanders. This is one of the weaker parts of his argument, but we must defer criticism of it for the moment. The main point is the implication that the differences in the illegitimacy ratios in different parts of the rural Lowlands — e.g. between Banff and East Lothian — were no proof at all of higher standards of female virtue in one part of the Lowlands as compared to another.

It was implicit in Strachan's argument that ante-nuptial pregnancies were normal in at least the rural Lowland working class. This receives a good deal of supporting evidence from others who knew the south of Scotland. Thus one minister asked two colleagues with parishes in rural Lanarkshire if they ever performed the marriage service for women who were also pregnant:

One replied, Oh yes, frequently. Well, I said, think and tell me when you did it last. On reflecting he answered, I really do not remember when I last married a young woman who was not in the family way. The other minister at once replied, No, I seldom, if indeed ever, perform the service where it should not have been performed long before'. (68)

Another said it was so important for border hinds to have a family to work alongside them that 'it is very usual for a couple to cohabit in order to ascertain whether the woman is likely to prove fruitful'. (69) Two sheriff-substitutes spoke in similar terms of the peasant morality of Berwickshire and Roxburghshire: 'the disclosures in filiation cases in my court exhibit a condition of unbridled licence as to a large extent the rule of life among the labouring class.' (70)

The evidence from the south-west in particular, however, suggests something different from (or rather, perhaps, additional to) norms of cohabitation with a 'steady' girl and pregnancy followed by marriage. Several observers noted that illegitimacy there seemed often to be hereditary:

Illegitimacy (is not) a true gauge of general impurity. My observations lead me to the conclusion that this is to a very large extent a hereditary sin. It can be traced through certain families. Very often a woman may have three or four illegitimate children, and the average is consequently raised. A frequent custom prevails of letting cottages to unattached women to procure field labour. These are mostly women who have been obliged to leave domestic service with illegitimate children and, I observe, they have an abandoned attitude and are, I fear, too often a temptation to young men in the district. (71)

Another commentator had analysed the parish of Monigaff in Wigtownshire, where between 1880 and 1893, out of 488 births 42 had been illegitimate, and two-thirds of those came from nine families.

Dr. Strachan next asked himself what might be the social causes and customs that would permit so high a rate of ante-nuptial pregnancies and illegitimacies in the rural working class. He listed five causes that tended to create a 'low tone of feeling regarding female purity' in the working-class. Three of them were overcrowding, the prevalence of swearing, and the 'coarse, indelicate freedoms' which prevailed between men and women in their everyday contacts at work and elsewhere. The other two were more interesting. One was the absence of any stigma on a girl who had slept with a man before marriage: 'previous unchasteness even with another individual, does not form a very serious bar to marriage'.

Here again Strachan was supported by a number of other observers, before and after he wrote, who also stressed that bastardy itself was not regarded as any kind of sin. In remarks intended to apply to the whole of the eastern Lowlands one reporter to the Royal Commission on the Employment of Women and Children in Agriculture stressed that the crimes of abortion and infanticide were unknown in the countryside, for 'there is indeed no pressure on the woman to commit any crime in order to conceal her lapse from virtue, as amongst her own class there is no feeling of indignation aroused in consequence of what they would call her "misfortune" '. (73) Another said, speaking of Roxburghshire, 'the stain of bastardy is little felt and forms no serious impediment to success in life'. (74) The Committee on Religion and Morals of the Free Church said 'the people hardly regard it as a sin. They seem to think that marriage covers all'. (75) William Cramond, in his remarkable pamphlet *Illegitimacy in Banffshire* written eighteen years after Strachan's articles, was able to illustrate these attitudes in the north-east by numerous quotations from replies he had received to a circular asking for views on the causes of local immorality.

Notwithstanding all our preaching and teaching this sin is not at all seen in its true light, in fact it is thought very little of — scarcely thought a sin at all, just a mistake, rather annoying and hard when the father does not take with the child and pay for it, but when he does it is not much better. There is no just sense of the soul-polluting, unmanly, unwomanly nature of the sin. — Parish Minister.

A woman once said to me with reference to her erring daughter, 'It was not so bad as if she had taken twopence that was not her own.' That woman was a fair type of the average church member in this district, neither better nor worse. — Free Church Minister.

In one instance it was put down to the 'will of the Almighty', a fatalistic idea which I fear is not so uncommon as one might think. — Parish Minister.

I have heard many a mother of this kind say, 'It's nae sae bad as steeling, or deein' awa' wi' the puir craters'. — A Bank Official.

A mother excuses her fallen daughter by saying, 'Puir thing, its a misfortune, but she'll get ower it', and the neighbours chime in and add 'It wad hae been waur if she had ta'en anything'. — Clergyman.

The only thing they seem to feel is if the father does not acknowledge the child. A woman who had five illegitimate children said to me that her mother said she was just the one to have them, as she always got a father.(76)

That these attitudes were not restricted to the north-east is made abundantly clear by the previous evidence, yet they remained very prevalent in that region. Lady Aberdeen founded a Haddo House Association for the promotion of purity in young female workers: it was renamed in 1881, with charming pre-Freudian innocence, the Onward and Upward Association. (77) Despite its efforts, the Free Church General Assembly was told in 1897 that still in Aberdeenshire 'breaches of chastity are taken very lightly'. (78)

Next, and most importantly, Strachan attributed working-class unchastity to distinctive habits of courtship which he plainly regarded as extraordinary, uncouth and detestable. It is, he said 'especially difficult to make the two classes understand the immense difference that exists between them. Working men will not believe that it is possible to court a wife without stolen interviews, with the lady sitting on the gentleman's knee, or enfolded in his arms, for hours in the dark; and they are totally incapable of conceiving that a kind look or a gentle pressure of the hand will yield delight a thousand times more exquisite than the coarser feelings in which they themselves indulge'. He explained to his middle-class readers how it was unusual for working-class lovers to meet in public: the ordinary thing was to meet after bedtime, at the back of a haystack or in a barn or an outhouse, or 'especially in the case of servant maids', in the girl's bedroom. Each meeting lasts for two or three hours, and is repeated weekly. A girl may 'pride herself on the number of such lovers she may have', and a boy 'not think it wrong to visit different girls after this fashion': as for the parents 'not even the most particular thinks there is anything wrong in this manner of courtship'. There was not, he was careful to stress, necessarily any immorality arising immediately from this: 'The upper classes would be astonished if they knew how long such visits were continued without a fall from virtue. In many cases they are so continued for years. In some ... no fall from virtue takes place'. In other words there was often heavy petting but not intercourse. But in too many cases, by this activity the 'outworks are dismantled, the citadel (left) defenceless', and 'they learn, when it was too late, what women can never learn too early or impress too strongly on their minds — that a lover's encroachments, to be repelled successfully, must be repelled and negatived at the very outset'. Hence the high rates of illegitimacy and ante-nuptial pregnancy.

This description of working-class courtship fitted in exactly with what other writers had written in a more sensationalised way about the midnight prowling of the bothymen and other undisciplined rural labourers, and, as Strachan himself pointed out, it fitted in with the traditional picture of peasant love 'among the rigs o' barley' that came down from Burns. The traditional so-called 'Bothy Ballads' of the Lowland farm-servant are full of descriptions of midnight visiting by bands of men or individuals. It was not really anything new and decadent: as an old peasant told William Cramond almost two decades later, it was 'bred i' the bane'. (79)

Despite this corroboration, however, it is difficult to believe that Strachan's account told the complete story of Scottish courtship. The evidence of oral history from the early twentieth century stresses rather that young people first met at dances or social gatherings of the family or community, and became closer acquainted first on walks or visits to the theatre and music hall (in late Edwardian times, the cinema). But once this stage was past, Strachan was probably accurate enough. Such a picture could even be reconciled with other evidence from oral history that girls of the working class often had very little biological knowledge or sex education outside children's gossip ('You got in a huddle and Jean was telling you all this yarn, what was going — what would happen — and — that was — that was all that I learnt'). One Free Church moralist put it in a nutshell in 1897:

> They do not mean to do anything wrong, but simply to take what amusement they can, and courting is an amusement, and they go into it as into a dream, from

which many awake too late, to find their lives for ever overshadowed with a dark remembrance. (81)

The only problem from the moralist's point of view was that the memory was not as dark as it should have been.

Strachan's picture, in summary, is of working-class girls distinguished from middle-class girls in the degree of their premarital sexual adventures, which often included intercourse and pregnancy, while the working-class man was distinguished by the fact that he was more likely to take sex *gratis* from willing girls of his own class than to buy it from a prostitute. It carries conviction only where it is most often corroborated by other observers — in respect of the Lowland countryside. It can be extended to the towns only with the qualifications we have discussed already. There were, however, certain other groups within the Scottish working class — the Irish immigrants, the Highlanders and the inhabitants of the northern islands — which he either does not consider at all or considers only in an inadequate way. To these we must now turn.

The Irish, the Highlanders and the Islanders

A case for believing that the Irish had, in their native land at least, an exceptional respect for premarital chastity has been strongly argued, with a wealth of convincing statistical and non-statistical detail, in Connell's brilliant essays. (82) It is abundantly confirmed by nineteenth century observations of Irish immigrant habits in Britain, though not of those of the unaccompanied males. As one commentator put it considering the behaviour of Irish labourers in Stranraer: 'We very much fear that our brethren of the Green Isle can lay no claim to the possession of that jewel (chastity) which is the brightest ornament of their women'. (83) The men, uprooted from their families, priests, and culture and herded into navvying teams under brutalised conditions, behaved notoriously badly. Indeed, sometimes Irishmen were guilty of precisely the same double standard as the middle-class Scottish male: Patrick Macgill in his remarkable autobiographical novels of life among Irish harvest workers in Scotland described how experienced men would go with Scottish prostitutes but condemn with horror a young girl of their own band who had been seduced by a farmer's son. (84)

But where immigrant Irish families were thick on the ground — as in Dumbartonshire and Renfrewshire or in the burgh of Greenock — illegitimacy rates were usually exceptionally low, and in mixed communities the Irish were seen to behave totally differently from the Scots. A Scottish tailor who acted as voluntary baillie in the village of Raploch in Stirlingshire had this to say of his Irish neighbours:

About the beginning of May they go with their families to the bark peeling ... they stay out about two months and sleep in wooden sheds, lying together as thick as bees, but there's no immorality among them; indeed they just behave to each other like a wheen children, you would think they had not the same notions as other folk. I have only known two or at most three Irish girls go wrong, and it was always with Scotchmen. (85)

Macgill's novels make the same point about the childlike relationships of young Irish immigrants towards each other, and in other contexts Mayhew speaks of the chaste nature of the Irish coster girls in London (surely a most unexpected tribute) and Keating of the same thing among Irish girls in the South Wales coalfield. (86)

It is difficult not to associate this with the nature of nineteenth century Catholicism in Ireland, with the great strength of the priests and the emphasis on the worship of Mary and the holiness of the virgin state. As Harriet Martineau succinctly put it: 'that great terror-striker, the confessional, is before the Irish girl, and sooner or later the sins must be told'. (87) But on the other hand it would be completely wrong to equate nineteenth-century Catholicism with universal chastity: Austria and Portugal, two of the most Catholic countries, also had two of the highest rates of illegitimacy in Europe. There may be particular reasons for this — for instance the very high cost of marriage in Portugal — and it would probably also be naive not to imagine that there is a relationship with the scarcity of land in Ireland. In the post-famine situation, with late marriage for the males and few holdings to go round, the teaching of the priests was reinforced by a quite separate economic sanction. For immigrant industrial workers into Scotland the economic situation was obviously of another kind, but the cultural and moral habit formed in Ireland would not immediately collapse.

The Highlands and Islands present a much more difficult picture to interpret. Taking the overall illegitimacy statistics for the Highland counties — Argyll, Inverness-shire, Ross and Cromarty, and Sutherland — together with Orkney and Shetland, one has the impression of an area intermediate in character between the Scottish Lowlands and Ireland: the illegitimacy ratio in Ross and Cromarty and Shetland, for instance, was generally about one third of what it was in Banff and Wigtown. Middle class observers, too, sometimes gave the impression that the sexual *mores* of Highland girls were not unlike those of Irish girls. For instance, one who had been inspecting the female bothies of the Lothians remarked:

> Those I saw were inhabited by Highland girls, whose modest character is well known, and I heard no complaint of the misconduct of farm bothy women. That it would be far otherwise if the bothy women were natives of the South of Scotland I can well conceive. (88)

Dr. Strachan claimed that 'a Highlander could not, in the presence of women, be guilty of the coarseness and indelicacy that is common among Lowlanders', and said that the Highlanders with whom he had discussed the matter all assured him that 'during their courtship they had never been in their sweetheart's company after ten at night', and they had expressed amazement at the midnight prowling of Lowlanders.

Some allowance must be made for the occasional Highland courtesy of telling outsiders what they think they would be most pleased to hear, yet there are other indications that parts of the Highlands may have been as Strachan saw them. Free Church and Church of Scotland reports from the 1870s and the 1890s, covering parishes in the west — for instance the Presbyteries of Mull and Skye on the islands, and Lochcarron, Tongue and Glenelg on the mainland — gave the impression that 'immorality' was rare or very rare: when there was an illegitimate birth, it was generally blamed on outsiders, or was said to have been the result of a girl going to the south to farm or domestic service. (89) Oral tradition sometimes points in the same direction. For instance, in the Catholic parish of Barra the Essex University team were told that bastardy cursed a family 'from generation to generation'; it was so rare that the informant could only recollect two instances, one concerning a girl who had emigrated south; courtship was fairly strictly controlled, both by teenagers being called early back home in the evenings by their parents, and by moral precepts like 'if you go with anybody to any lonely or out of the way place the devil is the third person'. (90) This appears to have strong overtones of the Irish situation.

On the other hand the Highlands cover a large area, and some parishes had very different reputations. Church reports were not so complacent about, for instance, Islay and Coll. (91) Tomintoul, like Barra, was a Catholic locality but here illegitimacy was as high as it was in the Lowlands of Banff to which it lay adjacent: 29 births out of 114 between 1861 and 1865 were of bastards, and as late as the 1880s it was being commented upon that this Catholic area was no better than its Protestant neighbours in its 'social morality'. (92) Again, there were remarks about certain parishes in the west considerably more adverse than the general run of outsiders' opinion:

> The Dumfriesshire shepherds, I believe, have had laid upon them the *onus* of introducing illegitimacy into the Highlands, and I must say that, if so, it has not suffered by the transplantation, seeming, as it does at the present day, to be indigenous to the soil. In Alvie, Glenshiel, Lairg, Croy and Edderton, the parishes wherein it attained unenviable superiority, the reputed fathers were thorough-bred Highlanders. Is there any part of Scotland in which illegitimacy exceeds the proportion of 18.18 per cent found in the thinly populated parishes of Alvie and Glenshiel? I rather think not. (93)

Nor can we disregard the very large body of traditional Gaelic songs which are on tape at the School of Scottish Studies, and which are not really specific to any one locality. One common and repeated feature concerns courtship at the shielings — the isolated upland pastures where the women and girls lived in summer making butter and cheese, and looking after the animals. Tales of visits to the shielings by bands of men, and of romps in the heather that followed, are as common a feature of these songs as tales of midnight prowling are of the Bothy Ballads in the Lowlands. It is certainly difficult to make this sort of evidence dovetail in with the remarks of Free Church commentators, for instance, the rarity of immorality in Presbytery of Glenelg, especially if one recalls that the Free Church regarded even dancing and loafing as tending to dangerous temptations.

In the face of all this conflicting but thinly spread evidence it may help to turn to two areas about which just a little more is known — the northern isles, and Lewis. Orkney and Shetland were particularly interesting in view of their low illegitimacy ratio (less than 5 per cent usually), combined with assertions by the church that local courtship practices were indecent and that ante-nuptial pregnancy was common:

> The absence of illegitimate births ... can hardly be regarded as a fair index of the real state of things ... while cases of illegitimacy are comparatively rare, cases of antenuptial fornication are not infrequent, and are little thought of, marriage being supposed to set all right. The system of courtship in many cases is conducted in a way which is very questionable. It is not easy to say at whose door the blame lies here. Young men and women and parents seem to be equally culpable. (94)

Nineteenth-century church sources do not explain what the courtship customs were, beyond saying they were long-engrained and hard to eradicate. Oral tradition, however, tells more. Some were of the shieling type: one informant described a 'flatchie carding' in Shetland: after six or so girls had been carding wool out of doors, they would spread pallets on the floor about midnight: 'this was a signal for the boys to come in, and they would come bounding in and spend the night rolling around with girls, jumping and rolling over them'. (95) This does not imply sexual intercourse. Others were associated with marriage celebrations: there are stories of a 'lang bed' in which the unmarried couples would all get together after the wedding party. A nineteenth-century account spoke of the 'members of each sex being alternately ranged along the floor on a huge couch of straw', but went on, 'the people enter quite innocently into these "barn bundlings" as they are termed, and ... the testimony of respectable persons who have taken part in them prove that nothing immoral occurs'. (96) There was also the custom of individual bundling, the couple remaining fully clothed, and often lying in bed with a bolster or deal between them: 'You know in other parts of the country except for Shetland, if a girl and a boy go to bed together it's for one purpose and one purpose only. But here in Shetland a girl and a boy would go to bed together as they might go for a walk'. (97) The implication once again, of course, is that they got into bed to pet: intercourse would not by any means necessarily follow. The church was certainly not quite fair in suggesting that bundling normally led to unchastity, still less to promiscuity.

What seems characteristic of Orkney and Shetland, however, is that parents (or employers) made little attempt to supervise the courtship of their teenagers and often did not know of it. This is illustrated by a story collected by the School of Scottish Studies concerning the wife of an Orkney farmer who accidentally disturbed a young man in bed with the maid early one Sunday morning, and then was obliged to go to great lengths to explain obliquely to the young man and the community at large that she was not a Peeping Tom and that it had been the merest accident she had disturbed the two of them: the community would attach blame to her, for interfering, not to the couple, for being in bed together. (98)

We shall never know how generally couples went beyond petting, but the Orkney and Shetland situation does illustrate a situation where you could have plenty of 'midnight visiting' and still get low illegitimacy rates. It may well be relevant that the islands were still essentially a peasant society where everyone knew everyone else and young men could not readily escape identification or their responsibilities to a pregnant girl. Correlation with the age of marriage is not very conclusive. While it is true that, in 1871 for example, men got married in Orkney and Shetland about eighteen months later than the national average, and women one year or two years later, in the Highlands (where illegitimacy overall was above what it was in the northern isles but below what it was in the Lowlands), men were on average over three years older than the national average, and women much as in the northern isles. These figures certainly do not support the contemporary view that delayed marriage led to a growth of bastardy.

The case of Lewis makes another interesting study: it presents a combination of enthusiastic membership of the strictest Presbyterian churches (there was much more adherence to the Free Church than in the northern isles), very low illegitimacy rates, and 'bundling' courtship customs. For the pre-nineteenth-century situation before evangelical religion got a foothold on the island, we have one extremely lurid description, which is worth quoting even if it contains only elemental traces of truth:

> In the part of the country we are describing, however, this frailty (intemperance) still prevails with the favourite fair, and her intercourse is frequently with so many men that the unfortunate girl is often at a nonplus where to fix with certainty; but she seldom fails to give up the gentleman or single man to save the married man and herself from the shame of doing penance in a white sheet. The rich man, indeed, finds a substitute by giving a little bribe, and a great many fine promises, both to the

woman and the ostensible father. As the poor young man cannot pay for substitutes the contending parties must (bring) the issue of their cause to an oath; and the affidavit of the suspected satisfied the accuser, and the bastard is as much esteemed as the lawfully begotten child.

The woman, if she is pregnant by a gentleman, is by no means looked down upon, but is provided in a husband with greater *eclat* than without forming such a connection. Instead of being despised, numberless instances can be produced where pregnant women have been disputed for, and even fought for, by the different suitors. (99)

Buchanan's description is suspect because he himself was a former missionary who had fallen out with the tacksmen on the island, and he undoubtedly wanted to blacken their name. On the other hand, even if we do not believe all his tales of drunken promiscuity, we must recognise that the account of peasant girls sleeping with gentlemen and being married off to advantage finds echoes, for instance, in the account of Lord Crawfurd and the girl from Arran (see above, p. 57), and in certain Gaelic songs extolling the virtues of bearing the tacksman's son. It is possible, at least, that such things were commoner before religious pressures began to be more puritan in the nineteenth-century, and perhaps before class pressures began to frown upon sexual collaboration of this kind.

Certainly, by the middle of the nineteenth-century Lewis had taken on its reputation for Godliness and good behaviour. Adherence to the Free Church was overwhelming: and by the end of the century many also adhered to the more extreme sects emanating from the Free Church. The island was famous for its Sabbath observance. It was equally famous for its very low illegitimacy ratio. Ross and Cromarty, indeed, vied with Orkney and Shetland for the distinction of the lowest county illegitimacy ratio in Scotland, but when Lewis is separated out from the mainland the record is even more remarkable: (100)

Illegitimacy ratio	Island of Lewis	Mainland of Ross & Cromarty
1880	2.1	6.3
1885	2.2	6.6
1890	1.9	6.4
1895	3.2	6.3
1899	1.9	7.0

Closer analysis showed, that, as in Shetland, the more rural the area the lower the ratio:

Illegitimacy ratio	Rural Registration Districts	Stornoway R.D.
1880	1.8	2.4
1885	1.5	3.2
1890	1.7	2.1
1895	2.8	3.7
1899	1.2	2.8

At the same time Lewis had a high birth rate: in the 1890s it varied between 32o/oo and 25o/oo, compared to a variation between 22o/oo and 19o/oo on the mainland of the county. There was no word in the various church reports of the period hinting at high levels of antenuptial pregnancies or of undesirable courtship customs. Could it be that nineteenth-century Lewis was a place where Dr. Strachan's beliefs in the 'modesty' of the Highlands were justified, and where the church ethic was for once properly followed by both sexes?

This may well be the correct conclusion, but when in the last quarter of the nineteenth-century others began to comment on such things it became clear that rural Lewis, no less than Orkney and Shetland, also had a long-engrained tradition of 'bundling' and courting at the shielings. For instance, an outsider who had stayed for a long period in Lewis wrote in 1874:

> Most of the unmarried young men pass the winter nights with their sweethearts. The want of light in most dwellings, the numbers of dark corners even in daylight, and the general habit among the people of throwing themselves down on the straw simply divested of their outer garment, gives every facility for courtship in the Hebridean fashion. As the girls are, at the same time, 'very kind', courting assiduously, and are possessed of far greater energy than the men, they acquire a great hold on their affections. (101)

Bundling, indeed, lasted until well into the twentieth-century in Lewis, but oral accounts of what actually happened explain it as carefully controlled. (102) Hebridean houses had only one room; with the whole family present, it was impossible for the parents not to know who was with the girl, and impossible for intercourse to take place. Similarly on the shielings the girls were accompanied by a few older women who exercised by their presence a restraining influence. On Lewis 'bundling' seems to have been a more acceptable courtship custom than walking out, for walking removed the control of other people over the lovers. The island, of course, was an extremely tightly-knit traditional society with a highly developed awareness of kinship, and the ethos that made social responsibilities very difficult to avoid: if a lad had made a girl pregnant and deserted her, his family would never have been allowed to live down the shame. At any rate the correlation in the rural districts between the normal practice of courting by 'bundling' and the very low rates of illegitimacy and (apparently) of ante-nuptial pregnancies, indicates that under some circumstances 'bundling' was perfectly compatible with chastity.

Conclusions

Some conclusions are easy, others must be speculative. First of all, the middle and upper classes had a distinctive code of sexual morality which involved the women in an extraordinary degree of premarital chastity, and in lack of physical contact even of a minimal kind until very late in courtship — even then it did not go far: the men, if they were not themselves chaste, pursued girls of lower social status for casual intercourse, which gave rise to a great deal of prostitution. It is not unreasonable to attribute the almost superstitious protection of women at least partly to the fact that marriage was, as well as a sexual contract, also a contract by which property was transferred. Dr. Johnson expressed it well in a conversation at Dunvegan: 'consider of what importance to society the chastity of women is. Upon that all the property in the world depends. We hang a thief for stealing a sheep, but the unchastity of a woman transfers sheep, and farm, and all from the right owner'. (103) Engels had essentially the same interpretation. (104) It is not, of course, necessary for everyone in bourgeois society to be aware of this foundation for the prevailing morality for it to be a valid explanation, especially as it was a morality backed (as far as the women were concerned) by the church. But when one considers the degree to which the unchasteness of middle-class men was tolerated, and the extent of the ensuing prostitution, it becomes obvious that we can hardly speak of the middle classes as a whole following the church ethic.

Secondly, in the towns, working-class morality was probably more heterogeneous than anywhere else. Some were heavily influenced by 'middle-class morality' — either those who were most firmly controlled by the middle-classes, like domestic servants, or who aspired in this and other respects to resemble the middle-classes, like shopworkers and craftsmen. Some took the tone of their behaviour from the rural areas from which they had immigrated — and in the case of the Irish this could place a high premium on female chastity, in the case of the north-eastern Lowlanders, rather a low one. Others lived, or partly lived, on the receiving end of prostitution. It seems impossible to discover any proletarian norm of urban society: this is probably because there was not one, but many.

In the countryside, morality varied according to region. In the Lowlands it would seem that sexual intercourse before marriage was common, and in some parts — the south-west and the north-east — for peculiar local reasons gave rise to exceptionally high rates of illegitimacy. In the Highlands and islands the situation is obscure and varied, but low illegitimacy ratios in the northern isles were associated with what the church, perhaps unjustly, considered to be 'licencious' morals, while even lower illegitimacy ratios in Lewis were associated with as high a regard for female chastity as in rural Ireland.

The one feature common to all these places, however, was that it was general to court after dark, indoors, and often in bed. Where parental surveillance was close, as in Lewis, a very high degree of chastity was nevertheless preserved. In other areas where peasant society was homogeneous and relatively stable, even if parental surveillance was not close, as in the northern isles, there were few illegitimacies because societal pressure could be brought to bear on fathers in order to prevent the desertion of pregnant girls whose children would then become a burden on the grandparents. But in the Lowlands, society was not of this kind — it was a world of farm labourers, not of peasants. In one area, the Borders and the Lothians where the bondager system prevailed, one might explain the frequency of sexual intercourse before marriage by the fact that couples wished to prove their partners' fertility, which was important for their job prospects where the basic work-unit was the family, not the single employee. This is perhaps premarital intercourse condoned by parents for economic reasons.

Nevertheless, this might not do as a general explanation of the frequency of antenuptial pregnancy in other parts of the Lowlands, and it is no explanation of higher illegitimacy anywhere — as the point of Border practice presumably was that the couple should marry if the girl was fertile. One cannot ignore, in an explanation of the frequency of ante-nuptial pregnancy in other parts of the Lowlands, the relative weakness of parental authority where the children of one sex or both lived away from home: the family cottage system of the south was replaced elsewhere by the bachelor bothy or the chaumer, where the young could do as they wished without danger of interruption, or the need to face mother and father in the morning. The chaumer system of the north-east, with the girls living away from home yet having constant occasion to mix with the young men who came into the house kitchens to eat, was the most unrestricted environment of all. Certainly farmers were not going to step in to exercise quasi-parental discipline in these matters — the collapse of paternal relations was a constant theme of church comment here and elsewhere in the Scottish Lowlands in the nineteenth-century. (105)

It is reasonable to assume that levels of illegitimacy will be related to the frequency of pre-marital intercourse in society, but that they will also depend on other circumstances. One must be the perceived need of society to enforce marriage for the sake of the girl and her child: another, the ability of society to do so.

The perceived need for marriage was obviously less if the unmarried mother could support herself without recourse to her parents: the burden of her child would then not fall on her kin, or on anyone else. This was certainly possible where, as over the Lowlands as a whole, the agricultural system provided some constant employment for single women in milking, hoeing and similar work: it was nowhere more possible than in Banff and Wigtownshire, where the chaumer system and the cottage let to an 'unattached woman' prevailed respectively, where there was much dairying, and a good deal of turnip husbandry. One commentator in the south-west noted that high levels of illegitimacy followed the line of turnip cultivation. (106) The girls were able to keep their jobs if they became pregnant or not: they were not an economic burden on their parents before, and they did not become one subsequently.

In any case, the ability of society to enforce marriage on the father of a pregnant girl was weaker in the Lowlands than in the Highlands. Both married and single labourers were notoriously mobile, moving restlessly from farm to farm and district to district, and relatively seldom settling down to a sojourn in one place over decades. This made it easy for an unmarried father to evade his responsibilities. Not only was there nothing abnormal in his leaving the district, but if rural society did not consist of a fixed cohort of families resident over generations it lacked a corporate memory which could rebuke the irresponsibility of neighbours. In the Highlands even the flight of a young man would not have saved his family from disrepute. In the Lowlands it was not likely the man or his family would stay in the locality to be remembered.

For these reasons, it seems, Lowland lovers in rural areas could get into bed together outwith the context of most of the social restraints that operated in, for example, the northern or western isles. In the Lowlands, therefore, and particularly (for local reasons) in the extreme south-west and the extreme north-east, a very 'unbourgeois' and even 'unpeasant' morality could grow up which not only accepted ante-nuptial pregnancy as normal, but which also accepted illegitimacy as conferring no stigma on mother or child, and did not regard refusal to accept responsibility by the man as a very grave sin.

Sexual morality in Victorian Scotland, then, was in practice largely a function of the authority relationship between parents and children, and the economic situation of both. Where parents were in a position to exercise control they often enforced sexual restraint and responsibility on their sons and daughters, or at least other people's sons were obliged to accept responsibility for what they did to daughters. This was especially true where illegitimate additions to the family imposed new burdens on an existing household. Conversely, where parents did not have this power (as over young theological students at College, or farm servants in a bothy), or where there was independent employment even for unmarried mothers (as in Banff), young people tended to experiment in a way that increased prostitution and illegitimacy. But in those areas where these things became common, working-class society tended to accept them as normal. Even from the middle class, there was no crusade for 'Victorian morality'; breaches in the church's code were visible everywhere, and if commentators from time to time raised their eyes to deplore them, no-one was prepared to unleash a campaign against fornicators, as they might possibly have done in the Reformation centuries. At root the Victorian moralist, like the Victorian businessman, was an individualist with a privatised vision: it was enough for him if he was pure, even if Sodom and Gomorrah were to be destroyed down the road.

REFERENCES

1. I am grateful for help from many friends and colleagues, but especially to Berrick Saul; to Ailsa Maxwell and Judith Gillespie of the Scottish Historical Demography Unit (Dept. of Economic History); to Emily Lyle, Alan Bruford, Donald Macdonald and John Macinnes of the School of Scottish Studies, Edinburgh University; and to Paul and Thea Thompson of the Oral History Unit, Essex University. They are not of course responsible for any errors of fact or interpretation here. I am also grateful to Kenneth Boyd, whose admirable Edinburgh (1973) doctoral thesis, 'The Theological Presuppositions of Scottish Church Pronouncements on Sex, Marriage and the Family; 1850-1914', was finished at the same time as this paper, but of which I have made little direct use. His work is certainly exempt from the strictures of this paragraph. Since the completion of the paper there has appeared James Bulloch, *The Church in Victorian Scotland 1843-1874* (Edinburgh, 1975), which has a section on these matters. I have not been able to make use of it. I should perhaps add that a further consideration of the Scottish illegitimacy statistics will appear in M.W. Flinn (ed.) *Scottish Population History from the Seventeenth Century to the Nineteen Thirties* (forthcoming).
2. See G.D. Henderson, *The Scottish Ruling Elder,* (London, 1935).
3. Joseph Mitchell, *Reminiscences of my life in the Highlands*, (1883), ed. I. Robertson (Newton Abbot, 1971), vol. I, p.237.
4. A.A. MacLaren, 'Presbyterianism and the working class in a mid-nineteenth century city', *Scottish Historical Review,* XLVI, 115-139.
5. See below p. 68.
6. Essex University, Oral History Unit (henceforth cited as Essex O.H.U.).
7. Ralph Wardlaw, *Lectures on Female Prostitution* (Glasgow, 1842), pp.57-8.
8. William Logan, *The Great Social Evil* (London, 1871), p.230. No doubt the usual view of the medical profession was for a long period the same as that of the former director of the student health centre in Edinburgh in the 1960s, encapsulated in the following report in the Edinburgh University medical students' journal *Synapse,* 17, No.2, p.11.

   Dr. Verney replied that to prescribe the pill for unmarried girls would be contrary to the dictates of his conscience and to the welfare of the community ... He felt it was the duty of women to maintain moral standards in sexual matters and deplored the current *mores* of the university. It is necessary to the male students to prove their manhood by the experience of sex. Earlier they had found this sexual outlet outside the university but now found it within the university, with an associated rise in illegitimacy and venereal disease in the student population. This Dr. Verney attributed to a decline of moral principles among the young women — in his day young women came to the university for education, not for fornication. In the tense and claustrophobic silence which followed Dr. Verney's last comment the sense of most of what he had said previously was forgotten.

9. *Statistical Account of Scotland,* vol. VI (1793), p.612.
10. See below, p.77.
11. Paisley Central Library: Andrew Crawfurd, 'Cairn of Lochwinnoch Matters', vol. 21, p.305. I am grateful to Dr. Emily Lyle for this reference.
12. See Alex Confort, *The Anxiety Makers* (London, 1967).
13. Wardlaw, *op.cit.,* p.138.
14. For example, *ibid.,* p.71.
15. William Tait, *Magdalenism, an inquiry into the extent, causes and consequences of prostitution in Edinburgh,* second edition (London, 1842), p.199.
16. See Alfred C.C. List, *The Two Phases of the Social Evil* (Edinburgh, 1861).
17. *Ibid.*
18. Elaine A. Corsie, 'Domestic Servants in Selected Parishes of Edinburgh 1871-91', M.A. Thesis, Department of Economic History, University of Edinburgh (this thesis is in the keeping of the Department). Also Essex O.H.U.
19. Wardlaw, *op.cit.,* p.94; Logan, *op.cit.,* p.110.
20. Tait, *op.cit.,* pp.32-3; see also Logan, *op.cit.,* pp.96-7, 118.
21. Tait, *op.cit., passim,* and pp.118-8; see also List, *op.cit.*
22. Tait, *op.cit.,* pp.227-8.
23. Isabella L. Bird, *Notes on Old Edinburgh* (Edinburgh, 1869), pp.22-3.
24. Tait, *op.cit.,* pp.2-10; Logan, *op.cit.,* p.72; Wardlaw, *op.cit.,* pp.31-2.
25. Logan, *op.cit.,* pp.92-3.
26. *Ibid.,* pp.107-10.
27. Tait, *op.cit.,* p.3.
28. *Ibid.,* p.185.
29. *The Autobiography of John Dunlop* (London, 1932), p.99. This refers to the 1830s.
30. List, *op.cit.,* p.4.
31. Tait, *op.cit.,* pp.2-3, 237, 245-7.
32. Scottish Record Office, RH, 15, 1856 at 20 May 1814: letter from Neil Ryrie, Edinburgh agent of Stein, Dewar and Co. distillers (Alloa), to the partners. I am indebted to Mr. R.B. Weir for this reference.
33. E.g. Thomas Chalmers, *Christian and Civic Economy of Large Towns,* vol. III, in his *Works* (Glasgow, 1838-42), vol. XVI, pp.107-8.
34. Anon., *The Great Sin of Banffshire* (Banff, 1859), p.l.
35. George Seton, *The Causes of Illegitimacy* (Edinburgh, 1860), pp.5-7.
36. Albert Leffingwell, *Illegitimacy and the Influence of Seasons upon Conduct* (London, 1892), p.147.

It may be imagined that a high level of illegitimacy in Scotland was due in some way to the popular view of what constituted a marriage: e.g. in Scotland, other things being equal, a declaration of marriage pronounced by a third person, before witnesses, with the consent of the couple, was popularly viewed as a marriage even if it did not take place with a clergyman officiating or in a church. But such unions, though 'irregular' in the eyes of the kirk, were valid in law, and registrars would not have entered the offsprings of such unions as illegitimate except by error or misunderstanding with the parents. It is unlikely to be a major source of difference either between regions in Scotland, or between Scotland and other parts of the U.K. or European countries.

37. E. Shorter, J. Knodel and E. van de Walle, 'The decline of non-marital fertility in Europe, 1880-1940', *Population Studies*, XXV, 357-94.
38. These and similar statistics have been compiled by the Scottish Historical Demography Unit, operating with SSRC funds at the University of Edinburgh.
39. *First Detailed Report ... of the Registrar General for Scotland, [1855]*. See also J.M. Strachan, 'Immorality of Scotland', *Scotsman*, June 7, 1870.
40. See *Free Church General Assembly Proceedings,* henceforth cited as FCGA), 1863, *Report of Committee on Houses for the Working Class.*
41. This was calculated by the Scottish Historical Demography Unit at Edinburgh University from civil registration material. See also W. Cramond, *Illegitimacy in Banffshire,* Banff, 1888, pp.17-21.
42. Cramond, *op.cit.,* pp.25-6; Seton, *op.cit.,* pp.12-3, 31, 33. *Fourth Report of the Royal Commission on the Employment of Children, Young Persons and Women in Agriculture (1867),* (henceforth *R.C. Agric. 1867*), P.P. 1870, vol. XIII, pp.25-6, 81.
43. *Fourth Report R.C. Agric. 1867,* pp.53, 55-9; Seton, *op.cit.,* pp.38-9.
44. *Fifth Detailed Report ... of the Registrar General for Scotland [1859].* Seton, *op.cit., pp.17-18.*
45. *Second Detailed Report ... of the Registrar General for Scotland [1856].*
46. *Royal Commission on Labour, 1893,* P.P. 1893, vol. XXXVI, Agricultural Labourer, vol. III, Scotland, pp.104, 113.
47. Cramond, *op.cit.,* pp.48, 52.
48. *Third Report R.C. Agric. 1867, P.P.* 1870, vol. XIII, p.52. See also Thomas Rees, *Miscellaneous Papers on Subjects Relating to Wales* (London, 1867), pp.29-36, and Leffingwell, *op.cit.,* pp.56-63.
49. F.C.G.A., 1864, *Report of the Committee on Houses for the Working Classes.*
50. *Ibid.*
51. *Fourth Detailed Report ... of the Registrar General for Scotland [1858];* Cramond, *op.cit.,* pp.31-2.
52. F.C.G.A.,1862, *Report of the Committee on Houses for the Working Classes.*
53. F.C.G.A., 1861, *Report of the Committee on Houses for the Working Classes.*
54. *Prize Essays and Transactions of the Highland and Agricultural Society,* N.S. vol. VIII (1843 ,)'Digest of Essays on the Bothy System', pp.133-144.
55. *Ibid.*
56. *First Detailed Report of the Registrar General for Scotland [1855].*
57. See F.C.G.A., *Reports of the Committee on Houses for the Working Classes* throughout the early 1860s, notably 1863.

84   SOCIAL CLASS IN SCOTLAND

58. Cramond, *op.cit.,* pp.61-5.
59. F.C.G.A., 1863, *Report of the Committee on Houses for the Working Classes.*
60. *Fourth Report R.C. Agric. 1867, P.P.* 1870, vol. XIII, Appendix, Part II, pp. 120-121.
61. Compiled by Scottish Historical Demography Unit at Edinburgh from Registrar General's material.
62. J.M. Strachan, 'Immorality of Scotland', *Scotsman,* 20 May, 2 June, 7 June 1870. All quotations are from this source without further reference.
63. J. Valentine, 'Illegitimacy in Aberdeen and the other large Towns of Scotland', *Report of the British Association for the Advancement of Science,* 1859, pp. 224-6.
64. Quoted in Leffingwell, *op.cit.,* pp.67-8.
65. Calculated from civil registration material.
66. Tait, *op.cit.*
67. Valentine, *loc. cit.*
68. Seton, *op.cit.,* p.38.
69. *Ibid.,* p.39.
70. *Fourth Report R.C. Agric. 1867, P.P.* 1870, vol. XIII, Appendix, Part II, pp. 194-6.
71. F.C.G.A., 1897, *Report on the Religious and Moral Conditions of Farm Servants.* See also *Church of Scotland General Assembly Proceedings* (henceforth C. of S. G.A.) 1895, *Report of the Commission on the Religious Condition of the People,* pp.747, 749. See also Cramond *op. cit.,* pp.49, 67-8 for traces of the same thing in Banff.
72. C. of S. G.A., 1895, *Reports of the Schemes of the Church of Scotland,* p.750. The problem of 'traditional bastard-bearers' is discussed by Peter Laslett and Karla Oosterveen, 'Long-term Trends in Bastardy in England', *Population Studies,* XXVII, 255-284.
73. *Fourth Report R.C. Agric. 1867, P.P.* 1870, vol. XIII, p.80.
74. *Ibid.,* Appendix, Part II, p.196.
75. F.C.G.A., 1863, *Report of the Committee ... on Religion and Morals.*
76. Cramond, *op.cit.,* pp.44-50.
77. I am grateful to Mrs. Margaret Somerville for drawing my attention to this: see following footnote.
78. F.C.G.A., 1897, *Report on the Religious and Moral Conditions of Farm Servants.*
79. Cramond, *op.cit.,* p.51.
80. Essex O.H.U., no. E.
81. F.C.G.A., 1897, *Report on the Religious and Moral Conditions of Farm Servants.*
82. K.H. Connell, *Irish Peasant Society* (Oxford, 1968).
83. A.C.C. List, *op.cit.,* p.4.
84. Especially Patrick Macgill, *Children of the Dead End* (London, 1914), and *The Rat-Pit* (London, 1915).
85. *Fourth Report R.C. Agric. 1867, P.P.* 1870, vol. XIII, p.66.
86. Henry Mayhew, *London Labour and the London Poor* (London, 1861), vol. I, pp.104-5. Joseph Keating, *My Struggle for Life* London, 1916), p.14.

87. Quoted in Connell, *op. cit.*, p.85.
88. *Fourth Report R.C. Agric. 1867, P.P.* 1870, vol. XIII, p.80.
89. C. of S. G.A., 1897, *Reports of the Schemes of the Church of Scotland,* pp. 942, 946, 951. F.C.G.A., 1870, *Report of the Committee ... on Religion and Morals,* pp.19-21; *Ibid,* 1873, pp.45-8.
90. Essex O.H.U.
91. C. of S. G.A., 1898, *Reports of the Schemes of the Church of Scotland,* pp. 887, 893.
92. Cramond, *op. cit.,* p.59. Calculations 1861-5 by Edinburgh University Historical Demography Unit.
93. Seton, *op.cit.,* p.32.
94. F.C.G.A., 1884, *Appendix to the Report on the State of Religion and Morals.*
95. Essex O.H.U.
96. R. Cowie, *Shetland and its Inhabitants* (Edinburgh, 1874), p.100.
97. Essex O.H.U.
98. I am grateful to Dr. Alan Bruford of the School of Scottish Studies for this story from his collection.
99. J.L. Buchanan, *Travels in the Western Hebrides from 1782 to 1790* (London, 1793), p.110.
100. *Report to the Secretary for Scotland ... on the Social Condition of the People of Lewis in 1901 ...,* pp.XCIX-CI, *P.P.* (1902), vol. LXXXIII.
101. W.A. Smith, *Lewsiana,* first published 1874, second edition 1886, p.79.
102. For this I am especially indebted to conversations at the School of Scottish Studies with Mr. Donald Macdonald of Lewis and Edinburgh.
103. James Boswell, *The Life of Samuel Johnson ... to which is added the Journal of a Tour to the Hebrides,* ed. P. Fitzgerald (London, 1897), p.593.
104. F. Engels, *The Origin of the Family, Private Property and the State* ed. London, 1942.
105. See for example, F.C.G.A., 1863, *Report of Committee on Houses for the Working Class;* F.C.G.A., 1897, *Report on the Religious and Moral Condition of Farm Servants;* C. of S. G.A., 1895, *Reports of the Schemes of the Church of Scotland,* (Commission on the Religious Condition of the People) pp.745-6. There is a full discussion in Kenneth Boyd's thesis cited in footnote (1) above.
106. *Royal Commission on Labour, 1893,* P.P. 1893, vol. XXXVI, Agricultural Labourer, vol. III, Scotland.

5. North-East Agriculture and the Labour Force, 1790-1875

Malcolm Gray

Agricultural 'improvement', as a comprehensive social movement, came late to the North-East of Scotland. In the 1790s the area was still notably backward with only scattered enclaves of land where any change had been made in the ancient manner of agriculture. But the movement, once started, was quick and general. By 1830, most of the farms consisted of compact and regularly shaped areas with isolated steadings standing at the convenient centres of the land which they served; approved rotations prevailed on even small holdings, with artificial grass and turnip forming regular series with the grain crops; two-horse ploughs, each with the one man in charge, performed the bulk of the cultivation and the one-horse carts moved about the new roads connecting the various parts of the farm and leading from farm to market or source of supply; the beasts fed solidly on the new crops and provided the soil with the dung that played so great a part in the new farming. Necessarily agricultural change had been accompanied by social rearrangements. A minority of farmers acquired considerably greater holdings of land than were anywhere to be found in the old system, while the class of small subtenants of land were largely squeezed out. The big farmers were bigger and some of the smallest tenancies that had supported a considerable proportion of the population had disappeared. Yet, on the whole, this part of Scotland did not fit the accepted stereotype of agricultural revolution resulting in the inflexible division of society into the two main classes of capitalist farmers and landless labourers. Families in which the main breadwinner was a landless labourer were comparatively few and most families were placed somewhere on a long and continuous scale from the small-holder with three or four acres to the farmer with over 300. Nevertheless the new agriculture was based on the use of a considerable wage-labour force. The North-East, in fact, had its own subtle solution to the problem of reconciling the hankering for land with the need for a force of wage-labourers. It is with the terms of that solution and with the manner in which it was achieved that this chapter will be concerned. The 'North-East' is defined as comprising the counties of Aberdeen and Banff, together with the parishes of Kincardine lying north of a line drawn westwards from Stonehaven. That is, it coincides with the geologically and socially distinct area enclosed to the south and west by the rich red sandstone districts of Kincardine and Angus on the one side and of Moray and Nairn on the other.

In the eighteenth century, the land was owned by a gentlemanly class, the lairds. Some of these were newly arrived in the position, being merchants or people of the professional classes from the towns, and some of the estates were very small, with no more than a dozen or so tenants, but nowhere had the working farmers secured ownership of the land which they occupied. Next below the owners of land came the tenants, working farmers who were secured in their position by the apportionment of land directly from its aristocratic owners.

In the main, in this area, the land was granted to the tenants in immediately usable units; there was no class of tacksmen living on the rents of a wide range of subtenants. A tenant might hold his land through the undivided control of a completely separate holding, or he might be embodied in a group sharing the resources of a common farm. The tenancy of land, however small the area, gave a man a certain standing and independence but the tenants varied a great deal in the size of the holdings which they controlled. True smallholders — with no more than five acres each — were fairly numerous but there were also found, in numbers far from negligible, men who had twenty times as much, with examples of holders all along the intervening scale.

In spite of the frequency of small holdings, a solid majority, amounting to about two-thirds of the tenants, employed labourers, maintained in their household or settled around the fam, to help them with the farm work; it was indeed common to have two or three such possible helpers. (1) Thus each farm had its own small internal stratification. The fact that those who at least occasionally worked as dependent labourers were more numerous than the independent tenants was due not so much to the size of the farming units, or to the wealth in land of the tenants, as to the laborious nature of the main farming operations. Even the smallest unit, if it was being used with efficiency, required a grouping of workers. The ploughing, for example, was performed by large teams of up to twelve animals, whether oxen or horses, and the simple maintenance of these animals was a severe call upon labour as well as upon resources for feeding, while the operation itself occupied two men to manage the cumbersome and slowmoving implement. Harvesting with the hook, or the sickle, required a large attendance, especially in a climate which underlined the importance of working hard when the weather was favourable. The North-East was also an area depending much upon its stock and, with the lack of any enclosure, herding was an important task, performed very often by young boys. Lack of roads, and consequently of vehicles for the carriage of goods and materials, was another factor making necessary the use of much labour for the working of even moderate holdings of land; much of the carriage had to be done by use of creels or currachs carried on the human back, and even where horses or ponies were called upon it was to be laden with panniers rather than to pull carts or wagons. Marketing of grain or bringing supplies, for example of lime, from outside the farm was another heavy drain on farm resources of manpower and of animals. Turf was much used in the farm and domestic economy, both for building and for making of dung, and cutting and carrying it occupied many days.

The digging with the spade, or cutting with the breast plough, a quantity of turf, provincially *muck feal,* the carriage of this to the dunghill, and then carrying the whole on horses' backs to the fields, occupied that part of the autumn that remained after harvest, and also that portion of the spring months which was not employed in ploughing the fields, or in sowing the different kinds of grain. (2)

But perhaps the heaviest call upon the labour resources of the farming unit was the cutting, drying and carriage of peats. This occupied a plentiful band, representing every household, through the entire period between Whitsunday and harvest. Added to the tasks of cutting and drying an amount of material which in its sodden state would weigh several tons, there was the cartage for distances up to ten miles on the backs of the work animals. The almost universal dependence on locally-cut peat placed its stamp not only upon the methods of farming — by preventing any farming operations during the summer months — but also upon the social structure. The comfort of all classes depended upon this commodity which could only be acquired by much labour. Consequently, proprietors required labour services of their tenants, consisting in large measure of the obligation to cut so many feet of peats; tenants in their turn turned to subordinates — whether subtenants or labourers — either to perform the services or to meet the tenants' own domestic needs. One of the definite marks of standing, going along with the holding of enough land to make for independence, was the ability to call upon subordinate labour for the tasks of peat-cutting for the combined needs of the proprietor and of the personal household.

Some of this subordinate labour was provided by the servants, both male and female. They were hired, at a fixed wage, to be at the full-time disposal of their masters for continuous periods of six months or a year at a time, and some, of course, would engage year after year. They were sufficiently numerous for a good half of all tenants to have one or more servants in their employ. (3)

Servants who were paid to be constantly at the master's service could not economically be used to meet those needs which swelled suddenly at particular times of the farming year; the farmer depended on a reserve of labour which he could call upon more occasionally, although at definite times of the year. Much of this need was supplied by subtenants.

> Every farm was skirted with a number of subtenants, who were bound to assist their masters, in spring and harvest, with their services, which was generally the greater part of the rent they paid for their possessions; and they were allowed to keep as many cattle and sheep upon the common pasture as they pleased ... Whenever the seed-time was over, all hands were employed till harvest, and even after harvest was over, in providing fuel, and in burning and in driving lime. (4)

There were many variations on this model but the basic relation of land given in return for service, compulsory at certain times of the year, was the main means by which labour was raised for the occasional farming tasks. Nearly always at some time of the year the subtenant was bound to work for his superior; but the labour might well be paid for at set rates, rather than simply stand in lieu of rent. Thus, in Udny, the subtenant

> works to the farmer in harvest, attends the plough during winter and spring, at which time he either receives his victuals in the farmer's house, or has allowed him two pecks of oat-meal a week. (5)

Or the unpaid labour of part of the year might be reinforced by paid labour when the farmer called upon the subtenant at other times. (6) In either case there would be a period of the year when the subtenant was free to work his own holding or to work 'for day's wages to different persons'. The livelihood of such cottagers, indeed, came from various sources. In Udny, a cottager would have

> a boll's sowing or two from the tenant; it is plowed to him; his cow is kept in summer with the farmer's cattle; and the straw of his corn from the croft maintains the cow during the winter. He has liberty to cut turf for himself, and sometimes a few peats ... What time he has to spare in summer from Whitsunday to harvest, he works for day's wages to different persons. His wife and children weave stockings ... until the boys are fit for herding cattle. (7)

Keeping the cow, evidently, in the main for the milk it would yield, was the central function of the 'croft' but, particularly where there was plenty of rough pasture, a small flock of sheep would be kept and the ownership of more than one cow may imply the rearing of cattle for the market. (8) In this fashion lived a large proportion of the population, combining day labour for wages, by which the larger farms were kept going, with the working of a holding and with the sale of the linen or stockings spun or knitted by the women folk.

The labourer might obtain the land, on which nearly every household was based, in another fashion — by renting a few acres directly from the proprietor. For this he paid rent and gave some small service to the proprietor but he escaped direct obligation to any working farmer. Nevertheless, possessed of no more than a few acres of land, he had to spend much of his time as a day labourer. A major difficulty in working such a small acreage of land was to find the means of ploughing it. A full plough-team could scarcely be justified for less than thirty acres. Sometimes, then, the crofter would keep two small horses which, yoked with two cattle, would perform, very roughly, the ploughing work; sometimes he would join with his neighbours to provide the plough and the beasts to pull it; sometimes he would simply pay an independent farmer to do the ploughing for him. (9) Such small tenants provided probably a small fraction of the necessary subordinate and occasional labour for the larger farms but they grew in importance through the eighteenth century, slowly displacing subtenants as a source of labour for large-scale farming. The movement towards the direct tenure of small holdings was connected, according to Keith (writing after 1800), with the growing profits to be made from spinning between 1760 and 1780. (10) By subdividing some of the larger farms proprietors were able, by levying rents, to tap some of this industrial income. Even so, the replacement of indirect tenancy was slow; and in any case did not affect the economic position of the holder who remained a man making much of his livelihood by wages earned very often on the larger farms. Thus in 1696 there were already large numbers of evidently small units, held directly of the landlord, which can only have provided a livelihood when combined with the wages of day labour or of plying a craft. (11) A century later some parishes are found with large bodies of crofters holding their land directly of the landlord. Thus, in Kemnay there were 'a good many small parcels of land, which we call crofts, held immediately of the proprietor, and renting from £1.10s to £3'; (12) such holdings were possessed by day labourers and mechanics. This is not an exceptional case, but it was more common for the farmer to find his labour still by subletting his own farm.

In all, in the rural society of the North-East in the 1790s the great bulk of the married men could still hold land, whether as direct or as indirect tenants. In Kemnay, where we have already seen a considerable body of crofters.

> there is no day labourer here who does not rent a small piece of ground, either of the proprietor or of a tenant, which enables him to keep a cow or two, to supply his family with milk, and to rear some young cattle almost every year. (13)

In Crimond, there were 'no villages in the parishes and no cottages to be let but such as have a piece of ground annexed to them'. (14) Even villages were laid out with plots of land attached to the feus and the villager lived much as did the isolated cottager. There were parishes, however, with landless groups. Monymusk had ninety-six tenants and eighty-five subtenants — 181 with land — and sixty-two with gardens only; (15) Keith Hall had 144 farmers and subtenants while sixty-four people had only a house, sometimes with a small garden. (16)

There was one landless group of some size — the servants who had neither land, gardens, nor even houses. This is, however, no exception to the rule that most families occupied land, for nearly always the servants were young unmarried men or women. Their roots lay among one or other of the groups of landholders. The households in which they were born and spent their early childhood — till they were old enough to take part in the herding — would be based in landholding and to some such position the servants would return when in their turn they married and set up household. How far, however, the servants were sprung from a particular group of landholders is not clear. Certainly one of the reasons for establishing so many small-holders was that such households would reputedly produce servants; and a man who had been born in a small-holding household to be followed by a number of years in service was unlikely to have the means in his turn of taking other than a subordinate position. It seems likely, although it cannot be clearly proved, that the servants were, in terms of their whole life-span, part of the class of small-holders, occupying subordinate positions in the rural order but generally with eventual access to small scraps of land.

The main social groups, then, consisted of householders with more or less land at their disposal. The range was wide, from the considerable numbers who had between fifty and 100 acres to the holders of three or four acres, and a primary distinction can be made between households in terms of how much land they had at their disposal. But social stratification was much more precise than was implied by the rudimentary measure of position on this continuous scale. There was a fairly clear distinction between the men who lived independently by farming and those who had to combine farming with labouring for wages — a pressure which usually brought them into direct dependence on the greater farmers; the differences implied in having more and less land became, at least intermittently, division between employer and employee. Such distinctions might occur between people who were on a par as regards the type of their tenure of land — both categories might hold their land directly of the same aristocratic landlord. But more commonly the distinctions were built into the system of tenure. The smaller holder received his land of the greater and was bound by the terms of that tenure to serve the greater as master. For the considerable proportion of the population in this nexus of tenure there could be no doubt about social position; they were firmly in one or other of the two main groups, sharply distinguished within a hierarchical structure, either of the employed or of the employing classes.

The labour of farming, then, was performed partly by the efforts, on their own behalf, of holders who had land enough to give them independence, partly by the aid of a numerous class of people — probably slightly outnumbering the independent farmers — who had small fragments of land but who also submitted to the explicit or implicit necessity of working for wages and who provided their sons and daughters to serve for a number of years as servants in the households and steadings of the greater men. The stratification at any given time was perfectly clear. The distinction between the farmer and the cottager or crofter — and most households came into one or other category — was a matter of common understanding. It was equated, for example, with the type of house that could be expected for a man in one or other of the two main positions. The cottager would have 'his family in the one end and a cow in the other end of some of the meaner cottages'. (17) The tenant on the other hand would have a cottage divided in rudimentary fashion into two chambers — the 'but' and 'ben' — while the cattle would be housed and the grain stored in the various outbuildings. Farms were generally small and the farmers poor, living in housing conditions far removed, for example, from those of the English yeomen, but they were clearly a cut above the cottagers whom they employed intermittently through the year. Whether families were perpetually fixed in the strata that were so evident at any given time is uncertain. There is evidence of a fairly quick pace of turn-over in the tenancies of particular farms and indeed in the tenantry of estates as a whole. But whether this represents the shifting of established tenants from one place to the other must remain in doubt. The fact that so considerable a number of tenants appear from time to time with names new to the particular rent-roll would seem to indicate either that families were moving from one estate to the other or that there was some recruitment of tenants from the lower ranks of the hierarchy. At the least it was not a completely static society in which given families remained in charge of the same farms — and in control of the same families of subtenants — generation after generation.

Until the last quarter of the eighteenth century, however, the change probably consisted of the movement of individuals up or down within a fixed structure. Then started considerable structural changes which altered the basic positions of large groups. This accelerating change was largely the result of a deliberate effort at a general re-shaping by the people of social power, and particularly by landlords. Nearly all the elements of the agricultural system came under radical scrutiny and criticism in the later eighteenth century. There were, in fact, three main tendencies in the adjustment of the agrarian layout by this improving generation. Farms were increased in size; subtenancies were crushed; and a large new category of smallholdings, deriving directly from the landlord, came into existence. These three tendencies, shifting the balances of the older systems, created the frame within which the main social groups found their new basis of livelihood and their relation with each other.

The increase in the size of farms was a tendency of limited result rather than a sweeping movement. The argument of improvers and publicists was generally that a farm had to be at least large enough to utilise fully the working capacity of a plough-team which would have to be maintained at high expense whatever the results of its labour; in the cropping and soil conditions common in the North-East this meant about seventy acres. But for the economic use of other items of farm equipment and for the efficient inter-relation of the different elements of labour and equipment, much greater size was desirable. Here and there, by the time of the Old Statistical Account, consolidations, implying the throwing of several units into one, had been achieved but, overwhelmingly, the general sense of the reports is of farming still being conducted in very small units. The late nineties, according to Keith, saw a more definite move to the creation of big units. (18) Growth could also come through the clearance and improvement of waste land added to the core of an already established but small farm. The typical unit may have been upgraded slightly in size, very often improvements of land within existing boundaries, but it remained such as could be worked by a single plough-team. Of the units above fifty acres — which excludes some smaller units which still ranked as independent farmers — considerably more fell below than above the 100-acre mark, and of these the great majority would only have the one plough. In 1875 Aberdeenshire's 55 per cent of farms in the range between fifty and 100 acres compares with 40 per cent for the whole of Scotland and 9 per cent in a big-farm county such as Haddington. (19) This, in fact, understates the predominance in numbers of the smaller type of farm for there were some of less than fifty acres which were designated as farms rather than as crofts. The typical farm in the North-East, then, was the 'one pair-horse' unit — that is the unit on which only one plough would be employed and the smallest type that was consistent with the independent and efficient use of up-to-date farm equipment. The parish of Old Deer shows, perhaps in extreme fashion, the predominance of the smaller units.

There are about five score of tenements that can be managed with greater or less ease by one plough; above thirty that require two ploughs; seven or eight that cannot be wrought by fewer than three ploughs, at least; and two which furnish sufficient employment for five, six or seven. (20)

The smallish holding, running to less than 100 acres and employing one plough, was strikingly more tenacious in the North-East than in many of the southern districts of Lowland Scotland; such units still provided the livelihood of a majority of the independent farmers. Yet the formation of a new stratum of farms of larger size had brought important changes of balance. Farmers with more than 100 acres were in the minority but they had considerable power. The North-East had very few farmers with more than 300 acres of arable land but by 1875 the men with between 100 and 300 acres had 59 per cent of the land in their hands (21) and employed some 65 per cent of full-time agricultural wage-earners. (22)

The abolition of holding by subtenancy was rapid and complete. Farmers were eager to put every possible acre into the new cropping schemes. 'The active spirit of improvement which recent years have witnessed in our farmers, and the common thirst for wealth, led to the removal from their farms of the cottars and subtenants'. (2 Thus, holders found the small subdivisions of their land-space a hopeless obstruction to the arrangement of the fields for regular rotations; the fields that were now being planned, indeed, would often be several times as large as the smaller subtenancies. The high grain prices after 1790 also increased the farmers' greed for land; acres under the wasteful regime of the small-holders represented loss of cash. But the subtenancies could scarcely have been terminated without some alternative means of ensuring a labour supply. In this, the emergence of the crofts, which we shall examine later, played its part. Another change which altered labour requirements was the declining use of peat as fuel. Partly this arose from the nature of the new agriculture which could not spare its labour during the summer months; partly it was enforced by the depletion of the reserve supplies; and partly it was encouraged by the improvement of inland transport which, together with the abolition of the duty on the coastal shipment of coal, brought the new fuel to the inland farms. Peat and its cutting had been closely connected with the older forms of tenure. When the pressure on the tenant to cut peat for his laird and for himself diminished, he in turn could dispense with some of his subtenants. Further, the diminution of the reserves made landlords think anxiously about the pressure of a large subtenant population on a limited resource. The substitution of coal for peats constituted a powerful reason for dispensing with subtenants.

These tendencies were already advanced enough to be the subject of frequent comment in the 1790s, but subtenants were then still accepted as a widespread and normal way of providing necessary labour, and in 1811 in Aberdeenshire there were said to be 'still too many large crofts which hold of the farmer and where the subtenants plough their own grounds'. (24) But things must have been changing rapidly by this time and by the 1830s there seems to have been little subtenure left. The evidence must here be largely of a negative type. In their nature, subtenancies do not appear on rent-rolls and it will only be by explicit mention that we know of their existence. But it is clear that in an era when efficiency and improvement were prized, any large group of subtenancies which were inevitably poorly cultivated would have been the subject of actual derisory comment. Yet in the many surveys and reports from the 1830s onwards subtenancy scarcely finds a mention. The leases in the nineteenth century, too, frequently contain a clause forbidding the subletting of land. (25) There can be no question that by the middle decades of the nineteenth century subtenants were very unusual.

Subtenants had at one time constituted probably a majority of families in the rural parishes and when farmers began to terminate their subletting it seemed to threaten the livelihood of a whole major class of society. Yet there is no sign of the growth of a large, and poor, landless class and only infrequent depopulation. The surgery on the social order, which was implied by this change, was far from radical. The North-East, in fact, retained its class of small-holders — with a key function in the working of the whole agricultural system — because of the creation, even as subtenants were being evicted, of a new array of holdings, known as crofts, small in size, but held directly of the landlord. This concerted move, which seemed to go so much against the agrarian tendencies of the time, was based on two considerations. Firstly, there was anxiety about labour supply for the larger farms. Crofts were seen 'as affording the means of supplying the large farmers with better labour than they would otherwise secure'. (26) This help accrued not only in the obvious form of crofters coming to work for day wages but also in providing sons and daughters who would become servants. 'I consider the crofts to be of great value for the purpose of supplying the country with a class of respectable servants'. (27) Secondly, the small tenant provided a convenient means of having waste land cleared. New small holdings could be created in the North-East even while existing farms were being enlarged and consolidated because the area, unlike the southern arable parts of Scotland, still had a big reserve of land to be brought into cultivation and which became worth cultivation when, through the middle two quarters of the nineteenth century, price and technical conditions gave a big boost to the types of agriculture fitted to the area. Thus it became common to mark out stretches of foothill or moorland in units to be held by tenants who would pay first nominal and then increasing rents as the small holding became more productive; by the end of the process the crofts would be assessed at rents which were higher relative to acreage than those of the greater farms. The resulting clusters or colonies of crofters are found in great numbers in certain parts of the area.

> There are a great many crofters especially in the upper districts of these counties. They have most of them been originally established for the purpose of bringing waste land into cultivation. In some cases the crofters have been originally squatters,

but in general, the waste which is for most part moorland is let to crofters leased at a very low rent, on condition of bringing it into cultivation. (28)

But even when there was no large area of moorland awaiting clearance, the landlord would find smaller sections on which more isolated crofts could be sited in ones or twos. (29) Here it was probably the question of labour supply that dictated layout. It is very common to find farms with one or two crofts of the same name attached to them; the relations between crofting — with its supply of men, women and boys seeking part-time work — and large-scale farming is almost explicitly stated.

At least till the middle of the nineteenth century the creation of new arable land, very often in the form of small-holdings, was proceeding fast in many parts of the North-East. In the northern parishes of Kincardine, for example, there is considerable increase of acreage between 1790 and 1810, and again between 1810 and 1830. (3 Many of the parishes throughout the area record increases in the 1830s and in the census report of 1851 it is common to find the comment, explaining the population trend of particular parishes, that waste-land has been brought into cultivation, the small-holder being often specifically mentioned as the agent. (31) The increase in arable did not stop in 1850 and all the north-east counties show increases in the area under crop and grass between 1855 and 1875. (32) But it is doubtful whether this last burst in the long process of expansion resulted in new small-holdings; indeed there are reports by this time of some crofts being taken into larger units and a slow decline in the number of holdings occurred between 1870 and 1880. (33)

The small-holdings that were created on the waste provided for many of the sub-tenants removed to allow the greater farmers to make more thorough use of their land. Evicted cottars and subtenants 'had no other resource left them but that of the crofters'. (34) Some of the direct tenants, who were displaced, as in the enlargement of holdings several units could be thrown together to make one, also might be accommodated with crofts.

In the more fertile and cultivated parts of Buchan, a system has prevailed of augmenting the number of large farms; and in consequence, diminishing that of the small. By the operations of this system, many of the small-holders, deprived of their possessions, were forced to betake themselves to the improvement and cultivation of a piece of waste land on the side of a hill, or on the margin of a moor or moss, given them by the proprietor at a nominal rent for a stipulated number of years, and afterwards to be paid for at value. (35)

These new crofts served their holders in much the same fashion as had the old subtenancies. The main object was still the keeping of a cow. This would now be done on the basis of a cropping scheme which obeyed the tenets of the improver; frequently the crofter was compelled to follow the same rotation, with roots, sown grass and oats, as the greater farmer. 'Their great ambition is to keep a cow which they contrive to do by raising a few turnips, potatoes and oats'. (36) On the bigger crofts, however, it might be possible to raise a few young cattle for the market and it was recognised as necessary to provide a small range of farm buildings as well as a cottage on even the smallest of holdings. Like the large farmer, the crofter had little permanent pasture and all his land had to be ploughed, yet none of the crofts were big enough to maintain or to employ fully a plough-team. Thus the crofter was forced to improvise in much the same way as had the subtenant under the old system. He might have his ploughing performed for a fee by one of the greater farmers; or he might join with a neighbour to provide the necessary two horses; or he might yoke an ox with a horse or pony, either on his own account or in conjunction with another of his kind. (37)

In one way, the crofter differed from the subtenant — he was under no fixed obligation to labour for anyone else. Yet the circumstances of his position forced him to combine working his land with labouring, and implicitly to provide the same sort of necessary labour reserve, subserving the needs of the superimposed order of capitalist farms, as had the subtenant whose obligation was so much more explicit. The rent was heavy — crofts paid more per acre than did the larger farms — and the subsistence inadequate (providing sometimes little more than a supply of milk), and the crofter or his family had to find other ways of earning money. Sometimes the labour required on the croft was very occasional and the holder was more of a labourer than a worker on his own account. 'A man who has a small croft of six acres can devote almost the whole of his time to working as a servant for hire'. (38) Sometimes the crofter would combine the working of his holding with carting work (which made it economic to keep a horse for farm work as well as giving him another source of income). (39) When the croft extended to twenty acres or more, as some of them did, the produce would be greater and the call on time would leave him free to take only occasional outside jobs.

The crofter was quite sharply differentiated from the farmer in common understanding and the basis of the distinction was evidently whether or not a man lived entirely from his own farm, or whether he had to do even occasional outside work. There was, of course, a general distinction of size between holdings designated respectively as 'farms' and as 'crofts'. But there was no definite break in the scale of size; a croft might be bigger and more highly rented than a farm, even on the same estate. In general, however, the distinguishing boundary lay somewhere around the thirty-acre mark and, in any case, most crofts were well below this size, while it was most difficult to live independently on less than fifty acres. While the distinction may appear to be somewhat arbitrary when it is picked out on this continuous scale, it was evidently well understood when it came to placing a man in his social position and there is no ambiguity about how the holdings were designated. The use of the terms and the classification of individuals, in fact, was a shorthand for a complex relationship between the two groups. The crofter was in part a labourer. Further, he was most likely to find work on a nearby farm and he became very often the direct employee of the farmer. Certainly, the farmers saw the crofters in this light, as employees ready to meet their labour needs. Not only did the smallholders work occasionally as day labourers but also they provided from their households the lads who would become their servants and ploughmen. 'The crofts supply labour to the farmers; some even engage as regular servants; many work as day labourers; their families make valuable farm servants'.(40) Thus the crofter was classified along with the labourer and the servant, in a social group quite distinct from that formed by the farmers who employed them.

The net effect of the elaborate shifts resulting from the formation of units adapted to the new husbandry, pursued in a period of expansion, was to re-establish the small-holding as a main source of livelihood for a large section of the population and as a key device providing labour for the larger farms. Yet while the new order of small-holdings was laid out partly with labour requirements in mind, there was no exact matching of the population settled on the crofts and the apparent labour needs of the farmers; accidents of local topography seem to have played at least as great a part as the deliberate shaping of a balanced social order. Thus in some parts crofts had proliferated beyond any obvious need for labour. The north-eastern section of the county of Aberdeen was one such area. The parish of Old Deer emerged with over 400 crofts to set against its 140 farms (41) and the nearby parish of Tyrie had crofts outnumbering farms by about two to one. (42) It is more usual to find a much narrower ratio between crofts and farms with something nearer to equality between the two groups. (43) In 1870, in Aberdeenshire, 48 per cent of holdings were definitely of croft type (being of less than twenty acres) and 31 per cent of farm type (being of more than fifty acres); (44) if even a small proportion of the ambiguous group of between twenty and fifty acres were classified as crofts the type would be left in a substantial majority.

Crofts and farms together provided land for a large proportion of the households whose main business was in agriculture. Thus in a sample of ten parishes, representing conditions in different parts of Aberdeenshire, there were 1686 holdings compared with 463 landless households depending solely upon agriculture.* In two of these parishes the number of landless families was over a third of the estimated number of all families engaged in agriculture, but in all other cases the proportion was less than a quarter and in two cases less than a tenth.

While the North-East was, by comparison with many parts of Scotland, an area of smallish, 'family' farms, it depended considerably upon the employment of full-time labourers. Even the one-plough units which formed the majority of all farms would have at least one man, other than the farmer, employed full-time. The greater farms, fewer in numbers, covered so much of the acreage that they provided the work for the greater part of the force of full-time employers. In Aberdeenshire, in 1851, some 70 per cent of labourers were on farms of more than 100 acres. (45)

The size and type of the full-time work-force attached to particular farms was determined by the need to use the work-animals efficiently. Work had to be arranged, in particular, to fit with the use of the two-horse plough, or ploughs, now to be found on virtually every farm. Horses were expensive to maintain and the only way they could pay for themselves was by work on the farm. Thus the team of two which was not in some way productive of result every day was incurring expense without return. To solve the problem of efficient use, the Scottish farmer allocated his horses in teams to ploughmen who would each have the sole duty of maintaining the working with a particular pair. It followed that such men had to be in constant attendance on the farm. Not only had he to be ploughing or in some way using his horses during the normal working hours but also there were the tasks of yoking, feeding and grooming which spread into the early morning and evening hours. Such a man must live on, or very close to, the farm steading and while he held the position he could not engage in any other work. The ploughman, then, was invariably a full-time servant, hired by the six-months or the year, rather than a day labourer; and every farm had to have at least one such man. The specialisation of the ploughman had other consequences for staffing; he had to concentrate on the horse-work and therefore every farm also had to have a man who would undertake

* See Appendix A. p.102.

the more miscellaneous tasks that provided a continuous load of work through the year. It was convenient to have at least one man ever-present on the farm to meet the changing needs of the day and season. On the larger farms, the general tasks were specialised into categories and the ploughmen fitted into a hierarchy of their own. Thus, there might be a grieve, first, second and third ploughman, cattle-men and orramen. On the smaller farms, of course, the farmer might himself hold the plough and he might have sons of convenient age who could be assigned the different functions. But such functions remained the same; two, three or even more, men had to work full-time, with specified functions on even the smallest farm and the great bulk of the men so occupied were hired as servants in an open labour market. North-East farming was based solidly in all its reaches on the hiring of men to give full-time service for the six months, or the year, in the terms of the contract.

Improvement tended to diminish some of the seasonal irregularities in the demand for agricultural labour. Ploughing was spread more evenly through the year, the horses were used on various other tasks of cultivation and haulage when there was no ploughing to be done, and the new tasks created for the summer months were scarcely less than those of the traditional months of heavy work in autumn and spring. Using this tendency, farmers of the North-East, like farmers in other parts of Scotland, tended to have a high proportion of their work done by servants hired on a long-term basis and housed on the farm. But there were still considerable irregularities which even the Scottish farmer could not conveniently absorb by using his full-time staff. It was convenient to use day labourers from outside the farm for some tasks. In particular, much of the harvest and summer field work such as weeding and thinning — and, later in the year, the lifting — of turnips would be done by men or women hired for short periods. Some of the farm work, too, depended on specialised skills for which the individual farm, unless very large, would not provide continuous work for one man; thus dykers and ditchers would also be hired on an occasional basis, working by the piece. And the harvest always needed additional help. Such occasional labour tended to be provided in the North-East by crofters and their families looking for the earnings they needed to supplement the produce of the croft.

Most of the full-time employees were young, unmarried men, nearly all engaged to live on the farm, having food provided in the farm kitchen rather than cooking for themselves in bothies. Thus, in a ten-parish sample, 70 per cent of those recorded as farm labourers were unmarried 'indoor' servants. (46) And in the category of ploughman — the key to farm working — the predominance of the unmarried was even greater. These indoor servants were overwhelmingly young, 73 per cent being under the age of twenty-five and 83 per cent under the age of thirty. Thus is explained the paradox that in a society in which land was widely available to agricultural households, a majority of all those engaged in agriculture were landless and full-time labourers. Aberdeenshire in 1871 had 15,000 servants and labourers to compare with its 12,000 holdings; yet we have seen it to be a county in which the majority of households were provided with land. (47)

The life-history of the individual might well be composed of periods as indoor servant, outdoor servant or labourer, and crofter and many could not clearly be described as landless labourers or as landholders. Their lives held large elements of both conditions. Boys would enter farm service at the age of fifteen or younger.

Few found their employment very close to home, their first and subsequent positions being generally outside the parish of birth, but they did not generally move more than a few miles; probably, that is, they could remain within the area served by the feeing market through which the farmers hired most, but not all, of the men and boys they needed. (48) The period of hiring was six months and frequent moves would follow the first engagement. The unmarried farm servants were notoriously inclined to flit, but their movements seem generally to have been contained within a fairly small area of, say, ten miles in diameter.

Farm service in these conditions was, for most of the men, but an episode in a life of varied conditions of livelihood; and employment as a landless labourer did not define the basic social position of a man in his life as a whole. For one thing, very often he would originate in a land-holding rather than a landless household. The crofts were widely reputed to be important and indeed necessary as a source of farm servants. Superficially the numerical relationship of landholding and landless households seems to bear this out. Some 60 per cent of the households in subordinate agricultural positions were based on small holdings. (49) But it should also be noted that these small-holders were generally of much higher age than the landless and it may well be that most of the families in the child-bearing age were landless. Perhaps a small majority of those subordinate agricultural positions would have spent their early childhood in the household without land; but some of these might well find themselves on a croft before they left the home. Thus a considerable proportion and perhaps an absolute majority would at some part of their childhood live within a household in occupation of land, drawing upon the ideas and ambitions of the small landholder. Whatever their later histories as servants, it is to be suspected that some ambition for a small piece of land would be implanted and that the idea of wage-earners acting in cohesion for common interest would be rejected. There followed the years of employment as an indoor-servant, living around the farm steadings and feeding in the kitchens of the farmers for whom he would successively work. In many cases he would be on a farm so small that he had at best one fellow with whom to make any sort of group. Even on the larger farms he found himself part of a rigid and stratified hierarchy with a very fixed order of precedence. It is possible, however, that ideas of common action did begin to form within such groups. But most of the groups of farm servants must have been somewhat evanescent. If the servant did not show a marked tendency to stay with one employer, neither did he stay in firm groups with his peers.

The farm servant group was also much eroded as the men got married. The majority tended to leave indoor service while still in their twenties, usually on the occasion of marriage. A study of individual parishes shows how sharply the numbers dropped in moving up the scale of age. The number aged between twenty-five and thirty-four was much lower than the number aged between fifteen and twenty-four and the drop was greater than could be accounted by natural attrition (to an extent shown by a comparison with numbers in these age-groups for occupied males in the population of rural Scotland as a whole). On the aggregate figures for all ten sample parishes, the upper age-group is seen to be 60 per cent short of what it would have been with normal attrition. For individual parishes the drop-out could be anything between one-third and three-quarters, but most parishes showed about two-thirds of the group ceasing to be indoor servants, above the age of twenty-five.

For a man leaving his position as indoor servant, that is well over half of the whole group, there was still left the greater part of a working life, and the employment he then obtained would form the main social position of his own life as well as supplying the starting point for his family. One possibility was that he would be allowed a cottage — a cottar-house — on a farm from which he could continue as full-time servant, exercising the full skill of the ploughman if he had been so trained. But cottages were notoriously few in the North-East. Many saw this as a social evil forcing the farmers to depend on unmarried men (with all their reputation for drifting) for the main work on their farms, and throwing an awkward barrier in the way of the servants themselves. Statistics reinforce the general impression of the difficulty facing ploughmen in any effort to find places in which as married men they might continue their craft. Thus, on 595 farms in various parts of Aberdeenshire there were only 368 cottar-houses. (50) It was particularly unlikely that he would continue as a ploughman, for the number of married ploughmen was very tiny compared with the unmarried; it could only be that large numbers left the craft of ploughman, generally round the middle twenties and nearly always on the occasion of marriage. A small minority of the men who had been ploughmen or servants of other sorts, housing on the farm, would continue in such positions through their lives by dint of securing a cottage on one of the farms.

Another possibility was that the servant, on marrying, would find a lodging or a house in one of the villages. Living away from the farm he would not be able to continue in the full-time employments for which the farmer demanded the constant presence of the labourer. He must depend then on work as a day labourer. But day labourers living at a distance from the farms were somewhat rare, possibly because the crofts were always able to supply such labour in abundance. Thus in the sample parishes, only 209 have been found living in the villages compared with the 368 in cottages on the farms.

An allied but less satisfactory arrangement was for the ploughman or general servant to continue to live on the farm and to maintain his family in lodgings in a nearby town or village, visiting it on Sunday, the only day of the week when he had freedom to move off the farm. The plight of the servant with his wife in lodgings at a distance was an evident scandal which received some attention in reports of the second half of the nineteenth century. Some villages appear to have been notorious in providing for this form of existence, and clusters of families in this condition are to be found in the records. (51) But when, in a diverse collection of parishes, the numbers are averaged, this is found to be a relatively infrequent arrangement; the majority of servants on marrying would find other ways of earning a living. Certainly, more would find cottages than would continue to live on the farm as married men.

Some of the men losing their positions as indoor servants would become outdoor employees, whether on the farm or in the villages, and this group gains in numbers above the age of twenty-five as compared with the control group for the population as a whole. But the gain in the number of outdoor labourers is in most cases considerably less than the loss in the number of indoor servants. In the parishes studied, the drop, after the age of twenty-five, in the numbers employed as agricultural labourers, was inconsiderable, but in eight others there was a significant falling-off with something between one-third and one-quarter lost from the original cohort. For the parishes as a whole the loss was 38 per cent. (52)

There remains the possibility that those ceasing to be labourers took over crofts, certainly the ambition of many a farm servant. The dilemmas and ambitions of the farm servants are somewhat wistfully expressed by one witness, himself an employer. 'My present farm servant has been with me eleven years. He is near forty years of age. He looks forward to having a farm. If he were to marry I should not continue him in my service.' (53) Yet this ideal solution only infrequently came about immediately. In our sample, the numbers holding crofts in the appropriate age-groups is far too small to indicate that this was for men below the age of thirty-five a solution to the dilemmas facing them at marriage. Only a small fraction of those who had ceased to be labourers had become crofters, at least within the same parish. The crofts, in fact, appear to have been taken very frequently by men over the age of forty-five. Indeed such was the gain in numbers of crofters at a relatively late stage of the working life that there were more than enough crofts occupied by men to have accommodated all who had started as servants or labourers. The gain came in part from the outdoor labourers, who in their turn may well have been men who had started as indoor servants, for beyond the forty-five year level the number of outdoor labourers in its turn drops unduly. But also some probably were coming from the ranks of the artisan population to combine the pursuit of a craft with the holding of a small fragment of land.

It seems likely, then, that a significant proportion of the men in agricultural service, who originally had come out of the homes of crofters or of agricultural labourers (servants and day labourers) would leave the land entirely, whether because they were marrying and therefore unable to continue in the craft they had learned, or because they had tired of the work and its conditions, or because they saw opportunities elsewhere, or because they had saved enough money for, say, emigration. This, indeed, may have been the typical occasion on which the men left the land. It is well known that there was a continuous movement from rural to urban parishes and from mainly rural areas such as the North-East to the industrial regions of the south of Scotland; emigration, too, sporadically occurred. Thus, in the decade of 1861 to 1871 nearly all rural parishes of the North-East showed some net out-migration, although in most at the same time the population was still increasing. (54)

Thus classification into the groups of crofter, servant, and day-labourer is nominal and transitory rather than significant of lasting social positions. Individuals passed from one group to the other. Men and boys from the households of labourers, out-servants and crofters gathered in a single group — comprising perhaps the whole of their generation — as lads still unmarried, being trained in the skills of working the land. Then, as each cohort advanced into their twenties, they would marry and spread out to take positions as out-servants, as agricultural day labourers, as crofters; or they would simply leave the land altogether.

Some of these shifts may have been made by individuals remaining within the bounds of defined groups of landholders and landless men. Some would begin as children in labouring households, would serve for a period as indoor servants, on marriage would revert to the position of outdoor servant and would bring up their children from the same position in life. Such individuals formed a genuine landless class. But they were probably few in number. In the first place, they have to be set alongside the men who would start in crofting households, who would in due course become indoor servants but then on marriage would move back to the crofts. At any moment of time the households with land well outnumbered those without. But this course of life, with crofting broken only by the pre-marital period as an indoor servant, was perhaps scarcely more frequent than the life which was that of the landless labourer from start to finish. Both these rigidly defined groups seem small compared with the group composed of individuals who would be mostly born into households with some land, would duly serve on the farms, would then work for a period as outdoor labourers, and finally would take a croft for the last part of the working life. Most individuals had substantial experience both of living within a household with some land and of labouring for a period longer than that simply of indoor service before marriage. Thus the groups of indoor servant, of outdoor servant or labourer, and of crofter all show a distorted age-structure; but the distortions seem to fit with each other. The peak of numbers of indoor servants comes before the age of twenty-five, of outdoor between twenty-five and thirty-four, and of crofters over forty-five. It is a picture which may well describe life-histories in which individuals move successively through these categories. Yet when all are aggregated into one distribution, the people in the middle age-groups are lacking. Some must have left the land altogether in that period, while the crofting group draws some strength with the flow of people from other occupations.

North-East agriculture changed greatly in the first three-quarters of the nineteenth century and particularly between 1800 and 1830. A solid phalanx of farms, each greater than any that had been known under the old order, took over the greater part of the land and the system of using the land implied great dependence on the full-time employee, even on farms of the smallest size. Yet a social structure in which the central feature was a nearly universal holding of land proved remarkably resistant and adaptable. The outlines of the class division between farmers who in the main were employers, and small-holders who earned much of their livelihood by labouring for wages remained very steady; the number of people born into landless households and becoming in their turn lifelong landless labourers increased, but only slightly; most men were still small-holders with a taste of fully dependent employment when they had been in farm service and possibly a few years of labouring to follow. The crofts created in the expansion of the first half of the nineteenth century supplied the labour necessary for the larger farms, not only in the shape of day labourers, but also in a supply of young men who would engage to be farm servants for a period of their lives. At the same time they ensured that the great mass of the population would have experience of holding land, whether as crofters or as farmers, and that the prevailing ideology would be that of the small-holder rather than of the landless employee. In general, society was segmented into two grades which were of roughly equal numbers — the farmers and the crofters with all their ramifications.

APPENDIX A : DISTRIBUTION BY AGE IN TEN ABERDEENSHIRE PARISHES*

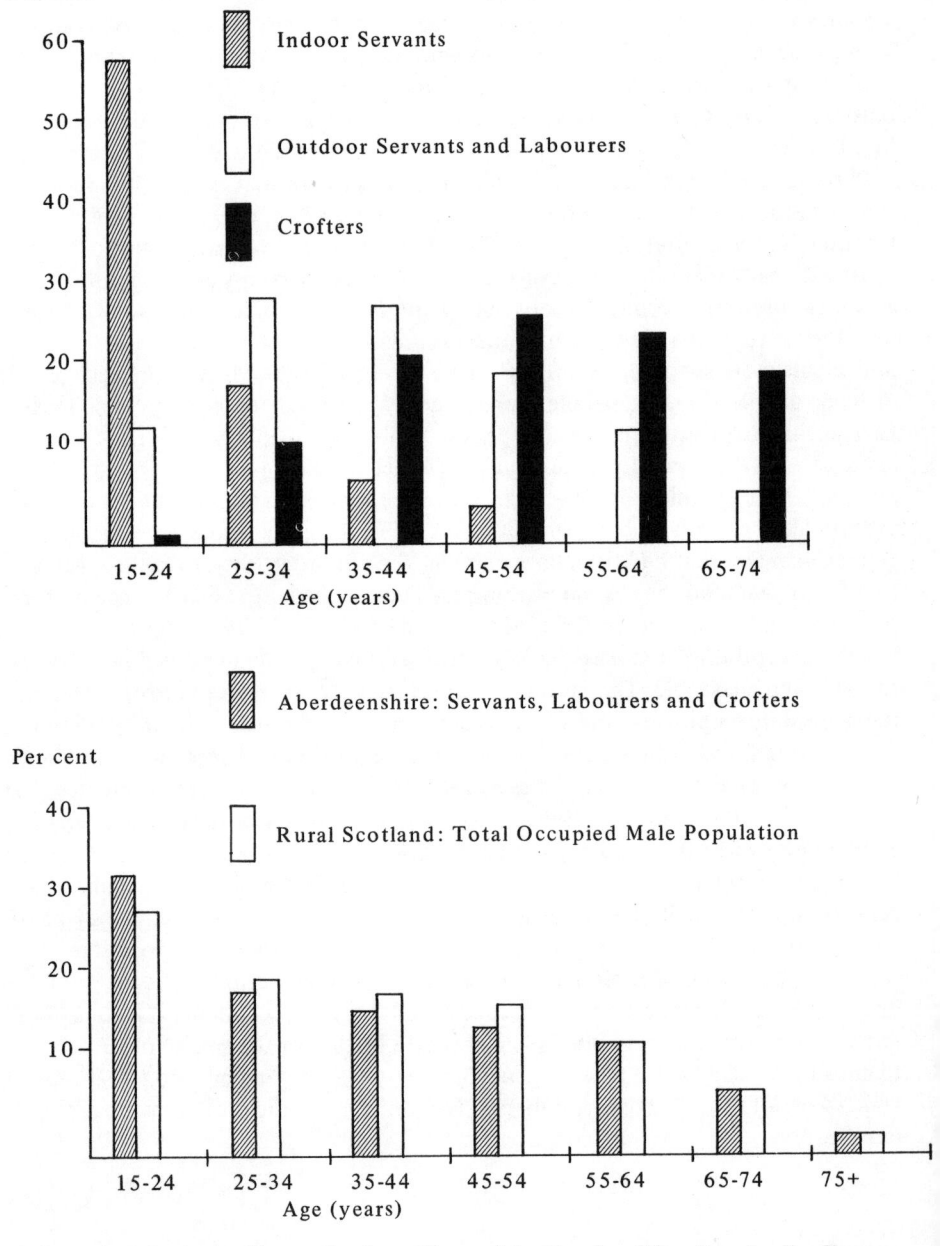

* Chapel of Garioch, Cluny, Cruden, Glenmuick, Huntly, Kinnellar, Leslie, Tarves, Turriff, and Tyrie.
Sources: 1861 Census, Enumerators' Books; 1871 Census Report, *P.P.* 1873, LXXIII

REFERENCES

1. John Stuart (Ed.), *List of Pollable Persons within the Shire of Aberdeen, 1696* (Aberdeen, 1844) gives a remarkably complete picture of the social structure prevailing in the Aberdeenshire countryside in the days before improvement.
2. George Skene Keith, *General View of the Agriculture of the County of Aberdeen* (Aberdeen, 1811), 513.
3. Stuart, *List of Pollable Persons.*
4. *Statistical Account of Scotland,* 21 Vols., (Edinburgh, 1791-8), (O[ld] S[tatistical] A[ccount]), IX, 562.
5. OSA, IV, 162-3.
6. OSA, V, 285.
7. OSA, IV, 162-3.
8. OSA, IV, 31.
9. Keith, *Aberdeenshire,* 149.
10. Keith, *Aberdeenshire,* 144.
11. Stuart, *List of Pollable Persons.*
12. OSA, XII, 205.
13. OSA, XII, 212.
14. OSA, XI, 416.
15. OSA, III, 73.
16. OSA, II, 529.
17. Keith, *Aberdeenshire,* 138.
18. Keith, *Aberdeenshire,* 148.
19. 'Agricultural Statistics of Scotland', T[ransactions of the] H[ighland and] A[gricultural] S[ociety], IV, 8 (1876), 303-8.
20. *N[ew] S[tatistical] A[ccount of] S[cotland]* , 15 Vols. (Edinburgh, 1845), *Aberdeenshire,* 155-6.
21. 'Agricultural Statistics', THAS, IV, 8, (1876), 303-8.
22. *1851 Census Great Britain,* P.P. 1852-3, LXXXVIII, Pt II, 'Occupation of the People', 1034.
23. James Black, 'Report on Cottage Accommodation in the district of Buchan, Aberdeenshire', THAS, III, 5, (1851-3), 95.
24. Keith, *Aberdeenshire,* 150.
25. *Fourth Report on the Employment of Children, Young Persons and Women in Agriculture,* P.P. 1870, XIII, App. Pt. I, 33.
26. *Ibid.* Pt.II, 12.
27. *Ibid.* Pt.II, 12.
28. *Ibid.* Pt.II, 18.
29. *Valuation Roll Aberdeenshire, 1859-60.*
30. See the reports for the parishes in north Kincardineshire in OSA and NSA which may be compared with the information compiled in George Robertson, *General View of the Agriculture in the County of Kincardine* (London, 1810), Table VI.
31. *1851 Census Great Britain,* P.P. 1852-3, LXXXVI, 'Inhabitants 1801...1851', 66-71.

32. 'Agricultural Statistics', THAS, III, 7, (1857-9), 204-7; IV, 8, (1876), 303-8.
33. S[cottish] R[ecord] O[ffice], A.F. 39/1/1.
34. Black, 'Cottage Accommodation', THAS, III, 5, (1851-3), 95.
35. *Ibid.*
36. *Fourth Report on the Employment of Children in Agriculture,* App. Pt.II, 14.
37. NSA, *Aberdeenshire,* 156; *Fourth Report on the Employment of Children in Agriculture,* App. Pt.I, 33.
38. *Ibid.*
39. *Ibid.,* Pt.II, 10.
40. *Royal Commission on Labour,* P.P. 1893-4, IV, *The Agricultural Labourer, Scotland,* Vol. III, Pt.I, 134.
41. NSA, *Aberdeenshire,* 152.
42. *Valuation Roll Aberdeenshire, 1859-60.*
43. *Valuation Roll Aberdeenshire, 1859-60.*
44. SRO, A.F. 39/1/1.
45. *1851 Census Report,* P.P. 1852-3 LXXXVIII Pt. II, 'Occupations of the People', 1034.
46. 1861 Census, Enumerators' Books.
47. *1871 Census Scotland,* P.P. 1873 LXXIII, 'Occupations', 296.
48. Most of the farm servants appearing in the Enumerators' Books are found to be working in a different parish from that of their birth and the parishes of origin are generally contained in a fairly small ring around the recording parish.
49. 1861 Census, Enumerators' Books.
50. 1861 Census, Enumerators' Books.
51. For example, Huntly and Strichen are reported as containing many families of farm servants who were themselves working as indoor servants. *Fourth Report on the Employment of Children in Agriculture,* App. Pt. II, 9, 13.
52. 1861 Census, Enumerators' Books.
53. *Report from H.M. Commissioners for inquiring into the Administration and Practical Operation of the Poor Laws in Scotland,* P.P. 1844, XXV, 748.
54. *1871 Census Report,* P.P. 1873, LXXIII, 'Births and Deaths', 556-7.

6. Class and Culture among Farm Servants in the North-East, 1840-1914

Ian Carter

Farm labourers sometimes appear as bit players in British sociology but they never play the lead. We have had to wait until 1972, and the work of Howard Newby, for the first serious sociological attempt to study the place in the class structure of hired labourers in agriculture. (1) For Newby, following Lockwood, such labourers are deferential traditionalists; 'individuals who endorse a moral order which legitimates their own political, material, and social subordination'. (2) The concept of deferential traditionalism is not well grounded. Lockwood acknowledges the origin of the concept in voting studies of working class conservatism, (3) and Kavanagh has shown how flimsy are the foundations for the concept in those studies. (4) It is ironic that Lockwood should thus derive a key concept from voting studies, when his recent work (with John Goldthorpe) has been devoted to giving the quietus to that other monster from the voting studies, embourgeoisified man. (5)

Lockwood identifies two social structural causes for deferential traditionalism — the worker's work situation and his local status situation.

The typical work role of the deferential traditionalist will be one that brings him into direct association with his employer or other middle class influentials and hinders him from forming strong attachments to workers in a similar market situation to his own. (6)

Deferential traditionalists typically live in local status systems based on interactional, rather than attributional, criteria. (7) This means that status is distributed not according to a single attribute of an individual — typically his income — but through interaction with the individual in a wide range of social settings. Thus a farm labourer may be accorded prestige for a particular skill-horticultural expertise, let us say — and will, in return, accept the legitimacy of (and hence his lowly position in) a system of unequally distributed political, social, and economic rewards. It follows that the only conditions under which an individual at risk of deferential traditionalism can escape that fate is when the constraints outlined by Lockwood are absent. Thus farm labourers can escape deferential traditionalism, and develop a radical social imagery, only when (i) the farm is run bureaucratically, and hence impersonal criteria of efficiency inhibit the development of close personal relations between farmer and labourer, and (ii) one-class villages inhabited by labourers — but with no farmers present — allow the labourers to maintain a radical definition of the situation within their own group. Under the conditions one may speak of an occupational community (8) and expect that 'proletarian' images of a class structure of two antagonistic classes will predominate. Such conditions are rare in agriculture, however; hence 'most commentators regard them (farm labourers) as deferential workers par excellence'. (9) Littlejohn gives an account of deference in the Border parish of Eskdalemuir.

> Judging from informants' accounts, attitudes of deference were more publicly displayed than they are now. Deference behaviour was more constantly and strictly

demanded of the labouring classes by the two farming classes, in the form of cap-lifting and 'sir-ing'. As the blacksmith said, 'It used to be terrible, always lifting up your bonnet, you barely had your bonnet on all bloody day'. A farm servant who neglected to give these signs of his position to any in the class above risked being branded as 'impudent' and fired from his job. (10)

But further north in Scotland one finds an area in which farm servants do not seem to have shown marked attitudes of deference. Compare the situation in Eskdalemuir with the comments of a retired Aberdeenshire farmer about the attitude of local farm servants: 'Oh, but there was aye a scant lack of real respect, what you would say reverence. It was just never overburdened. The familiar name that the farmer got was "the mannie", you see'. Evidence like this supports an impression to be gained from ballads, novels, personal reminiscences — in all of which the north-east is very rich — and interviews with retired farmers and farm servants, that farm servants in the north-east did not demonstrate marked attitudes of deference towards their 'betters' — whether farmers or lairds. Yet as we will see below, the north-east was an area where most farms were small in acreage and labour team size. Family labour provided a significant proportion of the labour force. The housing of unmarried male farm servants in bothies — which might be expected to promote the growth of an occupational community among farm servants — was not common in the area. Consequently, on Lockwood's argument, one would expect that northeast farm servants would approximate very closely to the ideal typical deferential traditionalist. This chapter is an attempt to explain this paradox.

The Hired Labour Force

We will be concerned with farm servants (11) in the counties of Kincardine, Aberdeen, Banff, Moray and Nairn between 1840 and 1914, that is between the effective completion of the agricultural revolution in the area and the changes — replacement of horses by tractors, break-up of estates — which gathered pace after the first world war.

One important feature of the agrarian structure of the north-east was the near balance between hired labour and family labour. The ratio of hired to family labour in 1891 was Kincardine 2.0, Aberdeen 1.4, Banff 1.2, Moray 1.7, Nairn 1.9. By comparison East Lothian, a county with a predominance of large farms, had a ratio of 13.4. (12) These aggregated county figures can be misleading, however, for they disguise significant differences in agrarian structure, as we shall see later.

The age structure of the labour force is also relevant. Figure 1 (opposite) shows the situation in Aberdeenshire in 1901 for male farm servants. The most noticeable feature of these distributions is that a majority of horsemen, cattlemen, and 'other servants' were under 35 years of age, while most grieves and foremen were over 35. Figure 2 (opposite) shows that most farmers were relatively elderly, too. These distributions give meaning to Joe Duncan's sardonic jibe that 'Agriculture is run by adolescent labour and senile management'. (13)

Most of the hired farm servants in the north-east in the second half of the nineteenth century were young unmarried men. These servants were hired by the half-year in the feeing market. Their wages were paid partly in money and partly in kind — food in the farmhouse kitchen (14) and lodging in a 'chaumer' in the farm

CLASS AND CULTURE AMONG FARM SERVANTS IN THE N-EAST 107

HORSEMEN

CATTLEMEN

OTHER SERVANTS

GRIEVES AND FOREMEN

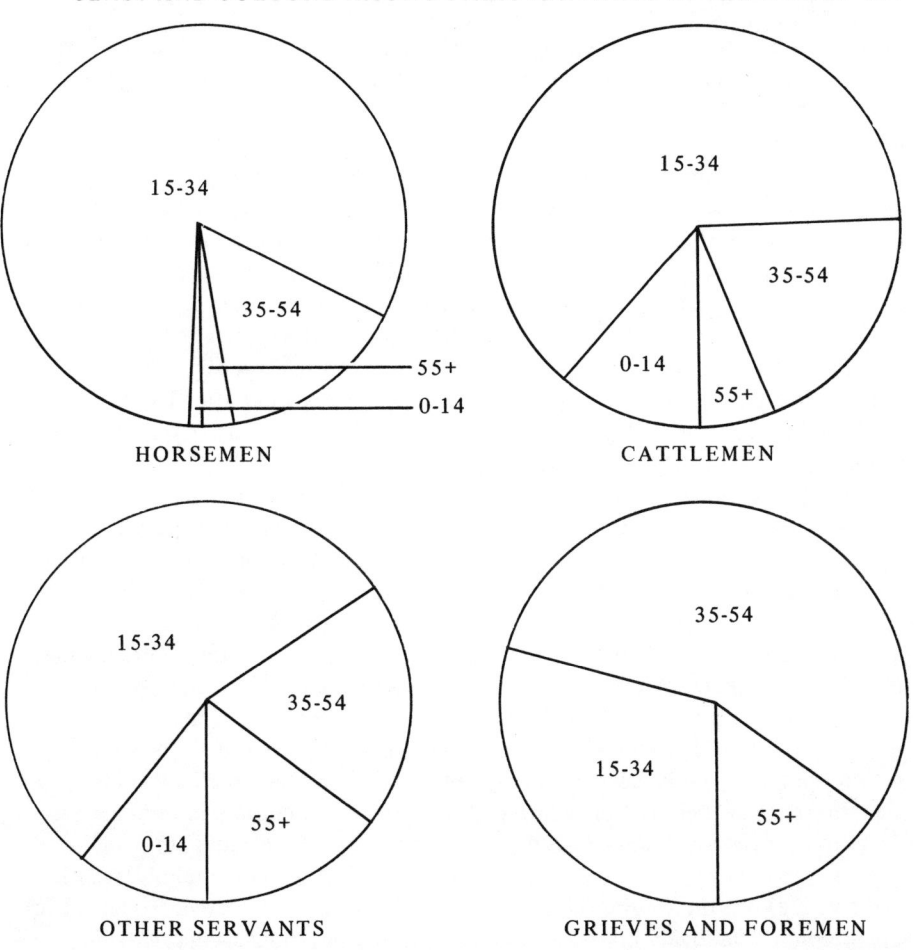

Fig. 1. Age distributions of male hired farm servants, Aberdeenshire, 1901. Source: Census (Scotland) 1901.

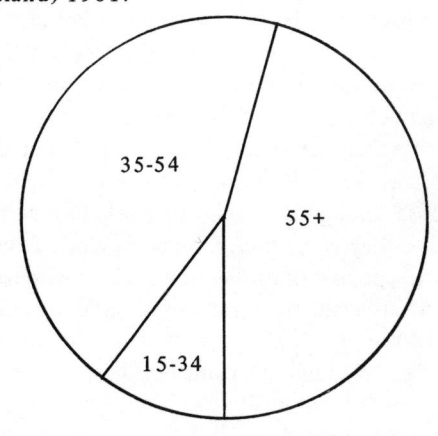

Fig. 2. Age distribution of farmers in Aberdeenshire, 1901. Source: Census (Scotland) 1901.

steading (the farm kitchen system), or an allowance of oatmeal and milk which the men themselves cooked, or failed to cook, in their section of the steading (the bothy system). (15) Bothies were uncommon in the north-east outside the old red sandstone areas of southern Kincardine and the coastal plain of Moray and Nairn, where the general run of farms was rather larger than in Aberdeenshire and Banffshire. This circumstance was most inconvenient for those clerics and proto-social scientists who, from the 1850s onwards, strove to demonstrate a causal connection between the putative breakdown of social control in the bothies and the astronomical rates of illegitimacy in the north-east. (16) But in 1849 there were only one hundred and twenty bothies in Aberdeenshire, occupied by five hundred and fifty men. (17) The 1851 Census shows a total of 10,953 male farm servants in the county. The number of bothies may have increased somewhat after 1850, but by 1871 the number was falling, (18) and by the end of the century it was declining steeply throughout the north-east. (19)

Married male farm servants were much less common than unmarried, though the balance between the two groups varied considerably from parish to parish, depending very largely on the policy of the landowner. The landowner usually let cottages for married farm servants with the farm, and it was his responsibility to build more cottages. Consequently it was only in those areas like the Haddo estates where a paternalistic landlord was willing to accept a low rate of return on capital invested in cottages in the interest of social objectives — in the case of the fifth Earl of Aberdeen, the extirpation of illegitimacy (20) — that the ratio of married to unmarried farm servants could rise. Married male farm servants were hired by the year in the feeing market, received wages in money and kind, and had a cottage on the farm rent free as a part of their fee. This tied cottage could represent a severe limitation on the freedom of action of the servant, as in England. (21)

Female field labourers were common in the north-east in the mid nineteenth century, (22) but their numbers dwindled as the century progressed. Female farm servants were effectively limited to the maids in the farmhouse — dairymaids, housemaids, and kitchen deems. They were perhaps the hardest worked servants on the farm, and they were the first group of farm servants to disappear. At the mid century the maids were often required to work 'baith oot an' in' — in the fields and in the house, (23) but by 1910 girls willing to engage as 'kitchie deems' were growing scarce, and they were no longer required to do field work. (24) By 1930 the maids had gone from agriculture. (25) Maids were always hired by the farmer's wife, usually through personal recommendation, though increasingly, as time went on, through register offices. They were under the control of the farmer's wife while working in the farmhouse, though if ordered to work about the steading — by cleaning lamps, for example — they came under the command of the farmer or (if the farm was large enough to support one) the grieve. They were fed and lodged in the farmhouse, which did not prevent the farm lads clambering over the roof or in at the window with priapic intent. (26) The all too frequent consequence was one main cause of the scandalously high illegitimacy rates of the area. (27)

Resistance to Unionisation

Having sketched in the nature of the hired labour force, we may now return to the problem of their lack of deference. One difficulty in an analysis of this lack of deference, particularly a historical analysis, is that one is attempting to study the social origins of attitudes — for deference is a matter of attitudes rather than behaviour. (28) One way in which those who assert that agricultural workers are almost inevitably deferential seek to circumvent this problem is by taking the failure of such workers to join trade unions as an indicator of deference, resulting from a work situation in which close personal relations between employer and worker inhibit the development of strong attachments among workers in a similar market situation.

It was not easy for men like Joseph Arch to organise farm labourers in southern England in the nineteenth century. Labourers worked in relatively small squads compared with industries like coal mining. A combination of farm labourers was more difficult to organise, and much less powerful, than an opposing combination of farmers. (29) Additional problems faced anyone seeking to establish continuing union organisation among farm servants in north-east Scotland. The individual bargaining between farmer and farm servant in the feeing market was inimical to the development of unions, (30) and thus when attempts were made to establish them, these unions were exceptional for the time in not seeking to negotiate for a specific wage. (31) The frequent flittings of unmarried male farm servants at the six monthly terms, and the rather less frequent flittings of married servants, added another obstacle to unionisation by inhibiting the development of strong and stable union branches. (32) It is not surprising for these organisational reasons alone, then, that attempts at establishing union organisation among farm servants in Aberdeenshire in 1872, 1880, 1886, and 1887 should have been unsuccessful. (33) It was not until 1912 that continuing union organisation among north-east farm servants was established. (34)

But not all the obstacles to unionisation were organisational. Some observers saw evidence of false consciousness. The Assistant Commissioner who surveyed the north-east for the Royal Commission on Labour in the 1890s found that farm servants throughout the area distrusted the Aberdeen-based union organisers. 'I could see plainly from the attitude of the representatives of the branch at Huntly that they distrusted their Aberdeen brethren'. (35) As late as 1926 James Leatham bewailed the false consciousness of the farm servants.

> When we read in the tales of Dr. Alexander of the sordid lives and mean outlook of the Aberdeenshire peasantry, we do not wonder that young men of spirit are hardly to be kept on the land. To get away to the city; and be policeman, carter, commissionaire, or shopman — such would seem to be the ambition of the farm-hand if we are to judge by the fulfillment. To remain on the land and try to make the life feasible to a man of some self-respect would seem to be beyond Aberdeenshire Sandy. Other counties make some show of organisation; and the result in improved conditions warrants, as might be expected, the efforts made. But the Aberdeenshire labourer, pluming himself on his self-imputed shrewdness, and absorbing the interested flattery of those who seek to keep him as he is, steadily resists all the efforts of those who would organise him into unions, with the improvement of his lot in view. (36)

Does the repeated failure of attempts to unionise north-east farm servants mean, as Leatham suggests, that those farm servants who did not vote with their feet and leave the land were all falsely-conscious deferential traditionalists, a lumpish lumpen proletariat without the insight or the guts to stand up in its own interests? I would argue that this was not the case, and my argument begins with an examination of the institution at which almost all male hired farm servants began their careers — the feeing market.

The Feeing Market

Feeing markets have had a bad press.

> ... Nothing can be more calculated to lower the moral position of the agricultural labourer than these degrading exhibitions. Upon the hiring day, nearly the whole rural population flock to the 'market'. Great numbers give up their places for no other purpose than to obtain the holiday. Assembled in the county town, they crowd its principal street, packed up in one dense and promiscuous mass, and there remain, like the men in the parable, 'idle in the market-place, waiting to be hired'. No attempt is made to inquire into character, and the labourers who thus exhibit themselves, like oxen, are judged like oxen by their physical appearance only. The long day done, the thoughtless lads and lassies compensate themselves for the tedium of the morning by evening orgies, which many of the women, at least, may have life-long cause to regret. (37)

The drinking and wenching that often marked feeing markets gravely disturbed respectable middle-class observers and farm servants writing for elite-sponsored essay competitions. (38)

But one finds objections made to feeing markets on grounds other than social control. One set of objections emphasised the unfortunate consequences of the markets for farmers. These arguments are summarised in the quotation above: the existence of the markets promoted unsettled habits among farm servants, (39) and the farmer — having no personal knowledge of the men in the market — had to hire a servant on the basis of personal appearance rather than on knowledge of the ability of the servant. (40)

Another set of objections argued the contrary case — that feeing markets were inimical to the interests of farm servants. There are two points here. Firstly, the inchoate setting of the feeing market was disadvantageous to farm servants as well as to farmers. A servant's reputation for good work was useless when all men were strangers one to another. (41) The second point emphasised the unequal power of farmers and farm servants in the negotiation. The ease with which farmers could combine to hold down the price of labour meant that a weak market position was an existential condition of the life of the farm servant. (42) Once the bargain was struck the contract between farmer and farm servant was systematically disadvantageous to the farm servant.

> The farm-worker is still a servant who enters into a contract of service of a binding nature and for a lengthy period...if he fails to fulfill his engagement, the farmer may confiscate any part of the wages that may be due to him, and may sue him for damages for breach of contract. If the farm-servant deserts his master and another farmer employs him before the date of the expiry of his engagement, the first master may sue the second for 'harbouring a deserter'. (43)

Attempts were made in the north-east through the later decades of the nineteenth century to replace feeing markets by register offices. These attempts came from the farmers and, in the case of male servants, were largely unsuccessful. (44) It was not until after the first world war that feeing markets began to be superseded as the principal means of hiring male farm servants in the north-east. (45) The resistance to the replacement of feeing markets seems to have come, in the main, from the farm servants.

...Raise a finger at the continuance of feeing markets, and you are, as it were, striking a blow at the liberty of the servants, which they will rightly resent. (46)

The liberty to be defended is, at one level, the liberty of a rare holiday for the farm servants, which they were naturally unwilling to forgo. But there is a deeper level at which the liberty of the feeing market was a valuable resource to be defended by farm servants, for it is by no means certain that the markets were disadvantageous to servants.

In the first place, farm servants were not always in a weak bargaining position in the market. A Banffshire farmer gave evidence to the Royal Commission on Labour that 'At present the men like to take the chance of the market'. A Moray farmer gave similar evidence: 'Men will not re-engage before coming to the market'. (47) This was rational behaviour in the north-east in the 1890s. The building of railways in the area, and the movement of labour out of agriculture, had created an acute labour shortage, with consequent high wages. (48) The farm servants pressed home their advantage in this situation. It became common for farm servants to make bargains with two or more farmers at one term, and then choose at their leisure which fee to accept. As a result of the prevalence of this bargain-breaking, a new institution developed — the rascal fair, held one week after the term-day, at which deserted farmers and servants who had not fancied any of the places at which they had contracted to work came together to make new bargains. (49) It is clear, then, that a weak market position was not an existential condition of the life of the north-east farm servant; such weakness was contingent on a labour surplus in the market. The fact that money wages for farm servants rose substantially between 1870 and 1900, while wage rates were stationary elsewhere in British agriculture (50) suggests that such a labour surplus was not common during these years at least. And in so far as one of the main functions of agricultural trade unions in southern England was to test the state of the labour market, (51) the feeing markets did not symbolise the difficulty in establishing unions — they were an alternative to unions.

Nor were feeing markets the inchoate gatherings that their critics maintained. There were taken for granted rules of conduct in the market, as interviews with retired farm servants and farmers show.

You never spoke first. You never approached the farmer. You always gave the farmer a chance, the initiative, to come and ask you. 'Are ye lookin' fer a fee, laddie?' And if you were you said 'Aye'. 'And would ye like to come to me? I've a place — ' wherever it was. Maybe you knew it, and maybe you didn't. You thought about it. He told you what you'd have to do, and the wages were the last thing to be spoken about.

The negotiations in the market were about more than money.

You see, it wasn't just the wages — there were other things that they thought they would like to make a bargain about, like when they would get a day off. You see, there was no half day on Saturday, and they would sometimes stick up for an extra day at the term. 'When we get hame, the nicht o' the term, or the nicht efter, ye'll gie us anither day?' — something like that. And some of them would say, 'We'll get St. Sair's Fair and we'll get Lowrin Fair, will we?' (52)

Once the bargain was struck it was sealed with a dram at the farmer's expense, and the farmer paid 'arles' to the servant. Arles was a sum of money — usually a shilling in the nineteenth century — paid as a manifest of the farmer's good faith and to assist the servant in moving his possessions (usually just his kist) to the new farm at the term.

But it was not just the understood rules of negotiation that put structure into the seemingly inchoate feeing market. More important was the fact that, contrary to the Victorian observers, many men in the market were known to each other, and a good reputation was important for both farmers and servants. Alex Mitchell was a farm servant in the Garioch and the Vale of Alford between 1855 and 1863. In his reminiscences, he mentions three specific occasions at the Alford market where he got a fee on the recommendation of someone else. One of these recommendations came from a farmer with whom he had been fee'd, while the other two came from former fellow servants. (53) A good reputation was a marketable commodity.

A man's reputation goes before him, and it was perfectly true even in the feeing market days, because a man who had a good name, well, he began to be known among the farmers, and he had a far better chance and would get a better wage.
And if a man had a bad name he would have trouble getting a fee?
Oh, there was no doubt about that, no doubt at all about that. And some of them, well, if there was anything against them, if men were plentiful and places scarce, they certainly would be unemployed. And no dole, or anything of that kind.

A good reputation was just as important for a farmer. As early as the 1790s the minister of Alford bewailed the fact that '...The dislike of getting what they call a bad word, among servants, generally ties up the farmer from applying for that redress which the law affords'. (54) The importance of a good reputation did not decline in the nineteenth and early twentieth century.

There's a story of a feeing market, that the farmer and the loon met, and argued a while. The farmer said, 'Weel, I'll along an' get your character, laddie'. And of course he got the loon's character and went back to fee the loon. 'Ah', the loon said, 'But I've got your een, an' I'm no comin'!'

A farmer who was known to have a bad chaumer, or whose farm was known to be 'an ill-fed place' would have to pay higher wages to attract servants in the market. The need for a farmer to have a good name in the market gave rise to the unique cultural production of the north-east — the bothy ballads. Not all the ballads to do with farm life have to do with the iniquities of farmers, of course. Some rejoice in the willingness of the kitchie deems to welcome the amorous attentions of the male servants; others record the welcome introduction of labour-saving machinery; a large group record pride in strength or skill. But the archetypal 'Drumdelgie' pillories the largest farmer in Cairnie for driving his hired men too hard and 'Newmill' attacks the farmer's wife for her meanness in feeding the men.

The breid was thick, the brose was thin,
And the broth they were like bree;
I chased the barley roon the plate,
And a' I got was three. (55)

Sometimes the author of the song was a servant at the farm, like 'The Poet Clark' who wrote 'Sleepytown' and was remembered by a fellow servant as 'awfu' learnt'. (56) But there were also specialised ballad-writers; Alex Mitchell remembered of

CLASS AND CULTURE AMONG FARM SERVANTS IN THE N-EAST

the Garioch in the 1860s that 'If there was a disagreement at any farm, they (the farm servants) sent Johnnie (Milne) particulars, and he would compose verses and sell them at the feeing market'. (57) The feeing market was the setting for which ballads critical of farmers were written.

> Come all ye jolly ploughboys,
> I pray you, have a care,
> Beware o' going to Swaggers,
> For he'll be in Porter Fair.
>
> He'll be aye lauch-lauchin'
> He'll aye be lauchin' there;
> And he'll hae on the blithest face,
> In a' Porter Fair.
>
> Wi' his fine horse and harness,
> Sae weel's he'll gar ye true;
> But when ye come to Auchterless,
> Sae sair's he'll gar ye rue. (58)

The necessity of establishing and maintaining a good reputation was the central element of the social relations of farming in the north-east. But along with this particularistic phenomenon one finds informal collective institutions among farm servants.

Informal Collective Institutions Among Farm Servants

1. *The clean toon.*

The clean toon was a situation where all the servants on a particular farm left at one term day. It emerges occasionally in official reports, (59) but observers from outside the class of farm servants found it inexplicable. Joe Duncan saw it as a part of the usual unsettled pattern of life among farm servants.

> Where there are a few of them on a farm and any changes are to take place at the term, the other young men become unsettled and they decide to have a 'clean toon' — that is, every man decides to leave. (60)

But interview material suggests that the clean toon was a more interesting phenomenon than this — that it was called only when the most senior hired servant left the farm. Once that happened, however, every servant had to leave.

> *What happened if the grieve didn't bide? Was there always a clean toon if the grieve left?*
> In the old days there was, yes. In the old days there was always a clean toon. I rejected this, because once I had to leave because of this, and I didn't want to leave. I think it was a foolish thing.
> *But you did leave?*
> Oh yes, you had to leave.
> *What would have happened if you hadn't left?*
> Well, it was an unwritten law. You had to leave.

Ballad evidence supports this conclusion. In 'The Ardlaw Crew', about a large farm in the parish of Longside, the entire hired labour team, seventeen strong, is preparing to leave at the next term day.

> But now our gaffer's leavin',
> And nae langer can we bide,
> So we'll gang to the hirin's,
> Baith Strichen and Longside. (61)

To understand the quasi-class nature of the clean toon we have to understand the position of the grieve in the social organisation of the farm (or, on smaller farms which had no grieve, the foreman) as the most senior hired servant. William Alexander noted the crucial influence of the occupant of this position in regulating conduct among his fellow servants.

...It depends entirely upon the character of the man who happens to be 'grieve' or 'foreman' upon the farm, what the behaviour and style of talk indulged in at meals, and during the leisure time after hours, amongst the company of lads and young women who assemble in the kitchen shall be. His influence may be for good; but it may also be for evil, and the master is practically helpless to find it out or check it. (62)

The most senior hired man was the linchpin around which turned the social organisation of a farm with a hired labour force of more than a couple of servants.

A grieve is in the position of one who runs with the hare while keeping pace with the hounds ... He has to get a fair deal for his fellow workers and at the same time get fair work for his employer. (63)

One of the stories in 'David Toulmin's' recent splendid set of recollections of northeast farm life concerns such a grieve. Rab o' the Barnyards made sure that the other servants worked diligently, but 'borrowed' things from the farm to improve the lot both of himself and his fellow servants. (64) The farmer knew what he was doing, as did the other servants. But they all acquiesced. The most senior hired servant occupied the crucial mediating role between farmer and servants in the informal structure of social relations on the farm. To protect this key individual in his dealings with the farmer, there developed among the servants the collective sanction of the clean toon. The farmer knew that if at the speaking time (65) — for whatever reason — he did not ask the most senior hired servant to stay on, then he would have to replace the entire labour team.

2. *The Horseman's Word.*

The clean toon was a quasi-class institution operating among all the hired farm servants in the north-east. The second collective institution to be considered operated only among one group of farm servants — the ploughmen or horsemen. Horsemen represented about forty per cent of the male hired labour force in the north-east up to the first world war. The figures for 1861, for example, are Kincardine 39.2%, Aberdeen 39.9%, Banff 41.0%, Moray 42.6%, and Nairn 42.0%. (66) Horsemen were highly specialised; when not ploughing they used their pairs for carting on or off the farm. This specialisation was not resented by the horsemen; rather they resented being asked to do tasks not connected with horses. (67) The horseman's day revolved around working and looking after his pair. He rose at five o'clock, fed his pair, had his own breakfast in the kitchen at half past five, and by six had yoked his horses and was on his way to the fields for ploughing. At eleven he returned to the steading, fed his horses, had his own dinner and at one o'clock returned to the fields for a second five hour yoking. At six he returned, fed his horses again, and had his supper. His time was now officially his own, though he would probably look in to see his horses during the evening. The stable was — with the kitchen — one of the social centres of the farm. An alternative name for the bothy ballads is 'cornkisters', because the men sat on the corn kist (chest) in the stable while singing, their tacketty boots thumping out the rhythm on the front of the kist. Most chaumers in the nineteenth century were either a part of the stable or the stable loft. So the horseman's whole life was spent in intimate contact with his horses, and many developed a very high degree of empathy with, and skilled control over, their charges.

One marked feature of the social organisation of north-east farming was the existence of a rigid hierarchy among horsemen.

The etiquette of the bothy and stable was equalled in rigidity only by that of the court of Louis XIV. Each man had his place and was taught to keep it. For the second horseman to have gone in to supper before the first horseman would have created as much indignation as an infringement of precedence at Versailles. The foreman was always the first to wash his face in the bothy at night; it was he who wound the alarm clock and set it for the morning, and so on, and so on. The order of seniority was as strictly observed between the second horseman and the third, while the halflin always got the tarry end of the stick..... But the foreman had pride of place in everything. He slept at the front end of the first bed — that is, nearest the fire; he sat at the top of the table in the kitchen; he worked the best pair of horses; and he had the right to make the first pass at the kitchen maid. (68)

Interview material shows the negative sanctions used to protect this hierarchy.

I've been working in a different field from the foreman, and trying to be home when he came home. But I was home first, just by mere chance, and I was at the horse-trough with the orra beast when he came in about. He gave me a swearing — he said I had no damn business to be there until he came with his pair. I was supposed to stand back. This is the sort of thing that went on. He started harnessing his horses first. You were not supposed to take a collar from a peg until he did it. And at the same time you were supposed to be at his heels when he went out — you didn't have to fall behind just because of that. You had to be ready when he wanted you.

This fierce industrial discipline existed even when there were only two horsemen on a farm. The same kind of discipline does not seem to have existed among the other large group of specialised farm servants in the north-east-cattlemen. A cattleman would be allocated a number of beasts to look after, and he had to perform a wide range of tasks for them. He might well have sole responsibility for a particular byre and its inmates. He tended to work irregular hours. A man might be tending cattle from early morning to late at night, but there would be long periods when he was not needed in the byre. Thus the cattleman enjoyed a relatively high degree of autonomy in the work situation, and while one man would be designated head cattleman (first coo baillie) and could give orders to his second and subsequent cattlemen, in practice the relations between coo baillies tended to be cooperative rather than competitive.

The situation of the horseman was very different. He enjoyed little autonomy in the work-situation, since his work schedule was timed to make maximum use of his horses and so maximise the return on these expensive pieces of capital equipment. Furthermore, since the most important part of a horseman's work — ploughing — was highly specialised and was lying in the fields open to the inspection of any passer-by, the relations between horsemen were fiercely competitive. The setting where this competition came out most clearly was the ploughing match.

Nobody who knows anything of ploughmen at all can deny they are, after their own fashion, a vain community. By being vain we mean that there is a certain display about them, and an inherent wish to outstrip their fellows in the same rank of life. At ploughing matches and other agricultural competitions they can be seen throwing their whole souls into the contest, not so much for the small pecuniary prizes as to have it said they were the victors. (69)

The ploughing match was the setting where the ploughman showed his skill in public. James Allan remembered a championship ploughing match at Balhaggarty, Inverurie in 1872 at which nineteen thousand spectators — mostly farmers and farm servants — paid for admission. (70) 'The Ploughing Match' shows the making and breaking of reputations, and the characteristic cultural emphasis on pulling down to size any individual who threatened to be too successful.

> The Champion plooman stood the test,
> But young D.E. cam' oot best,
> And O.P. grew some lang faced,
> That day amon' the ploomen.
>
> The judges cam' frae far and near,
> Tae pit them richt they had nae fear,
> But some wad say their sicht was peer,
> That day amon' the ploomen. (71)

It was reputation that was at stake in the ploughing match. But the horseman cashed in his reputation in the feeing market. If he was to gain promotion in the hierarchy of horsemen from halflin to third or second horseman and then, hopefully, to foreman, then he had to have a name as a good horseman. And his mobility chances were not blocked at foreman. Grieves were recruited almost exclusively from the ranks of horsemen. So if a horseman wished to make a career in farm service, then a name as a skilled ploughman — which presupposed skill in handling horses (72) — was a valuable property. It is here that the Society of the Horseman's Word comes in.

For a secret society the Society of the Horseman's Word has generated a considerable, if scattered, literature. Opinions differ as to its origin. Some trace it from pre-existing horse cults and see the Society as a relic of a submerged pre-Christian culture. (73) Another view sees the Horseman's Word as a transfer from the much older Miller's Word. (74) Whatever the origin, however, the Society of the Horseman's Word was very strong in north-east Scotland. It may have had its epicentre in the north-east, for the initiation ceremony was a finely tuned adaptation to the cultural milieu of the area, in which the supernatural was never far removed from the everyday world. The whole arrangement of the ceremony accentuated the inverted Christian — witchcraft ideology of the Society. The initiate had to bring with him to the midnight ceremony a blasphemous north-east version of the Sacrament — a loaf of bread, a bottle of whisky and (in different accounts of the ceremony) a sum of money or a jar of jam. The ceremony was conducted by a 'minister' using a bushel of corn as an altar. The horseman had to answer a parodied Catechism. (75) The climax of the ceremony came when he had to 'shak' the Aul Chiel's hand' — alternatively a stick, a heated spade, or a stirk's foot smeared with phosporous to make it glow in the dark — to the accompaniment of the sound of chains dragged along the floor. Stories are told of loons driven mad by the experience; and although the Society may not have come from the Miller's Word, great care was taken to cash in on the uncanny reputation which millers had in the north-east. To be initiated into the Horsemen's Society was to 'gang through the c'affhoose door'. The chaffhouse was a part of the water-driven threshing mill to be found in most north-east farm steadings — and the part of the steading which, by association with milling, had an unsavoury reputation. (76)

The effect of the initiation ceremony was heightened by the fact that the typical initiate was an adolescent. The Horseman's Oath stipulated that no man under sixteen years of age was to be given the Word, (77) but this injunction was frequently broken. (78) It was not the precise age that was critical, but the stage in a farm servant's career. A loon went through the c'affhoose door when he first came to control horses.

> First I got on for baillie's loon,
> Syne I got on for third (horseman),
> And syne of course I hid to get,
> The Horseman's gripping Word.
> A loaf o' breid to be ma' piece,
> A bottle for drinking drams,
> You couldna' get thru' the c'affhoose door,
> Without yer Nicky Tams.

The promise of the Word for a loon was control of two sets of unruly creatures — women and horses. (79) Control of women might have been of immediate concern to the newly made horseman, but control over horses offered the possibility of establishing a name as a skilled horseman which was a marketable commodity. There is literary evidence that to have the Word enhanced the reputation of a horseman among his fellow servants. (80)

The initiation ceremony was a multifunctional institution. It allowed an opportunity for wild horseplay (sic) among ploughmen; it also ritualised the bawdry of the local culture, (81) which caused Gavin Greig to suppress or bowdlerise some of the ballads which he collected; it also acted as a means of transferring quantities of whisky from young horsemen to their elders (which the youths would recoup from new initiates, in chain-letter fashion). But the main function was to bind the young horseman into a tight fraternity. He was taught special signs, handshakes and passwords by which he could tell if other horsemen had the Word. Thus, although possession of the Word might promote the individual advancement of a horseman, the essence of the Horseman's Society was collectivism.

> *And who told you that you had to go through the c'affhoose door?*
> Oh, just the rest of the servants, you see. They would just come on you, and say, 'There's going to be a Horseman's meeting. Are ye willing to come for a nicht to be made a horseman?'.

Sometimes the summons was even more secretive. An envelope containing a single horse hair would be delivered to the loon. But the social pressures to join the Society were equally strong. Interviews suggest that an attempt was made to recruit all the young men in an area who had become eligible for membership. Once inside the Society a number of sanctions could be used to elicit conformity from the made horseman. The initiation ceremony itself provided effective sanctions. The initiate bound himself to accept a singularly unpleasant fate should be reveal the secrets of the Society to a woman, a madman, or similarly unreliable folk.

> ...May my flesh be torn to pieces with a wild horse and my heart cut through with

a horseman's knife and my bones buried on the sands of the seashore where the tide ebbs and flows every twenth-four hours so that there may be no remembrance of me amongst lawful brethren so help me God to keep these promises. (83)

Further, by going through the initiation ceremony, the horseman might well believe that he had cut himself off from 'respectable' society, had joined an organised deviant group. (84) The ceremony was kept as quiet as possible, which would reinforce this impression. A farm-steading as far away from a public road as possible and separated from the farm house was a preferred venue, the ceremony did not begin until the lights had gone out in the farm house, and no singing was allowed. These were wise precautions, for stories are told of the heavy fines imposed on men caught by police at initiation ceremonies; though whether the fine was for trespass or administering oaths is unclear. (85) Another sanction available to control a newly made horseman was herbal. The young horseman could call on his more senior comrades in the Society for assistance in controlling unruly horses (86) — and that assistance might well take the form of herbal medicines, the existence and utility of which Evans has demonstrated very effectively for East Anglia. (87) But most of this medicinal knowledge was limited to a relatively few senior horsemen. It could be used to assist young horsemen, but it could equally be used to control a horseman. Evans quotes an example of such control from East Anglia.

Sometimes, however, a young or recalcitrant horseman went out of his turn. There would then be a fine row. But nothing much was said. On a chosen morning the head horseman would place one of the inhibiting substances on the harness of the offender's team or on the door post leading from the horses' stall. The offender was then 'in a true muddle'; his horses refusing either to go near the harness or go past the post. (88)

This kind of medicinal knowledge can be found in the north-east in manuscript books written by horsemen. One can speculate that this degree of knowledge was limited, as in East Anglia, to an inner core of the Society, which was probably largely co-extensive with the Ministers of the Word.

It seems reasonable to see in the Society of the Horseman's Word a collective response on the part of a large group of specialised farm servants to the new agrarian structure of the north-east in the nineteenth century. Like illegal trade unions in nineteenth century England, the Word represented solidarity with other horsemen — 'I shall attend to all signs and summons within a distance of three miles unless I be detained by a cause of necessity such as a house on fire or riding for a doctor or a woman in travail'. (89) But, as in England, (90) the Word also represented solidarity against the employer — 'I further vow and swear that I shall not give nor see it given to a farmer nor a farmer's son unless they are serving the same as myself nor to a grieve that is not working horses'. (91) The Horseman's Society was theoretically antagonistic to the class of farmers. We have no evidence of whether this ideological antagonism was converted into collective action against particular farmers, or whether the Society was a purely defensive institution. This is one of many topics concerning the social relations of north-east farming where more research is needed.

Conclusion: Class and Culture in North-East Farming

On the arguments of David Lockwood and Harold Newby which we reviewed at the beginning of this chapter, farm servants in the north-east of Scotland between 1840 and 1914 ought to have been deferential traditionalists. They ought to have endorsed a moral order which legitimised their own political, material and social subordination. The structural correlates of deferential traditionalism were certainly present. Farm servants had a work role that brought them into direct association with their employers. They occupied positions in interactional status systems; the crucial importance of a good reputation for a farm servant shows that his status position was defined by many factors, income alone being relatively unimportant. It would be a foolish man who, after the embourgeoisement studies, would take voting behaviour as a simple index of the underlying perceptions of the world of an individual or group; but if one trusts another simple index — extent of unionisation as a measure of deferential traditionalism — then on the face of it the lack of successful continuing union organisation among north-east farm servants before 1912 again suggests marked deferential attitudes.

And yet the evidence — scattered, discursive and qualitative as it is — does not support this conclusion. North-east farm servants seem not to have borne a close resemblance to the ideal typical deferential worker. How can we explain this paradox?

The failure of unions among farm servants before 1914 can be explained, at least in part, by asking what unions could have done for farm servants. Two of the main functions of unions were performed by other institutions. There was no need for unions to test the state of the labour market, for the feeing markets already did so. The need for unions to promote a collective defence against farmers was obviated in large part by the need for a farmer to maintain a good reputation, and by informal collective institutions among farm servants like the clean toon and the Society of the Horseman's Word.

Attributes of the male hired labour force may also go some way to explain the lack of deference on the part of the farm servants. In particular, one has to pay attention to changes over time in the life situation of agricultural workers. It may well have been the case in the arable districts of south-east England that a large proportion of a cohort of young farm labourers entering agriculture in 1850 would be hired farm labourers for the rest of their working lives. This was not true in the north-east of Scotland, as Mr. Malcolm Gray shows in the preceding chapter. (92) The majority of the cohort would have moved on by middle age to inherited or newly rented crofts or small farms, to cities and towns as carters, railway workers, policemen or a host of other occupations, or to the colonies. This career pattern made for a relatively weak dependence of the farm servant on the farmer.

This dependence was weakened by another factor, too — the high proportion of unmarried farm servants in the north-east. Observers urged an increase in the proportion of married servants throughout the nineteenth century, arguing that married men were more dependent on the farmer, hence more easily controlled by him and more closely identified with his interests, than were unmarried men. (93) Unmarried male servants in the north-east shifted very frequently from farm to farm. 'He wasn't married until he was thirty-five and except for three years when he worked at home, never stayed more than six months at one place. It wasn't done.' (94) Alex Mitchell generally moved every six months in his career in farm service and could only explain why he left farms where he was happy by saying 'it was expected of you'. (95) Observers put this frequent flitting down to bad housing conditions (96) or to generally 'unsettled and nomadic habits' among the servants. (97) But it had the effect, whether intended or not, of limiting the hold which a farmer could establish over a servant. The frequent implication that flitting was expected of unmarried servants suggests that this limitation of control was not unintended. But the frequent flitting had two other important consequences. Firstly, it allowed a farm servant to widen his experience of different kinds of farming and so increase his skill. (98) Secondly, it meant that the servant would have experience of different sizes of farm and hence of large and small labour teams. Thus although the clean toon, for example, was more likely to occur on a farm with a largish labour team, frequent flitting meant that a servant would almost certainly be on such a farm at some time in his career. Thus the informal collective institutions among farm servants, generated on larger farms, would percolate through the entire male hired labour force. If the argument that frequent flitting did limit the control which a farmer could exercise over his servants is true, then it is not surprising that servants should have resented suggestions to limit their liberty by closing feeing markets.

These points take us some way towards an understanding of the lack of deference among farm servants in the north-east. But they do not provide an adequate explanation. The most important explanatory factor is cultural. Mr. Gray shows that the result of the complex transformation of the land tenure system in Aberdeenshire in the eighteenth and early nineteenth centuries was an agrarian structure in which most holdings in the county were of small acreage, but most of the arable land was worked in larger farms, on which hired labour played an indispensible part. (99) But these larger farms were embedded in a cultural milieu which had survived relatively unchanged from the days before the agricultural revolution. The agrarian north-east remained a peasant society on Shanin's criteria:

1. The peasant family farm as the basic unit of multi-dimensional social organisation.
2. Land husbandry as the major means of livelihood directly providing the major part of the consumption needs.
3. A specific traditional culture related to the way of life of small communities.
4. The underdog position — the domination of the peasantry by outsiders. (100)

A number of features familiar to us from studies of other peasant societies are present in the north-east. There is the typical peasant hunger for, and attachment to, land. (101) There is the importance of the establishment and maintenance of a good reputation, in which process gossip plays a crucial part. (102) There is the emphasis on maintaining social solidarity by gossiping about anyone who threatens to be too successful and so challenge that solidarity.

> The pedigree of anyone who has 'got on' is carefully recited, just to reduce him to his ancestral level... A lively interest in his neighbour's affairs finds an outlet in the enjoyable pastime of gossip: a fine art in the farms and villages of the North East. (103)

But above all there is the culture.

The culture of the north-east was arcadian. The Golden Age lay in the past, not the future.

The novelists regard the old order with mingled understanding, sentiment, and admiration. Their sense of the past is strong: and it is a man-made past...The farming that intrigues them is always at least one generation in the past. (104)

This arcadian cultural emphasis has been noted in many peasant societies, and is usually explained as general conservation. (105) But work by anthropologists has tended to discredit the idea of peasant conservation; if one considers the situation of peasants in their own terms, then what appears to an observer to be irrational conservation becomes rational behaviour in pursuit of desired goals. (106) Thus the seemingly irrational desire of north-east farm servants in the eighteen nineties to continue to be paid largely in kind (107) seems more rational when one realises that money inflation at the time was making the customarily defined amount of oatmeal paid as part wage steadily more valuable.

The most important cultural prescription for social relations between farmers and farm servants in the north-east was the requirement that certain customary expectations should be fulfilled by farmers. Rev. A. Gray provides an admirable summary of the cultural stereotype of a good master.

He gives them just and fair wages. He does not grab and grind them down below what their labour is worth. While working his work he takes care that they get good, wholesome, well-cooked food. He sees that their sleeping apartment is commodious, comfortable, and suitable for civilised men. He does not oppress and injure them by overwork, or by keeping them out in all kinds of weather. (108)

The anti-farmer bothy ballads, as we saw earlier, are concerned with offences against this cultural stereotype by particular farmers. No opposition to farmers as a class comes over in the ballads in the published collections. (109)

We may conclude that north-east farm servants showed few signs of deferential attitudes as defined by Lockwood and Newby because of the heavy constraints of a peasant culture whose stereotyped hero was a crofter or small farmer who acted in accordance with culturally defined customary expectations. (110) The large farmer was never accepted to be *ipso facto* more admirable than the small farmer; why, then, should farm servants — a large proportion of whom sprang from crofting or small farming stock — defer to him? Lockwood's argument does not hold in the north-east for a paradoxical reason; it was the overwhelming importance of inter-actional status in the area that *prevented* the emergence of deferential traditionalism among farm servants.

We have been considering five Scottish counties. Other parts of Scotland — and England and Wales — will share more or fewer features with the north-east. Feeing markets were widespread throughout northern and western Britain. The Horseman's Word had a different, and more limited, distribution. The bothy ballads are unique to the north-east. More local studies are needed. Without such studies we will always run the risk of making inadequate generalisations about agricultural workers in Britain.

REFERENCES

1. H. Newby, 'Agricultural workers in the class structure', *Sociological Review*, 1972, 20, 413-439.

2. C. Bell and H. Newby, 'The sources of variation in agricultural workers' images of society', *Sociological Review,* 1973, 21, 233.
3. D. Lockwood, 'Sources of variation in working-class images of society', *Sociological Review,* 1966, 14, 153.
4. D. Kavanagh, 'The deferential English: a comparative critique', *Government and Opposition,* 1971, 5, 333-60.
5. D. Lockwood and J. Goldthorpe, 'Affluence and the British class structure', *Sociological Review,* 11, 133-163; J. Goldthorpe, D. Lockwood, F. Bechnofer and J. Platt, 'The affluent worker and the thesis of embourgeoisement: some preliminary research findings', *Sociology,* 1971, 1, 11-32.
6. D. Lockwood, *op.cit.,* p.253.
7. Ibid. p.254.
8. C. Bell and H. Newby, *op.cit.,* p.238.
9. Ibid. p.231.
10. J. Littlejohn, *Westrigg: the Sociology of a Cheviot Parish* (Routledge & Kegan Paul, London, 1963), p.57.
11. We are concerned with farm servants, not farm labourers. Farm servants worked long engagements of six or twelve months. Farm labourers were hired by the day. Labourers were an insignificant part of the labour force in the north-east.
12. Calculated from data in Census (Scotland) 1891.
13. J.F. Duncan, 'Organising farm workers', *Journal of Agricultural Economics,* 1935-7, 4, p.253.
14. For material on the diet of farm servants see J. Cruickshank, 'Changes in the agricultural industry of Aberdeenshire in the last fifty years', *Scottish Journal of Agriculture,* 1936, 19 pp.230-4; A. Fenton, 'The place of oatmeal in the diet of Scottish farm servants in the eighteenth and nineteenth centuries', *Studia Ethnographica et Folkloristica,* 1971, pp.87-101.
15. This clear distinction between the farm kitchen system and the bothy system oversimplifies a complex reality. It became more common as the nineteenth century drew to a close for bothymen to have their food cooked — in the bothy — by one of the maids from the farmhouse or the wife of a married farm servant. To some observers this was merely a less reprehensible form of the bothy system, while to others it was a new institution — the out-kitchen.
16. The Rev. Dr. Begg was the moral entrepreneur who got this crusade moving; the best attempt at analysis, rather than peroration, is a sensitive pamphlet by William Cramond, *Illegitimacy in Banffshire: Facts, Figures and Opinions* (Banffshire Journal, Banff, 1888).
17. W. Watson, *Remarks on the Bothie System and Feeing Markets* (G. Davidson, Aberdeen, 1849), p.3.
18. H.G. Reid, *Past and Present* (Edmonston & Douglas, Edinburgh, 1871), p.197.
19. PP 1893, xxxvi, pp.115, 119, 122, 126, 137, 139; W. Diack, 'The Scottish farm labourer', *Independent Review,* 1905, 7, p.320.
20. Rev. E.B. Elliott, *Memoir of Lord Haddo, in his latter years fifth Earl of Aberdeen* (Seeley, Jackson and Halliday, London, fifth edition, 1869), p.387. Aberdeen saw only a three per cent return on capital invested in building cottages in the eighteen sixties.

21. H. Newby, *op.cit.*, p.421.
22. PP 1867, xiii, 34.
23. Ibid.
24. A.R. Mortimer, *Notes on Farm Kitchen Work* (Elgin Courier, Elgin, 1910), p.52.
25. J.F. Duncan, 'Farm workers in the north-east, 1851-1951', *Scottish Agriculture*, 1951.
26. J.R. Allan, *Farmer's Boy* (Methuen, London, 1935), pp.32, 46-7.
27. The most understanding — though still disapproving — account of the plight of a pregnant deem is by William Alexander: 'Bawbie Huie's Bastard geet' in W. Alexander, *Life Among my Ain Folk* (D. Douglas, Edinburgh, 1882), second edition, pp.204-230.
28. E. Shils, 'Deference', in J.A. Jackson (ed), *Social Stratification* (Cambridge University Press, Cambridge, 1968), p.116.
29. H. Newby, *op.cit.*, p.16.
30. J.P.D. Dunbabin, 'The incidence and organisation of agricultural trade unionism in the 1870s', *Agricultural History Review*, 1968, 16, p.122.
31. G. Evans, 'Trade unionism and the wage level in Aberdeen between 1870 and 1920', *unpublished PhD thesis, University of Aberdeen*, c 1950, section 3, ch B, part a (thesis unpaginated).
32. G. Evans, 'Farm servants' unions in Aberdeenshire from 1870 to 1900', *Scottish Historical Review*, 1952, 31, p.31. See also K.D. Buckley, *Trade Unionism in Aberdeen 1878-1900* (Aberdeen University Press, Aberdeen, 1955), pp.30-1.
33. G. Evans, 'Farm servants' unions...'
34. J.H. Smith, *Joe Duncan: The Scottish Farm Servants and British Agriculture*, RCSS University of Edinburgh and the Scottish Labour History Society, Edinburgh, 1973, chapter 3.
35. PP 1893, xxxvi, pp.113, 133.
36. J. Leatham, 'An Aberdeenshire classic — centenary of Dr. William Alexander', *Trans. Buchan Field Club*, 1926, 13, pp.128-9.
37. Anon, 'The Scottish farm labourer', *Cornhill Magazine*, 1864, 10, pp.619-20.
38. J. Alexander, *Prize Essay on the Present Condition of Farm Servants in Scotland* (W. Bennett, Aberdeen, 1852), p.9; A. Fraser, 'Essay', p.11 and 'Bone and Sinew', 'Essay on the Present Condition of Farm Labourers', p.61, both in *Essays by Agricultural Labourers on the Condition and Improvement of their Class* (A. Brown, Aberdeen, 1859).
39. R. Molland and G. Evans, 'Scottish Farm Wages from 1870 to 1900', *J. Royal Statistical Society*, 1950, 113, p.221.
40. A. Harvey, *The Agricultural Labourer* (A. Brown, Aberdeen, p.22); Anon, 'The Homes of the Working Poor', *Poor Law Magazine*, 1859, 1, p.260; W. Watson, *op.cit.*, p.4.
41. 'Bone and Sinew', *op.cit*, p.61.
42. W. Watson, *op.cit.*, p.4; H. Newby, *op.cit.*, p.415.
43. PP 1917/18, xiv, p.162. For an analysis of the implementation of these legal provisions see G. Houston, 'Labour relations in Scottish agriculture before 1870', *Agricultural History Review*, 1958, 6, 28-41. See also W. Diack, *op.cit.*, p.327.

44. PP 1867, xiii, pp.36-7; A. Forbes Irvine, 'Report on hiring markets by a committee of the society', *Trans. Highland and Agricultural Society,* 1873, 4th series, 5, pp.312-3: PP 1893, xxxvi, p.130.
45. J.H. Smith, *op.cit.,* pp.61-2.
46. 'An Agricultural Labourer', *Duty to Farm Servants* (W. Bennett, Aberdeen, 1859), pp.9-10.
47. PP 1893, xxxvi, p.122.
48. R. Molland and G. Evans, *op.cit.,* p.226.
49. W. Alexander, 'The peasantry of north-east Scotland', *United Presbyterian Magazine,* 1884, 1, p.428; PP 1893, xxxvi, p.110.
50. R. Molland and G. Evans, *op.cit.,* p.226.
51. J.P.D. Dunbabin, *op.cit.,* pp.120-1.
52. The differences in the bargains struck, and the considerable element of — and variation in — payment in kind as part of the total wage makes it impossible to make precise statements about average earnings among farm servants. See R. Molland and G. Evans, *op.cit.,* pp.223-3.
53. A. Mitchell, *Recollection of a Lifetime* (privately printed, 1911), pp.42, 45, 49-50.
54. *Old Statistical Account,* 15, p.469.
55. G. Greig, *Folk-Song of the North East* (Buchan Observer, Peterhead, 1909), Article 92.
56. G. Greig , *op. cit.,* second series, 1914, Article 133.
57. A. Mitchell, *op. cit.,* p.35. For the activities of such ballad-writers at Paldy Fair in Kincardine see C.A. Mollyson, *The Parish of Fordoun* (J.R. Smith, Aberdeen, 1892), pp.79-80.
58. G. Greig, *op. cit.* Article 138. Porter Fair was the great feeing market at Turriff. Ballads may have been written for specific occasions in specific feeing markets, but they could affect a farmer's reputation for a good distance around. Gavin Greig collected versions of 'Sleepytown', about a farm in the Garioch parish of Kennethmont, from Maud, New Deer, Bruckley and Fyvie. Maud is some twenty-five miles from Sleepytown as the crow flies.
59. PP 1893, xxxvi, p.122; PP 1935-6, vii, pp.11-12.
60. J.F. Duncan, 'The Scottish agricultural labourer' in D.T. Jones, J.F. Duncan, H.M. Conacher and W.R. Scott (ed), *Rural Scotland During the War* (Clarendon Press, Oxford, 1926), p.191.
61. G. Greig, *op.cit.,* Article 92.
62. W. Alexander, 'Peasantry of north-east Scotland', p.427.
63. J.R. Allan, *The Seasons Return* (Robert Hale, London, 1955), p.61. The structural position of the grieve or foreman of a farm echoes that of the foreman in industrial settings. See C. Fletcher, 'Men in the middle: a reformulation of the thesis', *Sociological Review,* 1969, 17, 341-54.
64. 'David Toulmin', *Hard Shining Corn* (Impulse, Aberdeen, 1972), pp.26-36.
65. The speaking time was shortly before the local feeing market. At this time the farmer asked those servants that he wished to keep if they would stay. As in the market, the farmer had to ask the man; the man could not ask the farmer if he might stay.

66. Calculated from data in *Census (Scotland)* 1861.
67. Anon, 'Hints by the Banffshire ploughman', *Farmer's Magazine,* 1806, 7, p.54.
68. J.R. Allan, Farmer's Boy, p.113. Note the confusion between bothy system and farm kitchen system.
69. Mr. Watt (Stonehaven), 'The condition of the labouring poor', *Poor Law Magazine,* 1859, 2, p.231.
70. J. Allan, 'Agriculture in Aberdeenshire in the sixties', *Deeside Field,* 1927, 3, p.31.
71. G. Greig, *op.cit.,* Article 163.
72. For an account of the great skill of Kincardine horsemen — and their pride in that skill — see G. Robertson, *Rural Recollections* (Edinburgh, 1929), p.422.
73. T. Davidson, 'The Horseman's Word: a rural initiation ceremony', *Gwerin,* 1956, 1, pp.71-4; G.E. Evans, *The Pattern Under the Plough* (Faber and Faber, 1966), p.235.
74. W. Singer, *An Exposition of the Miller and Horseman's Word, or the True System of Raising the Devil* (J. Anderson, Aberdeen, sixth edition, 1865).
75. For one version of this chatechism see W. Singer, *op.cit.,* pp.35-6.
76. See 'Neil Roy' (A.D. Russell), *The Horseman's Word* (Macmillan, London, 1895), pp.92-9. This novel mixes a conventional Victorian plot about the dangers of aspiring to move out of one's class with acute observation of the forms of social organisation among horsemen in the Banffshire parish of Grange.
77. For published versions of the Horseman's Oath from the north-east see G.E. Evans, *op.cit.,* pp.230-1, and *The Horseman's Oath, as written down by a Buchan horseman in 1908,* broadsheet published by the Scottish Country Life Museums Trust, 1972.
78. 'I do not remember the half that he said, but I had "never to reveal, but always conceal, never give the 'word' to a boy under a certain age'. Well, *I* was a long way under that age.' A Herd Loon, *The Kingdom of Forgue* (G. & W. Fraser, Aberdeen, 1905), p.67.
79. J.P. Collie, 'A study of the treatment of the life of north-east Scotland by Scottish novelists', *unpublished PhD thesis, University of Aberdeen,* 1954, pp.70-1. Singer quotes recipes for a horseman to be able 'to make a girl tell you her mind', 'to make a person dance', and 'to make a girl follow you' (W. Singer, *op.cit.,* pp.20-2). Perhaps the efficacy of the Word is the true explanation of the high rates of illegitimacy in the north-east!
80. 'Neil Roy', *op.cit.,* pp.132-42; H. Beaton, *At the Back o' Benachie, or Life in the Garioch in the Nineteenth Century* (Central Press, Aberdeen, second edition, 1923), pp.67-8, 119, 146.
81. H. Henderson, 'The oral tradition', *Scottish International,* 1973, 6, p.31.
82. Interview by Hamish Henderson, School for Scottish Studies, University of Edinburgh.
83. *The Horseman's Oath...* Here, as elsewhere, the Oath owes a great debt to Freemasonry.
84. H. Becker, *Outsiders* (New York, Free Press, 1963), pp.37-39.
85. The administration of bloodthirsty oaths — and other features — links the

86. H. Henderson, 'A slight case of devil worship', *New Statesman,* 14 June 1952, p.698.
87. G.E. Evans, *The Horse in the Furrow* (Faber and Faber, London, 1960), pp. 251-271.
88. G.E. Evans, 'The horse and magic', *New Society,* 14 March 1963, p.16.
89. From an unpublished version of the Horseman's Oath in the School of Scottish Studies, University of Edinburgh.
90. E.P. Thompson, *op.cit.,* p.531.
91. Unpublished version of the Horseman's Oath, School of Scottish Studies.
92. See pp.86-101.
93. H., 'An essay on the proper size of farms', *Farmer's Magazine,* 1801, 1, p.380; G. Robertson, *General View of the Agriculture of Kincardineshire or the Means* (R. Philips, London, 1810), p.423; J. Black, 'Report on the cottage accommodation in the district of Buchan', *Trans. Highland and Agricultural Society,* 1851, 3rd series, 5, p.98; Rev. A. Gray, *Talks with our Farm Servants* (R. & R. Clark, Edinburgh, 1906), pp.101-6.
94. Letter concerning a Banffshire farm servant in the Country Life section, National Museum of Antiquities, Edinburgh.
95. A. Mitchell, *op.cit.,* p.37.
96. T. Ferguson, *Scottish Social Welfare* (E. & R. Livingstone, Edinburgh, 1958), p.41.
97. W. Alexander, 'Peasantry of north-east of Scotland', p.428.
98. PP 1893, xxxv, p.120.
99. See pp.86-101.
100. T. Shanin, 'Introduction', to T. Shanin (ed), *Peasants and Peasant Societies* (Penguin, London, 1971), pp.14-15.
101. PP 1867, xiii, p.33. The most forceful literary expression of this deep attachment to land is Lewis Grassic Gibbon's essay 'The Land', in 'L.G. Gibbon', (J.L. Mitchell), *A Scots Hairst* (Hutchinson, London, 1967), pp.66-81.
102. F.G. Bailey, *Gifts and Poison: The Politics of Reputation* (Blackwell, Oxford 1971), pp.1-25.
103. J.P. Collie, *op. cit.,* pp.73, 74-5.
104. Ibid., pp.38, 50.
105. See, for example, K. Dobrowolski, 'Peasant traditional culture', in T. Shanin (ed), *op.cit.,* pp.277-98. For peasant conservation in lowland Scotland before the agricultural revolution see T.C. Smout, *A History of the Scottish People, 1560-1830* (Collins, London, 1969), p.123.
106. E. Wolf, *Peasants* (Prentice-Hall, Englewood Cliffs NJ), chapters 2 and 3; F.G. Bailey, 'The peasant view of the bad life', in T. Shanin (ed), *op.cit.,* pp.299. 231; Sutti, R. de Ortiz, *Uncertainties in Peasant Farming: A Columbian Case* (Athlone Press, London, 1973).
107. PP 1893, xxxvi, pp. 112, 131.
108. Rev. A. Gray, *op.cit.,* p.108.

109. Buchan takes one song — 'Depression' (G. Greig, *op.cit.*, Article 147) — to be a case of 'militant class-consciousness' (D. Buchan, *The Ballad and the Folk* [Routledge and Kegan Paul, London, 1972], p.264). But this is not a song of farm servants; it is a song of the opposition of farmers to landlords and their factors.
110. The archetypical hero is the name character of the classic novel of the north-east, William Alexander's *Johnny Gibb of Gushetneuk* (D. Douglas, Edinburgh, 1880).

7. Thrift and Working-class Mobility in Victorian Edinburgh

Robert Q. Gray

Various commentators have suggested that the diffusion of norms of 'self help' was an integrative force in the grossly inegalitarian society of Victorian Britain. Thus Bendix cites the writings of Samuel Smiles as representing 'the formulation of an entrepreneurial ideology' — an essentially bourgeois value system whose promise of individual opportunity in an open economic and social structure could appeal to the working class. (1) And Best points to the 'socially-soothing tendency' of 'the concepts of respectability and independence' which assimilated 'even the most widely separated groups ... through a common cult'. (2) In this chapter I attempt to analyse the prevalence among working class people in Victorian Edinburgh of those modes of behaviour prescribed by the norms of 'respectability and independence'. The available evidence is inevitably fragmentary in character; but it does suggest that the upper strata of the working class were likely to act in ways congruent with the norms under discussion, and even to legitimate this behaviour in the language of the dominant value system. This pattern is, I shall argue, explicable in relation to the social experience of the 'labour aristocrat' (3) which pre-disposed him to envisage a relatively long-run project of improvement in his personal situation. But to understand fully the significance of this we require a more rounded picture of artisan life, to set such behaviour as saving in the context of the total situation of the worker, and the kinds of opportunity available to improve that situation. Smiles himself implied that thrift had to be seen in relation to the problems of survival under the conditions of working class life; (4) and those conditions could generate solidaristic behaviour at variance with the dominant norms and values. The notions of 'respectability' and 'self help' articulated by the upper stratum of the working class have, therefore, to be interpreted, by analysing the complex interaction of personal aspiration and class identity.

This chapter is concerned, first, to establish that high levels of participation in savings institutions distinguished the 'aristocratic' upper stratum of the working class, and that the visible commitment to thrift, foresight and restraint was an aspect of the life-style of the 'respectable working man'. It is then necessary to pose further questions about the significance of this pattern, and especially about the extent to which it represents a wholesale adoption of middle class values and social perspectives. This demands some discussion of the place of saving in the daily life of the artisan, and the prospects of future change in his position open to him. The analysis will, it is hoped, throw some light on the alternative meanings of widely used words, the differential interpretation of norms and values. Any discussion of thrift and the life-style of working class 'respectability' must consider the important elements of class identity and class tension, as well as those elements drawn from a language common to the social perceptions of middle class and working class groups.

There is a good deal of impressionistic evidence of the special appeal to artisans of organizations catering for the small saver. At the Royal Commission on Friendly Societies (1872) spokesmen for various Edinburgh lodges gave the same broad picture; in the words of the Free Gardeners' secretary, the members were 'generally speaking artizans'. (5) Shareholders in the Co-operative Building Company consisted of 'masons, joiners, plasterers, plumbers, printers, and every trade in Edinburgh'. (6) The historian of St Cuthbert's Co-operative Association (the leading consumer co-operative in the city) similarly indicated the link between institutions of working class thrift and the upper stratum: 'The cabinet works of Messrs. J. & T. Scott almost adjoined the railway works, so that, at Haymarket alone, there was a large number of intelligent workmen to whom co-operation would naturally appeal.' (7)

A breakdown of membership for one friendly society lodge and account-holders at the Edinburgh Savings Bank adds some statistical support to the impressionistic evidence. (8) Table 1 shows a majority of artisans in the Oddfellows and in the Savings Bank at the earlier period, and they are still the largest single group of new account-holders at the later period. The under-representation of unskilled workers is likewise to be expected; they are out-weighed by the proportion of business and white collar groups in all three columns of the table. It should be emphasized that the figures only represent two institutions — a tiny and non-random sample of the local bodies catering for those who wished to save small sums from limited incomes. The data do, however, support, for the two organizations concerned, a widespread impression of high skilled worker membership in savings institutions.

Table 1. Social Composition of Oddfellows' Lodge and Accounts opened at Edinburgh Savings Bank

	Oddfellows 1850s-70s	Savings Bank 1865-9	Savings Bank 1895-9
	%	%	%
Professions	1	2	8
Business, white collar	11	22	25
Retail, warehouse employees	1	3	2
Manual — skilled	71	52	37
Manual — semi and unskilled	1.5	10	12
Manual — skill unclassifiable	3.5	2	1
Domestic service	4	5	8
Miscellaneous services	3.5	1	2
Other, miscellaneous	3.5	3	3
	100	100	98
N	202	1420	772

We also have statistical evidence, of a less direct and more problematic kind, for another aspect of 'provident' behaviour. Banks has shown how, in the Victorian middle class, men were expected to postpone marriage until their resources enabled them to maintain a certain style of married life. (9) This discussion apparently percolated through to the world of the artisan, at least in Edinburgh. The *North Briton* (a local radical paper with a trade unionist orientation) advised working men to follow the middle class example of later marriage; and the president of Edinburgh Trades Council (a joiner) deplored the habit of early marriage at the Royal Commission on Housing (1884-5). (10) An analysis of occupational differences in marriage patterns may thus have some relevance to my theme. Table 2 gives figures for the ages of grooms, from marriage certificates for all men in selected occupations marrying during 1865-9 and 1895-7. (11) The skilled trades (with the exception of printers and painters in the 1860s) do have smaller proportions of grooms aged 21 and under than the two unskilled occupations included (building labourers and carters). While it is perhaps dangerous to assume that this pattern reflects directly the discussion cited above, it is nonetheless likely that the later marriage of skilled men had some relationship to the hope of accumulating resources before embarking on married life.

Table 2. Age of Grooms in Selected Occupations, Edinburgh Registration District

	1865-9		1895-7	
	N (grooms)	% aged 21 and less	N (grooms)	% aged 21 and less
Printer	135	21	127	8
Bookbinder	31	16	27	18.5
Mason	187	9	167	15
Joiner	212	7	177	10
Painter	77	23	82	18
Engineer	100	11	98	10
Ironmoulder	23	13	29	10
Brassfinisher	39	18	34	3
Shoemaker	115	11	64	12.5
Building labourer	113	19.5	108	23
Carter	80	29	127	22
All skilled occupations	919	13	805	12
Semi and unskilled	193	23	235	23
All occupations	1112	15	1040	14

Saving and later marriage thus characterised the skilled section of the Edinburgh working class. This pattern had, moreover, a widely recognized cultural meaning; it formed part of the distinctive life-style of the 'respectable artisan'. In this perspective the behaviour under discussion must be seen in relation to the patterns of residence, standard of life, leisure activity etc., which underpinned the labour aristocracy's claim to belong to the 'respectable' section of Victorian society. (12)

It may be noted, first, that a closer occupational analysis of savings institutions indicates a concentration of men from unusually prosperous trades. The pattern here is similar to that for certain local voluntary organizations which, as I have argued elsewhere, (13) helped define the image of the 'superior artisan'. Thus trades with 'several' men in the Oddfellows include masons, joiners, engineers, shoemakers and gold-beaters; (14) with the exception of the shoemakers (15) these are all economically advantaged trades. Founder members of St Cuthbert's included joiners and cabinetmakers (three each) — trades which 'throughout the long history of the society... have been well represented on the board' — a wood turner, two blacksmiths, an engine-driver, a warehouseman and a foundry manager. (16) Table 2 shows, moreover, that the masons, joiners and engineers — all identifiable as 'superior' trades — are among those with the lowest proportions of grooms aged 21 and under; while the figures for the painters — a trade notoriously afflicted by unapprenticed men and casualisation — likewise suggest a link between behaviour patterns and the economic hierarchy of skilled labour. (17)

Turning now to the more impressionistic evidence on which we must rely for a picture of values and attitudes, we find an insistence on the special identity of the 'respectable artisan': 'Generally speaking, should you say that your society included the poor? — No; the members of our lodge are rather of a respectable class, — what are called respectable artizans.' (18) And a moralistic perspective is often in evidence in attitudes to those sections of the working class unable, or unwilling to act in the ways prescribed by 'respectability'.

> He met the objections of those who looked upon the Co-operative movement as a mere matter of £ s. d., as though the members had no higher aim than the gaining of a few shillings per year in the shape of dividend, losing sight altogether of the grand moral principles which lay at the basis of the movement, as it must be patent to every right-minded and thoughtful man that, if the Co-operative element were to pervade society more generally than it did at the present time, a vast amount of the misery and crime, consequent upon intemperance and improvidence, would be altogether unknown. (19)

The influence of economic individualism is clear enough in the fears expressed by the president of Edinburgh Trades Council that the provision of municipal housing 'would strike at that industry and enterprise that lies at the very root of our national existence.' (20)

The struggle to eradicate 'intemperance and improvidence' is a main theme in the early history of St Cuthbert's. There are a series of incidents concerning drink.(21) In one instance, some members took exception to another group adjourning to a nearby pub after meetings:

> While these men were known to be sober and respectable, this habit of adjournment was very unpalatable to other members of the committee....At last the matter was raised at a quarterly meeting, and, of course, provoked a storm. Mr. James Veitch led the attack; and, although not a teetotaller himself, he condemned the officials and those associated with them in no unmeasured terms for showing such a poor example while being leaders of social reform. (22)

Credit was another recurrent issue; although the membership repeatedly voted against an outright ban on credit, it is clear that the leadership opposed it, and in practice restricted it as far as possible. (23)

Differences in membership of savings institutions and in related patterns of behaviour can therefore be seen as part of more general cultural distinctions within the working class. It would, of course, be quite wrong to suppose that less skilled and prosperous groups did not set aside parts of their incomes for future contingencies; there is evidence that they did this whenever possible. (24) But the institutions catering for working class savers were themselves stratified, in a way that reflects a wider stratification of the manual working class. Alongside the local lodges of the big friendly societies — which tended, as we have seen, to draw their membership from skilled workers — were several small, local, and often 'unsound' societies; (25) these, as well as work- or neighbourhood-based arrangements of a less formal kind, might cater for the less prosperous skilled men and the unskilled. There were, it should be emphasized, obvious actuarial reasons for this differentiation; but the demands of financial soundness often enough coincided with those of a socially homogeneous membership, 'respectable' conduct and cultural exclusiveness. Thus the district secretary of the Oddfellows reported that a 'better class' had entered the Order since the introduction of sound actuarial principles and higher rates; the 'poorest class' were excluded. (26) The question of credit in St Cuthbert's probably had similar implications, especially in relation to the other great difficulty of the early years: that of getting members to use the store for all their purchases. (27) Such credit as the Co-op did offer was doubtless on a less generous scale than that of private traders, given the leading members' marked hostility to credit. Working people in need of credit would thus be obliged to make use of private shops; and even if their need for credit was occasional, shopkeepers would try to make it available only in return for consistent loyalty. (28) For St Cuthbert's to give credit on a scale comparable to the private traders would — as opponents of credit always argued — deplete the capital and make it hard to pay any dividend. From this point of view the accumulation of dividend by consistently buying from the store was one of the forms of saving adapted to the circumstances of the artisan; the interest accruing in the shape of dividend being a return on credit foregone as well as on the initial cost of a share. (29) The social stereotypes implied by the norms of 'provident' conduct were thus reinforced by the problems of financial viability facing any organisation that catered for the working class.

The practice of thrift was therefore bound up with the claim to belong to the 'respectable' section of society. But the concept of 'respectability' was an exceedingly ambiguous one — indeed its power in shaping images of the society was a function precisely of this ambiguity, of the many levels of meaning which its users might attach to the word. The same ambiguity surrounded such related catch-words as 'self help', 'social elevation', etc. To investigate the meanings of this cluster of concepts we must turn to a closer analysis of the part saving played in artisan life, and the kinds of change in his personal situation that the artisan might envisage.

The minimal definition of 'respectability', on which all users of the word might agree, consisted in retaining personal economic independence, and hence avoiding reliance on the poor law or charity. (30) And the provision of social security for the worker and his family was, of course, the most general reason for setting aside a part of current income. This might, as in friendly societies and trade unions, take the form of regular payments, for which specific benefits were provided, but which could be 'cashed' only if the claimant came into the relevant category of need; or it might take the form of generalized precautionary saving for the proverbial 'rainy day'. In either, or both these forms saving against sickness, unemployment, old age, death was certainly extremely common. It is, however, likely that the ability to commit regular payments to specific social security purposes — rather than to a fund of liquid assets — distinguished the more prosperous sections of the working class. (In this context it may be noted from Table 1 that the Savings Bank contains a far higher proportion of unskilled workers than the Oddfellows). On the other hand, friendly society benefits would rarely provide for more than a short period of sickness; those who wished to guard against longer term need would therefore have to undertake a range of savings commitments. (31) The distinctive feature of the labour aristocracy is not that they saved when others did not, but that they were able to save in several different forms, and thereby to protect their families against a wider range of contingencies.

A less general function of saving arose from the cost of tools in certain skilled trades. According to the *Edinburgh News* (1852) a set of masons' tools cost £2 to £2.10.0., while joiners' tools might cost as much as £10 to £25:

> But it is not difficult to perceive that in this case what appears to be a heavy affliction is in reality a social blessing; and that the habits of saving early acquired, and the possession of property gradually increased are of ... advantage to the progress and elevation of their possessor. (32)

In a brewery labourer's family studies by Paton (c1900) the son, an apprentice joiner, gave 5s. of his 6s. wage to his mother, who 'can count on 37s. a-week but she saves out of this to buy the more expensive joiners' tools for her son'. (33)

The system of rent payment in the city provided a third motive for saving. According to the president of the Trades Council, only the 'very poor class' paid weekly; yearly tenancies and half-yearly payments were the rule. (34) It was therefore presumably common to set aside money week by week for this purpose, as, for example, in the two cases reported in Paton's study where the co-op dividend was ear-marked for rent. (35)

The practice of thrift was therefore closely linked to the exigencies of nineteenth century working class life. Saving was, as we have seen, by no means confined to the aristocracy of labour; but it was probably only this limited stratum within the manual working class who were able consistently and successfully to maintain their family standard of life without falling into debt, going on poor relief, receiving charity, or otherwise suffering a loss of 'independence'. Their standard of life was, moreover, somewhat removed from that defined by prevailing notions of minimal subsistence; and the personal saving of labour aristocrats may well have helped underpin this superior standard. This is most evident with regard to housing, where a 'general desire among our artizans to be laird of their own house' (36) created a demand for owner-occupied houses of the better artisan type. Thus the Co-operative Building Company built dwellings for sale to the 'better class of working man'. (37) St Cuthbert's gave members loans towards house purchase from the 1880s; (38) and local mortgage companies were said to cater mainly, though not exclusively, for working men. (39) The purchase of a house - whether with accumulated savings, or on the basis of loan repayments – clearly implies a long-term financial commitment. And this trend to owner-occupation was itself only part of a general movement to new and superior housing (40) whose higher rents would in any case imply additional financial commitment.

More generally, it is likely that some artisans accumulated modest amounts of personal property, and of money deposited in savings banks, co-operative societies, etc. Thus, in the 1880s, the committee of St Cuthbert's between them held £1000 of capital, about ten per cent of the total. (41) Not enough is, or probably can be, known about financial arrangements in Victorian working class families; but the accumulation of personal savings – perhaps in the first instance the unintended consequence of strongly ingrained habits of thrift in conditions of improved real wages and economic security – no doubt had some connection with aspirations towards better housing, improved levels of consumption in furnishing and dress, the acquisition of the trappings of 'self culture', etc. 'Respectability', which in one sense meant minimal family subsistence without falling into the condition of dependence, in another sense meant the pursuit of a more ambitious project of improvement in family standards of housing and consumption. In practice, aspirations of 'respectability' might operate in both senses at the same time; those artisans who were consistently able to guarantee the survival of their families also enjoyed improved standards of housing, general consumption, access to cultural facilities, etc. (42)

A further set of questions about the aspirations of the labour aristocracy is suggested by the frequent use of such terms as 'self improvement', 'social elevation', etc., often in conjunction with 'thrift' and 'respectability'. Does this cultural pattern imply the *embourgeoisement* of the stratum, a dissolution of their identity as manual wage-earners through the wholesale adoption of middle class values and perspectives (including notably a perspective of individual ascent out of the ranks of the manual wage-earners)? (43) When labour aristocrats talked of 'elevation', did they hope to rise with, or out of their class? As a first step to answering this question we clearly need some account of the changes in occupational position which labour aristocrats might experience. In the absence of any adequate statistical data for nineteenth century social mobility, all that can be offered here is a general descriptive account of the range of opportunities available — this has, however, the important advantage of fixing attention on the social location of those occupations into which skilled workers or their children might move, and on the crucial issue of whether *occupational* mobility in fact constituted any real change in *social* position. It will be argued that, although there were important possibilities of occupational mobility, these did not constitute a long step out of the social world of the artisan; the struggle to maintain a 'respectable' life-style, and the wide economic range within the skilled working class were more important referents of the notions of 'elevation' held by the Victorian labour aristocracy than the prospect of moving into non-manual or non-wage-earning occupations.

Those types of mobility to which analysts of the twentieth century class structure have drawn attention — from manual to non-manual employment, or from employee to employer — must be set in the context of mobility within the skilled working class. This is probably one of those facets of working class life so obvious to contemporaries, that it has been overlooked by historians. Yet in any investigation of living standards the researcher quickly becomes aware, not merely of the wide occupational differences in the nineteenth century working class, but also of the wide range of economic experience within the various trades. Every skilled trade contained, on one hand, a group of casually employed low-paid men; and on the other hand, a group of regularly employed men earning superior rates. The average economic position of the trade as a whole was largely a function of the relative size of these two groups within the trade. Apart from fluctuations in employment there was often a wide apread of individual wage-rates; the payment to men just out of their apprenticeships of an 'improver's' wage, instead of the full journeyman's rate was, for example, a common grievance, even in such prosperous trades as bookbinding. (44) In these circumstances it is likely that the typical ambition of the skilled worker was to enter, and remain in the more desirable sections of his trade. For those already in the favoured sections, there was a very real fear of falling — through some loss of efficiency from a long period of illness or unemployment, (45) accident or ageing — into the depressed and casually employed section: this fear of falling, as is perhaps often the case with nineteenth century conceptions of competitive struggle, was as important as any hope of rising. The position of the skilled worker would thus depend on his efficiency, and sometimes on his versatility and the speed with which he could master new techniques, rather than simply on his occupation. As one technical handbook advised printing machinemen:

> If youths who do not know (and men, too, for they exist) would only endeavour to help themselves by studying the current literature of their trade...they might be able to help themselves forward very materially....Perhaps no one office has a specimen of every kind of printing machine...but there can be no harm in knowing something of the various kinds in the market. When a new class of machinery is introduced into an office one of the greatest difficulties the employer has is to get a careful man who is competent to take charge of it. (46)

Such a man 'has his situation secure, and his wages best'. (47) In the engineering trades blacksmiths sought experience in the 'more exact working shop of an engineer', after serving a traditional rural apprenticeship. (48) The artisan's ability to enhance his value to the employer, and to recover from such set-backs as sickness, unemployment, etc., so as to regain his former earning-power, might be heavily dependent on the savings he had managed to accumulate (if only in that they could help ensure that his nutritional standard did not decline too severely with the temporary loss of weekly income); the ability to transmit such advantages to his children (49) (for example, to keep them regularly at school and place them in good apprenticeships or sometimes non-manual positions) would reflect a similar pattern of cumulative economic advantage.

It therefore seems likely that when the artisan thought of 'progress and elevation' it was primarily this struggle for survival and promotion within the world of manual labour that he visualized. Those occupational opportunities that took him outside the manual working class can be regarded as relatively minor extensions of the hierarchy within that class, rather than as precarious toe-holds in the world of the middle class proper. (50) Thus the move into managerial and white collar posts in industry — and there can be little doubt, despite the absence of rigorous data, that such promotion was commoner in the nineteenth century than the twentieth — brought a larger income and greater security; but the ex-artisan continued to rely on his craft skills and experience as a journeyman, and probably retained his ties with the occupational culture of the trade. The emergence of industrial managers as a clearly defined middle class group (recruited largely through the educational system) has been a twentieth century phenomenon. (51) Thus printing overseers (works managers) were recruited from the journeymen compositors; (52) a joiner, as the 'comptroller general' of building works, might become a clerk of works, a surveyor, even (in the 1850s) an architect. (53) There is less information for other trades but the general importance, in most industries, of craft skills and experience, presumably favoured the appointment of ex-journeymen to managerial and supervisory posts.

The move from the status of journeyman to that of small master was still in the mid-nineteenth century of some significance as a form of occupational mobility — though we are again faced with a lack of rigorous data. Even at that period, however, there were important variations between sectors of industry; and there is also evidence that in all sectors ownership had become more concentrated towards the end of the century. The artisan's chance of setting up on his own account would clearly depend on such factors as the amount of fixed capital, the size of firms, etc. Table 3 therefore gives data for various locally important industries based on official statistics which are, however, to be treated with some caution. (54) The figures nonetheless accord

Table 3. Structure of Various Edinburgh Industries

	1871 (Factory Returns)		1901 (Census)		
	Steam h.p. per employee	Employees per employer	Employees per employer	% employers	% self-employed
Printing	0.10	47	74	1	0.2
Masons	0.08	18	14	7	0.2
Joiners	0.03	9	9	10	2.2
Painters	-	7	8	12	0.9
Engineering	0.14	83	43	2	0.65
Shoemakers	-	6	8	10	12

Table 4. Turnover of Business Names in Directories

	% of names surviving 10 years or more			
	1866	1868	1894	1900
Printers	58	61	73	76
Bookbinders	73	62.5	69	74
Masons	48	44	51	50
Joiners	55	53	67	60
Painters	59.5	69	81	82
Engineers	56	63	68	58
Shoemakers	51	48	43	39

with the pattern to be expected from other sources in suggesting that the building trades and shoemaking had lower levels of mechanisation, (55) smaller units and higher proportions of employers and self-employed than printing and engineering; and the consistency of the factory returns and the census may be taken as an indication that figures at least show the direction of differences between trades. Table 4 attempts to measure the stability of ownership as reflected in the trades sections of Post Office Directories. (56) Here again, the data are far from reliable (the likely exclusion from Directories of the more ephemeral enterprises being perhaps less serious than the possible distorting effects of variations in completeness, both at different dates and as between industries) but may nonetheless afford some indication of the *direction* of differences; a comparison of Tables 3 and 4 does suggest some association between industrial structure and the turnover of ownership. We can infer, then, that opportunities to start new businesses were far more open in the labour-intensive building and shoemaking trades; (57) the aspiration of becoming a small master would be less realistic for some artisans (including the highly 'aristocratic' engineers) than for others. It must also be remembered that in all trades the small businesses owned by ex-journeymen might be over-shadowed by far larger firms; and that movement from small master to wage-earner was possibly as common as movement in the opposite direction. This economic mobility did not therefore necessarily entail any wide or permanent social separation from the upper working class. We may finally note the apparent decline in turnover for the building trades, comparing 1866/8 with 1894/1900. This is of considerable interest, in the light of a widespread impression that firms were indeed becoming bigger, and ownership more concentrated in the hands of 'syndicates...formed by individuals who know nothing about the trade; they distribute their capital to drive men in the same way as steam is distributed to drive machinery.' (58) Whatever the chances for men in certain trades to set up on their own account, these may, by the end of the century, have considerably narrowed.

An important feature of the kinds of occupational mobility so far considered was that the ex-journeyman remained within his industry and continued to rely, in some measure, on his craft skills and working experience. There were also, in the second half of the nineteenth century, a range of white collar posts apparently recruited from artisans or their children. Thus it was widely assumed that pupil teachers in the elementary schools were recruited from this stratum. (59) For other, socially similar types of employment there is less evidence, though individual cases can be cited. William Paterson, former secretary of the joiners' union, became fire master of Glasgow; (60) and two other noted Edinburgh trade unionists became respectively a superintending school attendance officer and registrar for the Canongate district of the city. (61) These cases draw attention to the fact that labour and political activity was becoming, from the mid-nineteenth century, a channel of movement into non-manual occupations. Thus St Cuthbert's decided in 1873 to appoint store managers from among the membership, rather than hire them from the ordinary retail trade; while the first manager of the Scottish Co-operative Wholesale Society was the son of a prominent Edinburgh trade unionist and founder of St Cuthbert's. (62) Apart from this kind of employment in the institutions of the labour movement itself, it is likely that the growing role of its representatives on national and local bodies gave access to jobs in the public services. There were thus certain kinds of white collar employment open to the labour aristocracy or their children. But, as with the occupational mobility within industry considered above, it is unlikely that these white collar groups were socially far distant from the world of the artisan. Elementary school teachers, for example, occupied a distinctly marginal position in middle class society. (63) The occupations into which skilled workers might move are perhaps best seen as belonging to the fringes of an upper working class social world, rather than the lower reaches of a bourgeois one. (64) The career of William Paterson may again be cited, to illustrate the haziness at this period of social boundaries which have since become more clearly marked. The son of a small master joiner in Elgin, Paterson worked in various white collar jobs after leaving school, then served an apprenticeship in his father's business; coming to Edinburgh at the age of 20 (in 1863), he became first branch, then general secretary of the union, and ended his life, as already noted, as fire master of Glasgow. (65)

I would therefore argue that the aspirations of the aristocracy of labour must be seen as contained within their own limited social world, inextricably bound up with the conditions of manual wage-earning life (even if at the level considerably removed from that of most wage-earners). We may summarize this analysis by suggesting that there were two ways in which the social experience of the artisan might pre-dispose him to envisage a relatively long-term improvement in his personal situation. Firstly, the 'respectable working man' might look to rising standards in housing, dress, access to cultural facilities for himself and his family; the concept of 'social elevation' to which he was committed may have referred to certain kinds of status aspiration in the community, rather than to any projected change in occupational position. Secondly, artisans may have viewed their social world, in terms partly of the competitive struggle for survival and promotion, so often described in the popular homilies of vulgarized political economy. In this struggle, the resources the worker had managed to accumulate, his efficiency and versatility, level of technical (and even general) education, the quality of his tools, etc. might be crucial. But this was a struggle within the manual working class, rather than a scramble to climb out of it. Those forms of mobility that involved a move out of the manual wage-earning class may well have appeared less important than the great economic and cultural range within that class.

The appeal of dominant values of 'thrift' and 'self help' was thus a considerably more complex phenomenon than any simple process of *embourgeoisement*. The foregoing discussion has tended to concentrate on certain themes of ideology and behaviour, to ignore (as analyses of ideology often do) the complexities and inconsistencies of social experience and of the language used to structure that experience. The language of economic individualism co-existed with a strong sense of class identity — an identity underpinned by certain kinds of solidaristic behaviour. Those institutions, such as the co-ops, which catered for the thrifty artisan, embodied at the same time his class identity. Thomas Wright emphasized that the 'intelligent artisan', the man who looked to an improvement in the position of his class, was altogether commoner and more representative of the working class elite than the 'educated working man', the man striving to climb out of his class. (66) The desire for 'social elevation' could thus mean the elevation of the class — however narrowly and ambiguously membership of that class was conceived, and however much its elevation was taken to mean an acceptance of dominant criteria of social evaluation. Sometimes, perhaps usually, the aspirations of the labour aristocracy might refer to both class and individual simultaneously; the social standing of the class would be measured by the commitment of its individual members to 'respectability' and 'self improvement'. A founder of St Cuthbert's remembered how:

We opened with considerable spirit and enthusiasm, and some of us found a new relish in our butter, ham, and meal, in that it was turned over to us from our own shop, through our own committee. We were all yet working-men, but we began to have the feeling that we were something more, and would soon be business men, reaping profits we had for long been sowing for others. (67)

The outlook of the Victorian labour aristocracy cannot be understood without an appreciation of the ambivalence which lies behind their apparent commitment to certain pervasive values and norms of conduct. For these values and norms were re-interpreted within the upper working class social world; their meaning might change as they became embodied in distinctive manual working class institutions. The practice of thrift and the associated claim to 'respectability' were intertwined with a real and growing sense of class identity.

REFERENCES

1. R. Bendix, *Work and Authority in Industry,* New York, 1963 (Harper Torchbook edn), pp.99-116.
2. G. Best, *Mid-Victorian Britain, 1851-75* (London, 1971), p.256.
3. The concept of 'labour aristocracy' is of course problematic. I attempt to establish its validity with reference to Victorian Edinburgh in my unpublished thesis, 'Class Structure and the Class Formation of Skilled Workers in Edinburgh, c1850-c1900', Edinburgh University PhD, 1973; see also R.Q. Gray 'Styles of Life, the "Labour Aristocracy" and Class Relations in later Nineteenth Century Edinburgh', *International Rev. of Social History,* Vol.XVIII, 1973, which discusses more fully the material for the Oddfellows also presented above, table 1.
4. Cf. A. Briggs, *Victorian People* (Harmondsworth, Pelican 1965), pp.136-41.
5. *Royal Commission on Friendly Societies, Second Report, pt.ii,* PP 1872 XXVI, q 9655; and cf. q 9877, q 10032.
6. Ibid., q 9013.
7. W. Maxwell (ed), *First Fifty Years of St. Cuthbert's Co-operative Association Ltd., 1859-1909* (Edinburgh, 1909), p.24.
8. Table 1 is based on: list of members' occupations in *City of Edinburgh Lodge No. 1 Branch of the Scottish Order of Oddfellows,* n.d., c1940 (duplicated); occupations from 10% random sample (adult males only sampled) of 'declaration forms' of new account-holders at Edinburgh Savings Bank, I am indebted to Mr. T. Donoghue and Mr. N. Steel respectively for allowing me access to these sources. The Oddfellows' list of occupations is not precisely dated, but said to refer to the '1850s to 70s'; some trades said to have 'several' members are counted as five each (probably an under-estimate) — even excluding these trades of unknown size altogether, skilled manual = 67%. The occupational classification used is fully discussed in appendix 1 of my thesis. In Table 1, I have combined the business and white collar groups detailed in that appendix; other groups detailed in the appendix but not listed in Table 1 are included in 'Other, miscellaneous'.
9. J.A. Banks, *Prosperity and Parenthood* (London, 1954), esp. ch.3.
10. *North Briton,* 29 June 1859; *Royal Commission on the Housing of the Working Classes (Scotland),* PP 1884-5 XXXI, q 19275.
11. I wish to thank the Registrar General for Scotland and his staff for facilitating this analysis of marriage certificates, and Mr. P. Morse for his help with computing work.
12. For a fuller discussion of this life-style see R.Q. Gray, *op.cit.*
13. Ibid.
14. *City of Edinburgh Lodge, op.cit.*
15. Shoemakers were, on the other hand, the largest single skilled trade at this period and their representation is therefore not surprising.
16. Maxwell, loc.cit.
17. The argument of this paragraph rests on evidence regarding economic conditions presented in ch.3 of my thesis.
18. *RC on Friendly Socs., op.cit.,* q 9659 (secretary, Free Gardeners).

19. Maxwell, *op.cit.*, pp.46-7.
20. *RC on Housing, op.cit.*, q 19188; and see also the same witness's views on marriage cited above, note 10.
21. Maxwell, *op.cit.*, e.g., pp.49-78.
22. Ibid. p.91.
23. Ibid., pp.32-3, 88-90, 116-7.
24. See, e.g., the family budgets in D.N. Paton *et al.*, *A Study of the Diet of the Labouring Classes in Edinburgh* (n.d. c 1900), *passim*.
25. The *North Briton* constantly warned readers of the dangers of the 'yearly' type of society, e.g., editorial of 21 May 1860; cf. R. Roberts, *The Classic Slum* (Manchester, 1971), p.64.
26. *RC on Friendly Socs., op.cit.*, q 9302-3.
27. Maxwell, *op.cit.*, e.g., pp.34, 92.
28. Cf. F. Bechhofer and B. Elliot, 'An Approach to a Study of Small Shopkeepers and the Class Structure', *European Journal of Sociology*, 9, 1968, p.194; Roberts, *op.cit.*, pp.60-2.
29. Co-op prices may also have been higher (if only because goods of decent quality were supplied) but I have no data on this.
30. Cf. Best, *op.cit.*, pp.256-63.
31. For the short-term nature of support by friendly societies see *RC on Friendly Socs, op.cit.*, q 9708-29 (assistant inspector of parochial board of St. Cuthbert's parish, Edinburgh).
32. 'The Condition of the Working Classes in Edinburgh and Leith', *Edinburgh News*, 2, 9 Oct. 1852 (subsequent references to this newspaper are all to this valuable series of articles).
33. Paton *et al.*, *op.cit.*, pp.30-1.
34. *RC on Housing, op.cit.*, q 19176-7.
35. Paton *et al.*, *op.cit.*, pp.23, 26.
36. *RC on Housing, op.cit.*, q 19185.
37. Ibid., q 19071.
38. Maxwell, *op.cit.*, p.139.
39. *RC on Friendly Socs., op.cit.*, q 9073.
40. For a fuller discussion of residential trends see R.Q. Gray, *op.cit.*
41. Maxwell, *op.cit.*, p.125.
42. The alternative meanings of Victorian 'respectability' as it affected the working class are discussed in: G. Crossick, 'Dimensions of Artisan Ideology in Mid-Victorian Kentish London', unpublished paper (duplicated), Urban History Conference, 1973; F. Reid, 'Keir Hardie's Conversion to Socialism', in A. Briggs and J. Saville (eds), *Essays in Labour History, 1886-1923* (London, 1971), p.22.
43. For a critical analysis of concepts of *embourgeoisement* with reference to more recent years, see J.H. Goldthorpe and D. Lockwood, 'Affluence and the British Class Structure', *Sociological Rev.*, 11, 1963.
44. See, e.g., Minutes of Edinburgh Branch, Bookbinders' Consolidated Union (in National Library of Scotland), 16 June 1887, 10 Sept. 1894.
45. 'The Journeyman Engineer', *The Great Unwashed* (London, 1868), pp.282-3.

notes the loss of efficiency and earning-power after a period out of work.
46. 'Old Machine Manager', *The Printing Machine Manager's Complete Handbook and Machine Minder's Companion* (London, 1889), pp.vii-viii ('machine manager' in printing referred to skilled manual workers, not managers in the usual sense).
47. Ibid.
48. *Edinburgh News,* 13 Aug. 1853.
49. That advantages were transmitted in this way is, of course, implied by any hypothesis of structured stratification within the working class, such as the concept of 'labour aristocracy'.
50. Roberts, *op.cit.,* pp.5-6 indicates with reference to his youth in Edwardian Salford the social barrier between the 'jumped-up working class' and the 'middle class proper'.
51. See S. Pollard, *The Genesis of Modern Management* (Harmondsworth, Pelican, 1968).
52. O. Gordon, *A Handbook of Employments* (Aberdeen, 1908), p.316.
53. *Edinburgh News,* 9 Oct. 1852.
54. Table 3 is calculated from: *Return of Factories,* PP 1871 LXII; census occupation tables, *Census of Scotland, vol. III,* PP 1904 CVIII. In both sets of figures occupations originally given separately (printers-bookbinders-lithographers etc., engineers-foundries etc.) are combined, since many firms carried on these operations together (this may lead to some double counting in the factory returns though obviously not in the census). The discrepancy in the figures for employees per employer in engineering (columns two and three) is probably because the relevant census categories cover many small-scale metal-working trades excluded from the factory returns. In the census 'builders' described as employers have been added to the numbers of employers listed under the specific building trades included.
55. Steam-power is not strictly speaking synonymous with mechanization; it may, however, be taken as a rough guide in the absence of more adequate measures.
56. Samples of names from the various trades were taken from the Directories for the years mentioned, and traced through subsequent Directories. The years were chosen to give a cyclical peak and trough year from both decades (though there appears to be no consistent cyclical effect).
57. The painters are an exception, with little fixed capital, small average firm size, but lower turnover than the other building trades; but this may be a reflection of the depressed condition of the trade.
58. Associated Carpenters and Joiners of Scotland, *Annual Report,* 1895 (in Webb trade union coll., LSE).
59. E.J. Hobsbawm, *Labouring Men* (London, 1964), p.274; G. Sutherland, *Elementary Education in the Nineteenth Century* (Historical Association pamphlet London, 1971). J.S. Scotland, *The History of Scottish Education, vol. I* (London, 1969), pt. III, suggests that the Scottish situation was similar to the English, so far as elementary schools in large cities were concerned; but systematic comparative work is lacking.
60. I. MacDougall, *The Minutes of Edinburgh Trades Council, 1859-73* (Edinburgh, Scottish History Society 1968), p.xxiv.

61. Ibid.; W.H. Marwick, 'Municipal Politics in Victorian Edinburgh', *Book of the Old Edinburgh Club,* 33, 1969.
62. Maxwell, *op.cit.,* pp.106-7, 27-8, 94.
63. See Sutherland, *op. cit.*
64. I argue this point with reference to the associational patterns revealed by voluntary organization membership in R.Q. Gray, *op.cit.;* cf. Roberts, *loc.cit.*
65. Biographical sketch, *Reformer,* 6 May 1872; MacDougall, *loc.cit.*
66. 'Journeyman Engineer', *op.cit.,* pp.6-20.
67. Maxwell, *op.cit.,* p.27.

8. The Political Behaviour of the Working Class

James G. Kellas and Peter Fotheringham

The growing literature on Scottish political history from the nineteenth century to the present has paid particular attention to working-class political behaviour and radical movements. (1) Political scientists, working from recent survey material and census data, are starting to build up a picture of voting behaviour in Scotland, including of course the behaviour of working-class voters. Taking these two efforts together, it is possible to provide a guide to the problems and features of Scottish working-class politics, and to suggest some continuities. In this chapter, general problems of working class politics since the middle of the nineteenth century will be examined, in order to isolate certain characteristic features which appear to be present. There will then be a discussion of contemporary voting behaviour.

Scotland has always had a distinctive social and political system, and in Marxist terms, may have undergone its 'bourgeois revolution' at a unique point in time, compared with England and the nineteenth-century European nations. (2) Its class structure and class consciousness should therefore be separate, though with an ever-increasing assimilation in the face of the demands of the power structure and economy of the British state. After 1707, the upper and upper-middle class (though never the main part of the bourgeoisie) were drawn into the English Establishment through intermarriage, English education and British industrial enterprise, and the working class joined trade unions and parties with British organisations, especially when the employers and law-makers were British.

Nevertheless, working-class politics in Scotland never became entirely British in character or aims. This is because nationalism, religion, the geographical separation of Scotland from England, and parochial interest, kept Scotland apart. While these themes are inter-connected and overlapping, it is analytically possible to treat them separately.

Nationalism:

Here nationalism means the political aims of independent statehood, parliamentary devolution or administrative decentralisation for political ends. These are of course often seen as incompatible with one another, and most Labour leaders in recent years have attacked nationalism, while showing increasing sympathy for devolution. Working-class cultural nationalism is evident in Scotland, in the form of national consciousness and football patriotism. But this has never been expressed as political nationalism.

Scottish working-class movements (unlike those in Ireland) have never seen themselves as operating within a Scottish (as distinct from a British) class system, nor have they sought to create one. Thus appeals to nationalism from socialists take

---

* Historical aspects have been assessed by James Kellas and contemporary electoral behaviour by Peter Fotheringham.

the form of attacks on a metropolitan capitalist power centre and are in support of a 'national liberation' movement. For example, the Scottish Communist Election Programme in February, 1974:

> There is no contradiction in demanding a Parliament in Scotland to deal with Scottish affairs and at the same time advocate (sic) strong organisations of the British working class for industrial and political struggles. It is an essential condition to counter the highly organised forces of monopoly capitalism. (3)

This kind of appeal is widely scattered through time, from Keir Hardie and John Maclean to Jimmy Reid.

According to Tom Nairn (4), no nationalist movement of any significance was possible in Scotland throughout the nineteenth century because of the lack of drive from the bourgeois intellectuals, who alone could be the instigators of such a movement. The Scottish Labour leaders tried to annex the Home Rule movement, and Dr. Gavin Clark, the Crofter MP and vice-president of the Scottish Parliamentary Labour Party, promoted Labour policy on Home Rule through motions in the House of Commons. From that time, the Labour Party in Scotland included a nationalist or devolutionist wing, though its Westminster aspirations soon outweighed its separatism. At the Scottish Labour Party Conference in March 1974, David Lambie, MP for Central Ayrshire, found few sympathisers for his assertion that only in an independent Scotland could socialism be attained. (5)

The Scottish Trades Union Congress is more committed to devolution than is the Parliamentary Labour Party. Established in 1897, the STUC was formed in circumstances which

> reflected the uneasiness in Scottish trade union circles about the 'remoteness' of London, the inability of people there, including trade union people, to understand or be interested in the Scottish scene, especially with regard to the unfair interpretation by the Sheriff Courts of the law as it affected workpeople and their dependents. (6)

The practical concerns of the STUC, dealing with the Scottish legal system and Scottish employers, involve administrative and legal machinery rather than union-related nationalism, and purely Scottish trade unions have declined rapidly in number since 1918. Perhaps as a reaction to TUC prominence in British politics, the STUC has supported a strong devolution policy, (7) and it even convened a 'Scottish Assembly' on unemployment in February 1972 and January 1973 (abandoned when it was captured by the SNP). But there seems to be little evidence that rank-and-file unionists are more nationalist or devolutionist than non-unionists, or that they are discontented with the ways in which the British unions handle their interests. (8)

Working-class nationalism in Scotland has thus affected principally the 'peak organisation' leaders of the trade union movement, and is part of the parliamentary movement's heritage, though now an extremely divisive one. Communist leaders are more nationalist, in campaigns such as UCS (1971), and Jimmy Reid's 1974 election campaigns. But despite a loss of Labour working-class votes to the SNP since 1966, working-class nationalism is generally related to culture and football, not politics. Moreover, the appeal of nationalism for Scottish Labour MPs is much weaker now than it was before 1929, and is associated with the 'main opponent', the SNP. The sources of the strengths of the SNP at the present time are complex, and will be dealt with later (pp. 158-159).

Religion:

It is not surprising that religion is a strong force in Scottish labour politics, for Scotland is a rich field of religiosity. Chartist and Labour churches were particularly evident in Scotland. (9) The 'spin-off' temperance movement had a large part to play in the lives of the Chartists, Keir Hardie, William Gallacher, and Edwin Scrymgeour (Prohibitionist MP for Dundee, 1922-24, 1929-31). Glasgow's Labour Party maintained a 'dry' council-house estates policy until 1965.

The legal power of the Church of Scotland in education and poor law relief produced a system which mixed religion with social justice. Thus school board and parish council elections confused working-class interests with those of the churches. The anti-collectivist nature of the Scottish poor laws, backed by Free Church notions of Christian charity, made state action much more difficult to achieve in Scotland. This is an attitude still propagated in the immensely popular *Sunday Post,* read by 80% of Scottish adults (though not underwritten by them politically). One legacy of the Kirk's efforts in education, however, was to produce a strongly educational drive among the radical activists, from the Chartists to John Maclean. Unfortunately little of this is evident today.

The working class in Scotland is divided in religious affiliation (or tradition) between native presbyterianism and semi-alien Roman Catholicism. (10) There is evidence that the latter has always had a greater hold on the working class than the Church of Scotland, (11) and Catholic political activities are as important to the working class as are those of the Established Church.

Closely linked to religion is ethnic origin and region. Most Catholics and Orangemen have Irish ancestry (but not Irish birth), and live in west central Scotland, where politico-religious divisions and bitterness are strongest. Anti-Irish feeling permeated much nationalist thought till recently, but anti-English feeling is now as strong. (14)

The religious and ethnic divisions within the Scottish working class affect its political behaviour, whether in voting, trade union activity, or local government. In voting, the significance before 1918 of the 'Irish vote' is difficult to measure. John McCaffrey has shown (15) that the Irish vote in Glasgow at that time was small, probably under 50% of those Irish qualified to vote under the household franchise. Nevertheless, in some Glasgow constituencies (e.g. Blackfriars-Hutchesontown and Camlachie) an organised Catholic vote could influence results, and it *was* organised. Catholics were often instructed to vote Liberal rather than Labour to avoid splitting the Home Rule vote. (16)

This may have held back the progress of the Labour Party in Scotland. Few Catholics braved the ire of their priests to join John Wheatley's Catholic Socialist Society (1906). (17) But some branches of the United Irish League favoured Labour, as when George Barnes was given Irish support in Blackfriars-Hutchesontown in 1906, and won. (18)

The link between socialism and atheism in the minds of the priests persisted until a fundamental change took place in 1918 in the position of the Roman Catholic schools. By the Education (Scotland) Act of that year they were transferred to the directly-elected (by single transferable vote) Education Authorities, which immediately became the cock-pits of ecclesiastical politics. But it soon emerged that the Labour

Party was prepared to put 'Rome on the Rates' more readily than the conservative-presbyterian Moderate Party, and from this was forged the Labour-Catholic alliance in Scottish municipal politics. With the (temporary) removal of the Irish issue from British politics in 1922, the Catholic vote lost its Home Rule connotation, and came behind the Labour Party. This was consolidated in common -interest campaigns relating to rents and unemployment. (19)

That this alliance is essential to Scottish Labour Party interests today is shown by the attitude of Scottish Labour MPs to divorce law reform, abortion and Catholic schools. Humanists, civil rights exponents and secular school advocates in the Labour Party found that they could make no progress against the Catholic interest in the party during the campaigns for divorce law reform and against denominational state schools between 1970 and 1972. (20)

The strong electoral support given by Catholics to the Labour Party in Scotland has been well noted by political scientists, and is discussed below (p 157). It can be seen that Labour's initial disability in the face of the ethnic-religious factor has been handsomely made up in terms of votes, but not entirely. There remains the Orange working man, about whose political activities in Scotland little has been written. It is perhaps no accident that Unionism was stronger in the west of Scotland after 1886 than in many parts of Britain, though Orangeism, important as it was, contributed only one element in that political revolt which included businessmen, solicitors and professors. (21)

The ILP was subject to Orange attacks in the early twentieth century, (22) and as late as 1972, Orangeism in Coatbridge (60% Catholic) was said to have inflated the 'Conservative and Unionist' vote and representation on the Council. (23) But other accounts have noted a decline in Orange influences in Scottish politics, (24) and the contemporary troubles in Northern Ireland have had remarkably little effect on Scotland. This indicates that Catholics and Protestants in Scotland are equally anxious to isolate themselves from the Irish Question.

The trade union movement suffered at first from ethnic-religious divisions, and the extensive immigrant Irish labour in the Scottish mines contributed to the lack of strong miners' unions in the west of Scotland, compared with north-east England. But the fragmentary nature of Scottish mining, and disputes among leaders, may have had as much to do with this. (25) At any rate, in political terms nothing was to emerge from Scotland like the 'Lib-Lab' miners' MPs from Northumberland and Durham and elsewhere in England, and the Scottish miners' unions wielded negligible parliamentary or even industrial power. Miners' leaders such as Alexander Macdonald, Keir Hardie and Robert Smillie, had to go to England to find seats as Labour or Lib-Lab MPs.

No Lib-Lab pact was made in Scotland at the election of 1906, and the Scottish miners sponsored seven unsuccessful candidates between 1900 and 1906, under the banner of the Scottish Workers Representation Committee. In each case, the miner candidate came third after Liberal and Unionist. The absence of pacts in Scotland has been attributed to greater class polarisation, leading to Liberal-Labour hostility. (2 There is truth in this, but Scottish Liberalism was able to project itself at this time as a working-man's creed, and it linked up to presbyterianism in preferring the ideals of libertarianism to ideals of class representation and collectivism. In any case, few workers had the vote before 1918, and the polarisation persisted, to grow even more pronounced in the First World War and after.

After the vote was extended in 1918, Glasgow turned quickly towards Labour, with 'class' voting emerging more strongly than in London. In part this was the result of religious factors discussed above, but it was also related to the failure of the Liberal Party in Scotland (unlike London) to retain strong working-class support, perhaps because of the right-wing sympathies of local Liberal Associations (most backed Lloyd George's Coalition between 1918 and 1922). According to Michael Kinnear, (27) it was not until 1935 that London split along class lines to the extent that Glasgow did in the local elections of 1921 and 1922.

Geographical separation and parochial interest:
The vagaries of Scottish labour politics can be related to the geographical separation of Scotland from England. The separate radical movements in Scotland, such as the Chartist, anti-Corn Law, Scottish Labour Party, Trades Council, STUC, shop stewards, and now Nationalist, are idiosyncracies which can be partly explained by organisational imperatives. Distance from the industrial centres in England, and from London, makes separate organisations in Scotland necessary, and communications (including the media from Chartist broadsheets to TV) focus on them, as being the most accessible. Hence separate Scottish Labour Parties existed from 1888 to 1894 and from 1900 to 1909, and a new 'Scottish Labour Party' was formed in December 1975. The Labour Party (Scottish Council) Conference is important today.

But this shades imperceptibly into parochial interest. Scotland is divided from England not just by geography but by a whole host of interests. These interests form alliances with the political parties, and the Labour Party is particularly dependent in Scotland on two of these interests. As we have seen, one is the Roman Catholic Church, in membership twice as strong in Scotland as in England. Another is the council-house tenantry in the large cities, also twice as numerous as its counterpart in England. Both groups muster at the polls to support their patron-party. (The relationship between council tenancies and voting behaviour is discussed below, on p. 156). Interchange with England would break down the very distinctive Scottish religious and housing patterns but distance and parochialism conspire against this. The sociopolitical lines are too well drawn between Scotland and England to be easily shaken.

The marked segregation of Scottish cities into council estates (working-class) and middle-class areas has grown more evident since the 1950s. This is as true of Edinburgh and Aberdeen as it is of Glasgow and Dundee. To compound this polarisation, comprehensive education along territorial lines further restricts the movement of that part of the working class which used to be 'creamed off' to the selective secondary schools to mix with the middle class. Thus class divisions are hardening in much of contemporary Scotland, a fact which is shown in contemporary voting behaviour.

Politically, polarisation benefits the Labour Party, and the collapse of the Conservatives and relative weakness of the SNP in the major cities demonstrates this. The Labour leaders are reluctant to change their policies in response to nationalism when so much vested interest in Scotland is still tied to them in the industrial centres. Even a Labour politician as anchored to Scotland as William Ross, puts his British connecticns well above any temptation to head a Scottish executive. (28) But it is only because the Labour Party has exploited traditional working-class and religious interests that it has kept its support in industrial Scotland. Elsewhere, where these interests are weakening, notably in the New Towns and small burghs of the east and Highlands, the Labour Party is losing support, and it has not yet found (or sought) an alternative clientele.

Class polarisation is linked to dogmatism. And the language of debate in Scotland is powerfully shaped by the polarisation of religious creeds and pupil-teacher relationships in the schools. Each can draw on a fund of authoritarianism and bitter dialectic which, when applied to social problems gives political debate a corresponding dogmatis It is easy to see why 'class war' ideologues flourish in Scotland, but why it is much less easy to make the transition from clientele politics to revolution.

'Red Clyde' militancy recurs in the mythology of Scottish history, but much of this can be accommodated, not in revolutionary terms (despite Walter Kendall), (29) but in craft parochialism, whether to resist 'dilution' from incoming workers (1916) (3 or to avoid the necessity to leave Clyde shipbuilding for alternative employment (UCS, 1971).

Probably the nearest thing to class war occurred in the Highlands, in the 1880s and early 1920s, (31) but the links with the urban class struggle were muted. (32) What remains today is the stronger working-class character of the Labour Party in Scotland (especially in Glasgow municipal politics), and the even stronger middle-class bias of the Conservatives and Liberals. But this polarisation is conservative politically, linked as it is to the static clientele politics just discussed.

The only challenge to this polarisation and clientelism so far has come from the SNP, which draws on an amorphous social base. (33) But it is far from a revolutionary party in a socialist sense, or even a working-class party in Keir Hardie's language. It is, however, a major challenge to the Labour Party's domination of working-class politics in Scotland, and is a key factor in contemporary Scottish voting behaviour. This behaviour raises further questions about the difference between Scotland and other parts of Great Britain, and leads us to look more closely at electoral and survey material.

Scottish electoral politics and the working class:

How distinctive are Scottish patterns of class structure, socio-economic conditions and voting behaviour compared to other national and regional patterns in Great Britain? In particular, do Scottish working-class voting patterns differ significantly from working-class behaviour in comparable social environments in England and Wales?

To answer such questions it is necessary to make use of existing measures of class structure, socio-economic conditions and political behaviour. Four major sources have been analysed. Firstly, the 1966 sample Census provides relevant socio-economic data at several territorial levels including the three nations comprising Great Britain, sub-national regions, conurbations and parliamentary constituencies as constituted prior to the redrawing of constituency boundaries after the 1970 election. Territorial differences in class structure are expressed in terms of the distinction between manual and non-manual workers by adapting the seventeen socio-economic groups based on occupation and employed by the Registrar-General in order to 'classify together people whose social, cultural and recreational standards and behaviour are similar'(34). It is assumed that the five clearly manual occupational categories, socio-economic groups 8, 9, 10, 11 and 15, can be identified with the working class and the seven clearly non-manual occupational categories, socio-economic groups 1, 2, 3, 4, 5, 6 and 13, with the middle-class. (35) The twelve groups comprised 92.6% of economically active males in the 1966 sample Census. (36) The remaining groups are difficult to place in class terms, e.g., 'personal service' workers, 'own account' workers other than professional, and members of the armed forces. The industrial structure of constituencies can be compared in terms of the industrial classification system described in Census publications; six industrial groupings are distinguished, viz., agriculture, mining, transport, distribution and civilian services, national and local government, and, under one rubric, manufacturing, construction, gas, electricity and water. It will be shown that the political affiliation of Scottish constituencies varies according to industrial structure. Another politically relevant social condition reported in the Census is housing tenure; the relative proportions of owner-occupiers, private tenants and council house tenants are available for individual constituencies.

The second source upon which this chapter relies is the Nuffield study of the 1970 general election which includes a statistical appendix, derived from the 1966 sample Census, listing for every British constituency the percentage of economically active and retired males in non-manual occupations, i.e., socio-economic groups 1-6 and 13. (37) This information has been included in Tables 3-6 below in order to compare the class structure and political affiliation of English and Scottish constituencies. Finally there are two sources describing voting behaviour and party support. Aggregate election returns at constituency, regional and national levels provide information concerning variations in support for political parties which can be related to the socio-economic conditions reported in the Census. There is also a limited amount of academic survey and opinion poll data linking party support in Scotland to social class and religious identification.

Three significant developments in Scottish electoral politics since 1959 are illustrated in Table 1. First, there has been an emphatic, sustained decline in support for the Conservative Party. The Scottish Tories won an average of thirty-three of the seventy-one Scottish constituencies in the five elections from 1945 to 1959 compared to an average of twenty-one seats in the five elections between 1964 and October 1974. Second, the major-party or two-party vote, i.e. the combined votes of the Conservative and Labour Parties, has dropped from 96.8% of those voting in 1955 (72.7% of the eligible electorate) to 60.9% in October 1974 (45.6% of the eligible electorate). The minor parties won only one seat in 1955 compared to fourteen in October 1974. Third, the Nationalist vote has increased from 2.4% in 1964 when fifteen seats were contested to 30.4% in October 1974 when every seat was contested.

The change in Scottish electoral politics had two principal consequences. The Labour Party was able to enter office in 1964 and February 1974 because Scotland sent more Labour MPs to Westminster than in 1951. And the major parties have been compelled to produce devolution schemes in an attempt to turn back the dramatic rise in support for the SNP which has destroyed at least temporarily the two-party basis of Scottish politics. The importance to the British political system of changes in Scottish electoral politics necessitates a more detailed analysis of the collective vote in Scotland.

150 SOCIAL CLASS IN SCOTLAND

Table 1. The Collective Vote in Scotland, 1945-1974
A. *Distribution of the Popular Vote*

ELECTION	LAB	CON	MAJOR-PARTY	LIB(1)	LIB(2)	SNP(1)	SNP(2)
1945	49.4	41.1	90.5	5	19(22)	1.2	9.7(8)
1950	46.2	44.8	91	6.6	11.5(41)	0.4	-
1951	47.9	48.6	96.5	2.7	24.8(9)	0.3	-
1955	46.7	50.1	96.8	1.9	31.2(5)	0.5	-
1959	46.7	47.2	93.9	4.1	19.4(16)	0.8	10.7(5)
1964	48.7	40.6	89.3	7.6	22.7(26)	2.4	10.9(15)
1966	49.9	37.7	87.6	6.8	22.2(24)	5	14.5(23)
1970	44.5	38	82.5	5.5	14.6(27)	11.4	12.2(65)
1974 (Feb)	36.6	32.9	69.7	7.9	18.1(34)	21.9	22.5(70)
1974 (Oct)	36.2	24.7	60.9	8.3	8.7(68)	30.4	30.4(71)

B. *Distribution of Parliamentary Constituencies*

ELECTION	LABOUR	CONSERVATIVE	LIBERAL	SNP
1945	40	30	0	0
1950	37	32	2	0
1951	35	35	1	0
1955	34	36	1	0
1959	38	32	1	0
1964	43	24	4	0
1966	46	20	5	0
1970	44	23	3	1
1974 (Feb)	40	21	3	7
1974 (Oct)	41	16	3	11

Notes and Sources

Two measures of Liberal and SNP support are included in Table 1. 'LIB(1)' and 'SNP(1)' indicate the share of the Scottish vote as a whole won by the two minor parties. 'LIB(2)' and 'SNP(2)' indicate the share of the vote won by each of the minor parties in the set of constituencies contested by the party. The number of constituencies contested is specified in brackets in column 'LIB(2)' and 'SNP(2)'. The SNP put up only two or three candidates in 1950, 1951 and 1955; hence 'SNP(2)' has not been calculated for these elections because a misleading impression of SNP strength would be given. Most of the statistics in Table 1 are reported in the Nuffield studies of general elections from 1945 to 1970. The 1974 figures have been calculated on the basis of constituency results as reported in *The Times*, 2nd March and 12th October 1974. 'SNP(2)' figures have been calculated from results published in F.W.S. Craig, *British Parliamentary Election Results,* 1950-1970, Chichester, Political Reference Publications, 1971. The seats won by the ILP in 1945 are included in the Labour columns because Labour won the seats from 1950 onwards. Similarly, seats won by two Independent Liberals and one Independent Conservative in 1945 are included in the Conservative columns.

Three distinct phases in recent electoral politics are apparent in Table 1, viz., 1945-55, 1959-66 and 1970-74. The two-party vote averaged 93.7% during the first phase when popular votes and seats were divided fairly evenly between the two major parties. In 1951 when both parties won thirty-five Scottish seats, the Conservatives attained office because their normal majority of seats in England and Ulster was superior to Labour's majority in Wales. In 1955 the Conservatives attracted almost exactly half of the Scottish vote and won thirty-six seats including seven of

Glasgow's fifteen constituencies.

The 1959 election marked the re-emergence of Labour as the majority party in Scotland in terms of seats, a position which Labour has maintained. A British swing of 1.1% to the Conservatives in 1959, which raised the incumbent Government's majority from sixty in 1955 to one hundred in 1959, was accompanied by a Scottish swing of 1.5% to Labour. Swing in Scotland since 1945 has frequently been either more strongly Labour or less strongly Conservative than in England. The Conservative vote in Scotland fell 3% in 1959 and has fallen in every subsequent election except 1970. Labour gained four seats from the Conservatives in 1959 and five in 1964. Labour's overall majority of four following the 1964 election was based on deficits of nineteen and twelve in England and Northern Ireland compensated for by majorities of twenty in Wales and fifteen in Scotland.

Labour's position as the majority party in Scotland reached a climax in 1966 when the party won forty-six seats — almost two-thirds of Scottish constituencies. The Liberals also gained seats and votes from 1959 to 1966, winning and holding onto Inverness (Russell Johnston) and Roxburgh, Selkirk and Peebles (David Steel). The Liberals also briefly held Caithness and Sutherland, Ross and Cromarty, and West Aberdeenshire.

The third post-war electoral phase began hesitantly in 1970 when the SNP, contesting all but six Scottish seats, raised its share of the vote to 11.4% and gained the Western Isles from Labour, the first Nationalist victory in a general election. The SNP won 21.9% of the vote in February 1974 and gained six seats — four from Conservatives (East Aberdeenshire, Argyll, Banffshire, and Moray and Nairn) and two from Labour (Clackmannan and East Stirlingshire and Dundee East). The SNP clearly replaced the Liberals as the third strongest party winning twice as many seats and a larger share of the vote per constituency contested despite running candidates in twice as many constituencies. The Labour and Conservative votes dropped 7.9% and 5.1% respectively and Labour thus won a higher share of the vote in England (37.6%) than in Scotland (36.6%) for the first time since 1955. The major-party vote fell beneath 70% and the Scottish two-party system was clearly undergoing a severe challenge.

In October 1974, the SNP became the second party in terms of votes, winning 30.4% compared to the Conservative share of 24.7%, though the SNP won five seats fewer. The two-party vote declined further to 60.9%, though Labour managed to win 58% of Scottish seats with 36.2% of the vote. The SNP gained four seats — three long-standing Conservative seats (South Angus, Galloway, and Perth and East Perthshire) and the relatively new constituency of East Dunbartonshire won by the Conservatives in February.

The principal justification for describing Labour as the majority party in Scotland lies in the distribution of seats. Labour's majority over the Conservatives among Scottish MPs has varied between twenty-six in 1966 and seven in 1959, averaging nineteen in the six elections between 1959 and October 1974. Labour's overall majority in Scotland has fallen from a peak of twenty-one in 1966 to eleven in 1974.

Labour's consistent majority since 1959 is based upon the capture of ten constituencies which had been predominantly Conservative. Only two of the ten are located outside west central Scotland, viz., Caithness and Sutherland which Labour won for the first time in 1966 (38), and Berwick and East Lothian which Labour has held since 1966 but for the period from February to October 1974. Labour has been successful since 1959 or 1964 in five Glasgow seats which the Conservatives had frequently won, viz., Craigton, Pollok, Scotstoun, Kelvingrove and Woodside. (39) The remaining Labour gains are Lanark, Rutherglen and West Renfrewshire.

Despite the decline in Labour's share of the Scottish vote since 1966 the Conservatives have won from Labour only two seats in the six elections between 1959 and 1974. Labour won Aberdeen South at the height of their electoral success in 1966, the Party's only victory in the constituency since it was created in 1950. Iain Sproat regained it in 1970. The Conservatives temporarily regained the marginal seat of Berwick and East Lothian in February 1974 but J.P. Mackintosh turned the tables in October. The Conservatives did win East Dunbartonshire in February 1974 following the redistribution of constituencies which reduced the number of Glasgow seats by two, (40) but lost the seat narrowly to the SNP in October.

Despite the fall in the number of seats since 1966 the size of the Scottish Labour Party's presence at Westminster was greater after the October 1974 election than at any point prior to 1964. The increase since 1955 in the number of Labour-held constituencies in Scotland forms part of the increasing electoral polarisation by type of constituency in Britain reported in the Nuffield election studies. (41) Labour won more seats in 1970 compared to 1955 in the major cities throughout Britain whereas the Conservatives won more seats in suburbia, smaller towns and rural areas. By 1970 the number of Labour seats had increased in Scotland and the North of England while the number of Conservative seats had increased in the Midlands and the South of England. Labour has won a majority of Scottish seats in eight of the ten elections between 1945 and 1974 — the exceptions were in 1951 and 1955. In contrast, Labour won a majority of English seats in 1945 and 1966 only, though Labour did win three more English seats than the Conservatives in October 1974. Labour has won a majority of Welsh seats in every election since 1935.

Trends in Scottish electoral politics thus provide part of the explanation of Labour's lukewarm attitude to any significant degree of devolution, especially if devolution were to be accompanied by a decrease in the number of Scottish constituencies in the Westminster Parliament. (42) The electoral advances of the SNP in 1974 raise doubts, at least in the short run, about the extent to which Labour would dominate either an independent Scotland or a Scotland governed in part by an elected assembly with the powers to take decisions in areas presently within the jurisdiction of Westminster and Whitehall. The implications for both British and Scottish politics of declining turn-out, temporarily arrested in February 1974, the sustained fall in the major party vote and a tendency towards electoral votability have become controversial issues in the literature on electoral politics. The idea that social class has been losing some of its intensity as the foremost influence on British voting behaviour is now a commonplace. Ivor Crewe has suggested that it 'seems plausible that strong partisanship diminished (in the 1960s) as both parties converged in policy and renounced traditional group appeals'. (43)

Recent trends in Scottish electoral politics therefore prompt two questions. Why has Labour been the dominant Scottish party since the 1959 election, winning consistently a higher proportion of constituencies in Scotland than in England? Do the electoral successes of the Liberal Party in 1964 and 1966 and the SNP in 1970 and 1974 point to a significant break in the links between the major parties and their class sources of electoral support? An answer to the first question is attempted below. The answer to the second question lies ultimately with the Scottish electorate.

Richard Rose has cited the 1966 Census statistics on 'social class' in support of the view that England, Scotland and Wales are essentially similar in class structure. (44) The variation across Britain in the proportions of economically active manual and non-manual workers is illustrated in Table 2. Wales had 4.6% and Scotland had 3.4% more manual workers than England in 1966. Scotland had a higher proportion of agricultural workers (3.5%) than either England (1.9%) or Wales (2.1%). Clydeside contained the highest proportion of manual workers after the West Midlands conurbation, while Greater London possessed by far the largest proportion of both non-manual workers and parliamentary seats. Labour's share of the major two-party vote in 1970 was related positively to the proportion of manual workers though Labour fared particularly well on Tyneside and on Clydeside and particularly badly in the West Midlands. Greater London was as favourable to Labour as the South-East Lancashire and West Midlands conurbations, though Labour strength was concentrated in Inner London (53.2% of the vote and 78% of the seats) rather than Outer London (41.4% of the vote and 36% of the seats). Labour's performance in Scotland and on Clydeside appears stronger relative to other areas when the major party vote is compared instead of Labour's share of the total vote.

Table 2. *Class structure (1966) and Labour's Electoral Performance (1970) in England, Scotland and Wales and Seven Conurbations*

	% Non-Manual	% Manual	Labour Share (%) All Votes	Labour Share (%) Major Party	No.of Seats	% won by Labour
England	32.8	57.6	43.3	47.2	511	42.3
Scotland	29.1	61.9	44.5	53.6	71	61.9
Wales	26.1	62.2	51.6	65	36	75
Clydeside	27.2	67.1	52	59.5	24	87.5
Tyneside	29.2	66.9	57.7	58.6	10	80
W. Yorkshire	29.2	65.5	48.9	54	23	69.6
Merseyside	30.3	64.6	47.7	50.8	15	60
S-E Lancashire	32.2	62.2	45.2	49.8	29	62
W. Midlands	27	68.8	45	47.6	27	55.5
Greater London	41.1	51.5	45.3	49	103	53.4

Notes and Sources: Agricultural workers have not been included in the manual column. The proportions of manual and non-manual workers (male) are to be found in the 1966 Sample Census, Economic Activity Tables, Part III, Table 31. Labour's electoral performance (1970) is reported in Butler and Pinto-Duschinsky, *The British General Election of 1970,* London, Macmillan, 1971, Appendix 1, pp.356-357.

Table 3 makes clear that there are more pronounced differences in social structure between England and Scotland at constituency than at national levels.

Tables 3 and 4 include details of the 1966 and 1970 elections in England but details of the 1970 election in Scotland only. This is because there were more changes in 1970 in England where 14.5% of the 511 constituencies changed hands. Only four constituencies (5.6%) changed hands in Scotland. And only one constituency, Aberdeen

Table 3. Labour share of English and Scottish constituencies by % males in non-manual occupations, 1966 and 1970

% in Non-manual occupations	English Constituencies %	English Constituencies (no.)	Scottish Constituencies %	Scottish Constituencies (no.)	Labour share (%) of Seats England 1966	England 1970	Scotland 1970
10-19.9	9	(46)	11.3	(8)	100	100	100
20-24.9	14.1	(72)	16.9	(12)	94.4	89	100
25-29.9	20.1	(103)	29.7	(21)	82.3	58	67
30-34.9	16.2	(83)	22.5	(16)	44.6	28	50
35-39.9	16.6	(85)	9.7	(7)	38.8	19	43
40+	23.8	(122)	9.7	(7)	13.9	6	0
Total	100%	(511)	100%	(71)	55.9	42.2	61.9

Source: Butler and Pinto-Duschinsky, *op.cit.*, Appendix 1.

South, changed between the major parties. Labour did better in England in 1966 than in any other general election except 1945, whereas in 1970 the normal Conservative majority was returned to Westminster. The fall in Labour-held constituencies from 1966 to 1970 was 14% in England compared to 3% in Scotland.

The share of Labour-held seats in both England and Scotland fell progressively as the proportion of non-manual middle-class workers increased, as is to be expected in the light of the conventional wisdom about social class and voting behaviour. Labour was supreme in constituencies in which less than 25% of males were employed in non-manual occupations. The Conservatives were equally dominant in constituencies where the non-manual element exceeded forty per cent. The Labour and Conservative parties each won a comfortable majority of constituencies in the 25-29.9% non-manual and the 35-39.9% non-manual ranges respectively. Constituencies in the 30-34.9% non-manual range were divided more evenly between the parties though the Conservatives won about 70% of such constituencies in England in 1970. Labour won a larger share in Scotland of constituencies where the non-manual component was less than 40%, with the exception of the 25-29.9% non-manual range in 1966.

Table 3 also demonstrates that there were more working-class constituencies and fewer middle-class constituencies in Scotland than in England. Fifty-eight per cent of Scottish constituencies compared to 43% of English constituencies could be described as strongly working-class with less than 30% of the male workforce employed in non-manual occupations. Conversely, almost 25% of English constituencies compared to a mere 10% in Scotland were above the 40% non-manual level. Such constituencies were overwhelmingly Conservative even though the middle class constituted more than half of the male workforce in only forty-five of the 122 English constituencies above the 40% non-manual level. Conservative dominance can be attributed to working-class conservatism. Labour won in 1966 only seventeen of the 122 English middle-class constituencies and only seven in 1970, six of which were located in Inner London. The normal Conservative majority in English constituencies is thus largely based on the Party's strength in the relatively high proportion of constituencies above the 40% non-manual level, constituencies which can be described as essentially middle-class in character. The Conservatives have won six of the seven comparable constituencies in Scotland in every post-war election. The seventh, Aberdeen South, was lost temporarily to Labour in 1966. Four of the strongly middle-class Scottish constituencies are located in Edinburgh (North, South, West and Pentlands), one in Aberdeen

(South) and one in Glasgow (Cathcart); the seventh is East Renfrewshire, essentially a Glasgow suburb, which had the highest proportion (52.2%) of non-manual workers in Scotland.

There can be no doubt that part of the explanation of Labour's superior strength in Scottish constituencies compared to England as a whole gives support to both the social class interpretation of voting behaviour and the British political homogeneity hypothesis, i.e., the higher proportion of Labour-held constituencies in Scotland is due in part to the differences between the two nations in class structure at constituency level. (45) There are still more strongly working-class constituencies in Wales, where Labour has been even more dominant than in Scotland. Two-thirds of Welsh constituencies in 1966 included a non-manual component of under 30%.

But why has Labour been winning a higher proportion of Scottish than English working-class constituencies beneath the 40% non-manual level? Table 4 distinguishes the political identity of Scottish and English constituencies according to the type of constituency (burgh/borough or county) and the distribution of manual and non-manual occupations. The formal distinction between the two types of constituency is based on local government status before reorganisation. Burgh constituencies are essentially urban or suburban in that the constituency boundaries are either entirely within the confines of one urban local authority which may form one constituency (e.g. Paisley) or several constituencies (e.g. the seven Edinburgh constituencies). Alternatively two or three urban local authorities may make up one parliamentary constituency (e.g. the large burghs of Stirling, Falkirk and Grangemouth). County constituencies include both urban and rural areas, and the distribution of the electorate between large burghs, small burghs and landward areas varies considerably; indeed a significant minority of county constituencies are largely industrial and urban in character. Though there are relatively more borough constituencies in England than in Scotland, this is due to the absence of Scottish towns large enough to constitute individual constituencies. Several Scottish county constituencies are named after the largest town which may dominate politically, e.g. Ayr, Kilmarnock, Hamilton and Rutherglen.

Table 4. *Burgh and County Constituencies by Non-Manual Occupations and Political Identity, England and Scotland 1966 and 1970*

Non-Manual Occupations	ENGLAND						SCOTLAND			
	Counties			Boroughs			Counties		Burghs	
	% of Seats	% LAB 1966	1970	% of Seats	% LAB 1966	1970	% of Seats	% LAB 1970	% of Seats	% LAB 1970
10-29.9%	15.2	73	55.1	28	98.6	88.8	32.4	65.2	25.3	100
30-34.9%	8.6	11.6	0	7.6	82.1	59	14.1	20	8.4	100
35-39.9%	10	15.7	3.9	6.7	73.4	41.2	7	40	2.8	50
40%+	9.6	2.4	0	14.3	12.2	9.6	1.4	0	8.4	0
TOTAL	43.4	32.8	20.2	56.6	73	59.1	54.9	49.2	44.9	78

Source: Butler and Pinto-Duschinsky, *op.cit.,* Appendix 1.

Table 4 indicates that Labour monopolised seats in the Scottish burghs up to the 35% non-manual level which comprised a third of all Scottish constituencies. The slightly higher proportion of comparable English boroughs were also predominantly

Labour but not to the same degree as in Scotland, even in 1966. There would appear to be greater political polarisation in Scottish burgh constituencies. Labour won fourteen burgh seats above the 40% non-manual level in England in 1966 but only one, Aberdeen South, in Scotland. In contrast the Conservatives have been winning only one Scottish burgh constituency, Glasgow Cathcart, with less than 40% in non-manual occupations compared to eighteen similar English constituencies in 1966 and fifty-two in 1970. Table 4 also emphasises the weakness of Labour in county constituencies above the 30% non-manual level. Labour won in 1970 only four of the fifteen Scottish county constituencies (East and West Dunbartonshire, Lanark and Rutherglen) but seven of the eight burgh constituencies (the exception was Glasgow Cathcart) in the 30-39.9% non-manual range. In 1970 Labour won only two of the 122 English county constituencies above the 30% non-manual level. The contrasting socio-economic characteristics of burgh and county constituencies in Scotland are illustrated in Table 5.

Table 5. Profile of Labour and Conservative Constituencies in Scotland, 1970

Indicator	Labour (44) Burgh (25)	Labour (44) County (19)	Conservative (23) Burgh (7)	Conservative (23) County (16)
Non-Manual Occupations	25.2	27.8	44.3	32.4
Employed in Manufacturing and Mining	58.6	61.4	43.8	36.5
Owner-Occupiers	20.4	22.9	45.8	37.5
Council Tenants	45.8	45.8	26.1	32.3

Average Proportions of Male Workers and Households

Sources: The 1966 Sample Census, General and Parliamentary Constituency Tables, No.4; Butler and Pinto-Duschinsky, *op.cit.*, Appendix 1.

Table 5 highlights the strong similarity in the socio-economic characteristics of the county and burgh constituencies won by Labour in 1970. Most Labour-held county constituencies lie in industrial areas, as indicated by the high proportions of males employed in manufacturing and mining, an average of 61.4% in county constituencies and 58.6% in burgh constituencies. Only one Labour constituency had less than 40% employed in manufacturing and mining, viz., Caithness and Sutherland, and only one other less than 55%, viz., Berwick and East Lothian. The proportion of males in burgh constituencies employed in manufacturing and mining ranged from 44.4% in Glasgow Kelvingrove to 68.6% in Coatbridge and Airdrie.

Conservative seats in Scotland are almost exclusively confined to middle-class urban constituencies (more than 40% employed in non-manual occupations) and rural county constituencies. Only one Scottish Conservative constituency outside the four cities included in 1970 a town of over 30,000 inhabitants, viz., Ayr; only two more included a town of over 20,000 inhabitants, viz., Perth (in Perth and East Perthshire) and Dumfries. The sixteen county constituencies won by the Conservatives in 1970 include eleven of the fifty most agricultural constituencies in Great Britain, five of which were won by the SNP in 1974. Scotland has relatively more agricultural constituencies, defined as 10% or more of the male workforce employed in agriculture, than England. In 1970, 28% of Scottish constituencies (twenty) compared to 13% of English constituencies (sixty-seven) could be so described. Labour did not win any of the English agricultural constituencies while the Liberals won two. In Scotland Labour won Caithness and Sutherland and Berwick and East Lothian. In only two Conservative constituencies in Scotland were more than 50% of the male workforce employed in manufacturing, viz., East Renfrewshire and North Ayrshire; in only two more did the proportion employed in manufacturing exceed 40%, viz., Angus South and Dumfriesshire.

The political consequences of national and regional variations in socio-economic conditions have been made explicit in Table 6 by comparing Labour's electoral record in 1966 and 1970 in Scotland and in three distinctive English regions, viz., the North-West, the West Midlands and Yorkshire. (46)

Table 6. *Comparison of Constituency Characteristics in Scotland, North-West England, the West Midlands and Yorkshire, 1966 and 1970.*

Constituency Characteristics		Scotland	Yorkshire	West Midlands	North-West
No. of Constituencies		71	55	54	79
% Labour 1966		64.8	71	59.2	69.6
% Labour 1970		61.9	65.5	44.4	51.9
% Agricultural		28	10	33	2.3
% Working Class (borough and county)		57.7	71	62.8	60.8
% Lab of Borough Seats, 10-29.9% Non-Manual	1966	100	100	92.7	100
	1970	100	92	87.6	83.4
% Lab in Borough Seats, 30-39.9% Non-Manual	1966	87.5	83.3	20	58.3
	1970	87.5	50	20	16.7

Sources: Butler and Pinto-Duschinsky, *op.cit.,* Appendix 1; the 1966 Sample Census, General and Parliamentary Constituency Tables, No.4. 'Agricultural' constituencies are defined as those with at least 10% of the male workforce employed in agriculture. 'Working-class' constituencies are those with less than 30% of males employed in non-manual occupations.

Labour parliamentary representation was strongest in Yorkshire and weakest in the West Midlands in both elections. Scotland overtook North-West England in 1970 as Labour's second strongest area among the four analysed here, as a result of heavy Labour losses in Lancashire. Labour's strength in Yorkshire was based on the combination of a high proportion of working-class constituencies and a low proportion of agricultural constituencies. In contrast, Conservative representation in both Scotland and the West Midlands was bolstered by the relatively high proportion of agricultural constituencies. The most significant development illustrated in Table 6 is the decline in 1970 in the number of urban constituencies with less than 40% non-manual workers won by Labour in the three English regions compared to the complete absence of change in similar constituencies in Scotland. Labour lost two seats in all to the Tories in Scotland, four in Yorkshire, eight in the West Midlands and fourteen in North-West England. Labour's stronger position in Scottish working-class and urban constituencies generally is emphasised in Table 6. In 1970 Labour lost fourteen English borough constituencies beneath the 30% non-manual level and another twenty in the 30-39.9% non-manual range. Labour losses included such heavily working-class constituencies as Brighouse and Spenborough and Keighley in Yorkshire, both Bolton and both Preston constituencies in Lancashire, and Oldbury and Halesowen and Birmingham Perry Barr in the West Midlands.

It can be concluded that Labour has been able to realise electorally its working-class political inheritance more comprehensively and at an earlier date in Scotland than in England. The reasons for Labour losses in England in 1970 include local conditions, e.g., the swing against Labour in Lancashire textile towns was 7.4%, nearly 3% higher than the average English swing. (47) This swing, based in part on the decline in the economic well-being of the textile industry, would account for some of the Labour defeats in Lancashire.

One clear national difference between English and Scottish constituencies is related to housing patterns. As noted above (p.145) there is much less home-ownership and much greater provision of council housing in Scotland than in England. There is evidence from statistical analysis of constituency election returns and from survey data to support the view that working-class individuals living in council housing are more prone to vote Labour than individuals who own their own homes or who live in privately-rented accommodation. (48) Almost 50% of people in England and Wales owned or were buying their own homes in 1966; in Scotland the proportion was 28%. Conversely 47% of Scottish households were living in council housing compared to 27% in England and in Wales. (49) Housing patterns may therefore provide part of the explanation of Labour's stronger hold on working-class urban constituencies in Scotland compared to England. However, an analysis of working-class constituencies retained and lost by Labour in North-West England in 1970 does not show that Labour lost constituencies where council housing was particularly low or home-ownerhip particularly high. In contrast the main social difference between Labour-held Craigton and Conservative-held Cathcart in Glasgow, essentially similar in occupational class structure, lay in housing patterns:

	Non-Manual	Manufacturing	Council Housing	Owner-Occupied
Cathcart	39.3%	52.4%	41.1%	33.3%
Craigton	37%	63.1%	64.4%	18.9%

The analysis of electoral politics has emphasised the importance of socio-economic conditions in the distribution of parliamentary constituencies between the two major parties. The relative weight of urban and rural seats, the occupational-class structure of constituencies and industrial conditions such as mining and manufacturing are largely responsible for differences in the political composition of regional and national delegations in the House of Commons. Accordingly, Scotland's preference for a majority of Labour MPs has been attributed to the stronger working-class elements in Scottish than in English constituencies. The Scottish Conservative presence in the Commons is increased by the relatively large number of agricultural constituencies. At the same time it has been pointed out that Labour does appear to possess a firmer hold on working-class constituencies in Scotland.

Survey evidence also suggests that there are differences in working-class political behaviour in Scotland, Wales and the English regions. Butler and Stokes and Rose have provided the most comprehensive regional analyses of class support for political parties. (50) Butler and Stokes analysed NOP data accumulated between October 1963 and December 1966. They found support for a 'two-nations' division within Great Britain; not Scotland in contrast to England but Scotland, Wales and the North of England in contrast to the Midlands and South of England. Working-class conservatism was at its lowest in Wales, a mere 15.2%. Both North-East England and Yorkshire had fewer working-class conservatives, 25.9% and 27.3% respectively, than Scotland with 29.5%. North Britain, including Scotland and Wales, had only 29.5% working-class conservatives compared to 37% in the Midlands and South of England.

Richard Rose, interpreting Gallup data obtained before the 1964 election, has pointed to 'the apparently high Labour support among the Scottish working-class' (51). Labour support among the Scottish working class (61%) is shown to be lower than in Wales (79%), Northern England (65%) and North-West England (63%) but higher than in the remaining English regions. Such regional comparisons are complicated by considerable variation in the size of the combined support for the major parties which ranged from 93% in Northern England to 79% in South-West England. When the Labour share of the two-party vote is calculated, support for Labour in Scotland appears slightly higher than in Northern England. The 1970 Gallup data suggested that working-class support for Labour in Scotland was higher (58%) than in any of the English regions apart from Northern England (66%). (52) As far as opinion poll data is concerned, both Wales and Southern England deviated more than Scotland up to 1970 from British class patterns of party support.

The electoral significance of religion in Scotland is difficult to estimate. Bochel and Denver found much more working-class support for the Conservative Party in Dundee in 1966 among adherents of the Church of Scotland (39.5%) than among Roman Catholics (6%) and individuals with no active religious commitment (13.5%). (53) Survey evidence has consistently suggested that about three-quarters of Roman Catholics support Labour. (54) A survey in Glasgow in March 1970 showed that one-third of the Labour support came from Roman Catholics. (55) Rose has attributed the 'apparently high Labour vote among the Scottish working-class' to the 'substantial minority of Roman Catholics in its composition'. (56) Yet, as argued in the preceding paragraph, it is not clear that the working-class Labour vote in Scotland was significantly higher in the 1960s than in other parts of North Britain. In addition there is little satisfactory information about the religious composition of electorates in individual constituencies so that it is not possible to calculate precisely the electoral consequences of religious divisions.

The electoral success of the SNP in 1974 constitutes the strongest challenge in a relatively large territorial division of Great Britain to the grip of the two major parties on their traditional sources of support. The Conservative vote in Scotland dropped from 38% in 1970 to 24.7% in October 1974 while the Labour vote fell from 44.5% to 36.2%. However, whereas the Conservative vote dropped by 5% in February and by 8% in October the Labour vote held firm in October. In addition, the Conservatives have lost eight seats to the SNP whereas Labour has lost three. The SNP came second to Labour in thirty-five constituencies in October 1974 and second to the Conservatives in five. The SNP lies second, less than 10% behind the major party in eleven Labour seats and four Conservative seats. The electoral future of the SNP depends upon two factors, viz., the extent of any rise in the SNP vote and the relative movement of voters between the two major parties.

The SNP gains from Labour in the Western Isles, Dundee East, and Clackmannan and East Stirlingshire can be explained in part by disputes within the local Labour Party. The personalities of the candidates contributed to the SNP's victory in East Stirlingshire in February 1974 when the Labour vote fell (14.6%) more sharply than the Conservative vote (8.7%). (57) The impact of the oil issue may have been a factor in Dundee East where the vote of both major parties dropped about 15%. The ability of the SNP to hold onto these two constituencies in urban, industrialised Scotland contrasts with the earlier failure of the Nationalists to repeat in general elections the by-election successes of Hamilton (1967) and Govan (1973).

The Conservative Party lost four seats to the SNP in February 1974 (East Aberdeenshire, Argyll, Banff, and Moray and Nairn). But these losses could be attributed mainly to tactical voting on the part of Labour supporters in traditionally safe Conservative seats. The Conservative vote dropped 5.6% in these constituencies compared to a 12.8% drop in the Labour vote. In Moray and Nairn, where Mrs. Ewing defeated the Scottish Secretary of State, Gordon Campbell, the Conservative vote dropped 5.7% and the Labour vote dropped 15.7%. Labour lost deposits in three of these constituencies. Nevertheless the fall in the Conservative share of the vote suggests that by no means all the SNP vote can be explained in terms of tactical voting. In October 1974, SNP gains from Conservative in South Angus, Galloway, and Perth and East Perthshire were based on a much higher fall in the Conservative vote than in the Labour vote. The Conservative vote dropped 7.9% in these three constituencies; the Labour vote dropped 2%. Tactical voting on the part of Labour voters in February and October may be part of the explanation of the SNP gains. But clearly many committed Conservative voters moved to the SNP.

In contrast, in October 1974 Labour held onto the few seats where the SNP lay within striking distance, viz., Govan, Stirling and Falkirk, West Lothian, West Stirlingshire and Hamilton. Apart from Govan, where the Labour vote rose 6% in October, the SNP vote increased between 5% and 8% but the Labour vote remained steady, rising 1.3% in Stirling, remaining constant in West Lothian, and falling 1.8% in West Stirlingshire and 0.6% in Hamilton. Accordingly the drop in the Conservative vote, which varied between 5.6% in Govan and 11.1% in West Stirlingshire, was not sufficient to defeat Labour. In October the net movement of voters between the major parties was clearly in Labour's direction in Britain as a whole, a condition which contributed to the SNP's failure to gain seats from Labour. In contrast, it has been assumed that in the indecisive February election the SNP attracted a larger proportion of Labour than Conservative support. (58) But, taking the two elections of 1974 together, it is clear that the SNP has made much greater inroads into Conservative than Labour support.

A review by I. McLean of the evidence concerning the sources of SNP support in its 1967-68 surge in municipal elections and by-elections emphasised that the SNP was drawing much of its support from individuals who had been too young to vote in 1966 or who had abstained. (59) There was some evidence that Labour was losing a larger proportion of its support than the Conservatives to the SNP. (60) Since 1967-68 the SNP vote has increased in two general elections and in the 1974 elections to the new local government authorities which came into operation in 1975.

The conventional wisdom has tended to the view that both the Liberals and the SNP have taken roughly equal shares of the vote from the two major parties, (61) especially in marginal constituencies. (62) An ORC poll two weeks before the 1974 (February) election indicated that the SNP was attracting similar shares of the lower middle class (17%) and working-class (16%) but a lower proportion of the upper middle-class (9%). (63) In May 1974, when 24% of an ORC poll stated an intention to vote SNP, there was very little variation in SNP support by class. (64)

Conclusion:

The evidence available from election returns, survey material and census socio-economic data confirms the continuing relevance to Scottish electoral politics of the three dominant themes discussed in the Introduction to this volume, viz., class politics, working-class conservatism and British political homogeneity. The 1960s and 1970s have added a strong element of Scottish nationalism. Regional differences in support for the Conservative and Labour Parties before 1970 have been attributed to parallel variations in socio-economic conditions, particularly the occupational class character of national and regional sets of constituencies. The major qualification of such a generalisation has been Labour's stronger grip in Scotland on working-class urban constituencies.

The historical parts of this chapter emphasised more strongly the distinctive features of Scottish politics. The themes of nationalism, religion and separate interest are only partly reflected in voting behaviour. But political action outside voting is more Scottish in character, and working-class politics must be understood in terms of attitudes, interests and decision-making as well as party affiliation. For example, it is clear that the Labour Party in Scotland operates within a context of religion, council-housing and nationalism which is significantly different from that prevailing in England.

To some extent, then, the historical and electoral methodologies appear to lead to conclusions differing in emphasis: the former more 'separatist' than the latter. The continuities of Scottish working-class history, as of Scottish society in general, mark Scotland off from England in many key areas of politics. It is possible, for example, to find many of the political cleavages and problems of the nineteenth century still present in Scottish politics today. Over the same period, however, electoral participation and party allegiances have changed considerably, and are subject to rapid fluctuations, the most recent being the rise in support for the SNP. It is therefore necessary to consider both electoral and non-electoral evidence when describing the political behaviour of the working class in Scotland.

REFERENCES

1. The best source for this literature is the *Journal of the Scottish Labour History Society* (1969-), and I. McDougall (ed.), *An Interim Bibliography of the Scottish Working Class Movement* (Edinburgh, Scottish Labour History Society, 1965). A completely new edition of this Bibliography is forthcoming.
2. Tom Nairn, 'Scotland and Europe', *New Left Review,* no. 83, Jan.-Feb. 1974, pp.70-71.

3. *Scottish Communist Election Programme,* 19 February 1974.
4. Nairn, *op.cit.,* p.81.
5. *Glasgow Herald,* 23 March, 1974.
6. STUC General Council, *Memorandum of Evidence to the Royal Commission on the Constitution* (Glasgow, May 1970), p.3.
7. STUC, *op.cit.* The STUC is at pains to avoid 'economic and political separation from the United Kingdom'. Preamble, s.6.
8. For a survey giving trade unionists' attitudes towards devolution, see Roger Brooks, 'Scottish Nationalism: Relative Deprivation and Social Mobility', Michigan State University, unpublished Ph.D. thesis, 1973, p.243. This shows 17.1% of Union members and 16.9% non-union members as SNP. Devolutionists and nationalists together were 36.5% of union members and 41.7% of non-union members. Trade unions which have supported devolution at the Scottish Labour Party Conference or STUC are the NUM (Scottish Area), TGWU and AUEW. But those opposed to nationalism and/or devolution are the Draughtsmen and the GMWU.
9. A. Wilson, *The Chartist Movement in Scotland* (Manchester, Manchester University Press, 1970), ch.11. W.H. Marwick, *A Short History of Labour in Scotland,* (Edinburgh, W. & R. Chambers, 1967), pp.75, 87.
10. Smaller religious denominations such as the Methodists, Congregationalists and Unitarians have never been so strong or as important in Scotland as in England. However, Keir Hardie was a member of the Evangelical Union, the predecessor of the Scottish Congregational Union, which was an 'anti-Calvinist sect with a strongly working-class membership in the west of Scotland'. F. Reid, 'Keir Hardie's conversion to socialism', in A. Briggs and J. Saville (eds.), *Essays in Labour History, 1886-1923* (London, Macmillan, 1971), pp.23-24.
11. A.A. MacLaren, 'Presbyterianism and the working class in a mid-nineteenth century city', Scottish Historical Review, vol. 46, 1967, pp.115-39; *Religion and Social Class* (London, Routledge & Kegan Paul, 1974). P. Sissons, *The Social Significance of Church membership in the Burgh of Falkirk* (Edinburgh, Church of Scotland, 1973), reported in *Glasgow Herald,* 30 July 1973.
12. K.D. Buckley, *Trade Unionism in Aberdeen, 1878 to 1900* (Aberdeen, Aberdeen University Press, 1955), p.55, describing Aberdeen Trades Council debate in 1881.
13. Dundee had a large Orange Walk on 7 May 1972, and Orangemen threatened to contest municipal elections when the use of a park was refused. *Glasgow Herald,* 6 March 1972, 5 April 1972. The Orange Order in Scotland is described in a two-part article in the *Scotsman,* 8, 9 July 1966.
14. J.E. Handley, *The Irish in Scotland* (Glasgow, Burns, 1964), p.352. For the view that anti-Irish feeling was absent from the nationalist movement in the 1930s, see G.S. Pryde, 'The development of nationalism in Scotland', *Sociological Review,* vol. XXIII, no.3, July 1935, pp.275-7.
15. J.F. McCaffrey, 'The Irish vote in Glasgow in the late nineteenth century: a preliminary survey', *Innes Review,* vol. XXI, i, Spring 1970, pp.30-6.
16. Handley, *The Irish in Modern Scotland* (Cork, Cork University Press, 1974), p.275f. T.W. Moody, 'Michael Davitt and the British Labour Movement, 1882-

1906', *Trans. R. Hist. Soc.*, 5th Series, vol.3, 1953, p.70.
17. K. Middlemas, *The Clydesiders* (London, Hutchinson, 1965) pp.37-40.
18. J. Paton, *Proletarian Pilgrimage* (London, Routledge, 1935), pp.199-200; Middlemas, *op.cit.*, p.34.
19. I.S. McLean, 'The Labour movement in Clydeside politics, 1914-22', Oxford University, unpublished D.Phil. thesis, 1972. Catholics continued to vote for Catholic candidates until the Education Authorities were merged in the local councils in 1929.
20. In 1970, Glasgow Corporation Labour Group refused to implement an integrationist resolution of the City Labour Party, *Scotsman*, 17 March 1970. Pressure at the Scottish Labour Party Conference similarly failed to convince the Scottish executive that any change should be made to the system of denominational schools. *Catholic and non-denominational schools*, Report to Scottish Annual Conference, The Labour Party Scottish Council, Glasgow, 1972. The Catholic educational interest is well summarised by R. Crampsey, 'Integration in schools won't end problems', *Glasgow Herald*, 30 June 1972.
21. J.F. McCaffrey, 'The origins of Liberal Unionism in the west of Scotland,' *Scottish Historical Review*, vol. 1, i, no.149, April 1971, pp.47-71.
22. Paton, *op.cit.*, pp.170-3, reporting Orange attacks on socialist meetings by shipyard workers. In the early years of this century Ulster immigration predominated, and Harland and Wolff opened works in Govan in 1912. This brought an influx of Orangemen to the area which may have made Govan a stronghold of working-class Toryism. The anti-Catholic bias of Rangers football team also dates from this time. See also Paton, *op.cit.*, p.186.
23. *Glasgow Herald*, 27 April 1972.
24. *Glasgow Herald*, 26 November 1971.
25. T.J. Byres, 'The Scottish Economy during the 'Great Depression', 1873-96, with special reference to the heavy industries of the south west', Glasgow University, unpublished B.Litt. thesis, 1962.
26. F. Bealey and H. Pelling, *Labour and Politics, 1900-6* (London, Macmillan, 1958), p.293.
27. M. Kinnear, *The British Voter*, London (Batsford, 1968), p.133.
28. At the STUC in April 1974, Ross violently attacked the 'shoddy' SNP and nationalism which divided Scotland. *Glasgow Herald*, 20 April 1974.
29. 'The only truly revolutionary tendency in wartime British socialism' is his description of the 1914-18 shop stewards movement on the Clyde. W.Kendall, *The Revolutionary Movement in Britain, 1900-21* (London, Weidenfeld and Nicolson, 1969), p.108.
30. McLean, *op.cit..* and J. Hinton, *The First Shop Stewards Movement* (London, Allen and Unwin, 1973).
31. H.J. Hanham, 'The problem of Highland discontent, 1880-5', *Trans. R. Hist. Soc.*, 5th series, vol.19, 1969, pp.21-65. N. Nicolson, *Lord of the Isles* (London, Weidenfeld and Nicolson, 1960), for Lord Leverhulme's troubles in the Western Isles in the early 1920s.
32. J.G. Kellas, 'Highland migration to Glasgow and the origin of the Scottish Labour movement', *Bulletin of the Society for the Study of Labour History*,

No.12, Spring 1966, pp.9-13.
33. J.P. Cornford and J.A. Brand, 'Scottish Voting Behaviour', in J.N. Wolfe (ed.), *Government and Nationalism in Scotland* (Edinburgh, Edinburgh University Press, 1969), p.26 for 1968 material. Brooks, *op.cit.*, for 1970 material, and the *Scotsman* and *Glasgow Herald* for surveys during 1974 and 1975.
34. The 1966 Sample Census, Economic Activity Tables, Part III, p.xvii.
35. Socio-economic groups 8, 9, 10, 11 and 15 comprise respectively foremen and supervisors (manual), skilled manual workers, semi-skilled manual workers, unskilled manual workers and agricultural workers. Socio-economic groups 1, 2, 3, 4, 5, 6 and 13 comprise respectively employers and managers (large establishments), employers and managers (small establishments), professional workers (self-employed), professional workers (employees), intermediate non-manual workers, junior non-manual workers and farmers (employers and managers).
36. *Ibid.*, Table 31.
37. D. Butler and M. Pinto-Duschinsky, *The British General Election of 1970* (London, Macmillan, 1971).
38. Caithness and Sutherland was won by the Liberals in elections between 1918 and 1935 and in 1964; the Conservatives held the seat from 1945 until 1964 though Sir D. Robertson ran as an Independent Conservative in 1959.
39. Craigton emerged as a new constituency, formed out of parts of Govan and Pollok, in 1955 when it was won by the Conservatives.
40. The Central and Bridgeton constituencies were combined to form the new Central constituency. Kelvingrove and Woodside were combined into the new Kelvingrove constituency. Labour won the new Lanarkshire constituency of East Kilbride but lost East Dunbartonshire in the reorganisation of Dunbartonshire into three constituencies — East, West and Central.
41. See 'The Results Analysed' by Michael Steed in Butler and Pinto-Duschinsky, *op.cit.*, pp.394-400.
42. See the rather inconclusive discussion on an appropriate number of Scottish constituencies in the event of some form of legislative devolution in the *Report of the Royal Commission on the Constitution*, Cmnd 5460, 1973, p.247.
43. Ivor Crewe, 'Do Butler and Stokes Really Explain Political Change in Britain?', *European Journal of Political Research*, Vol. 2, No. 1, March 1974, pp.47-92.
44. R. Rose, *The United Kingdom as a Multi-National State* (Strathclyde Occasional Paper number 6, Glasgow, 1970), p.18.
45. See p.8.
46. The General Register Office defines Yorkshire as the East and West Ridings, the York constituency and five constituencies in the Lindsey area of Lincolnshire. The West Midlands include Herefordshire, Shropshire, Staffordshire, Warwickshire and Worcestershire. North-West England includes Lancashire and Cheshire.
47. Steed in Butler and Pinto-Duschinsky, *op.cit.*, pp.395-6.
48. See R. Rose, *Politics in England Today* (London, Faber, 1974), p.167 and I. Crewe and C. Payne, 'Analysing the Census Data', in Butler and Pinto-Duschinsky, *op.cit.*, pp.416-436.
49. 1966 Sample Census, Summary Tables, No. 11.
50. D. Butler and D. Stokes, *Political Change in Britain* (London, Macmillan, 1969), pp.140-1.
51. R. Rose, 'Class and Party Divisions: Britain as a Test Case', in M. Dogan and R. Rose (eds), *European Politics: A Reader* (London, Macmillan, 1971), pp.169-70.
52. R. Rose, 'Simple Abstractions and Complex Realities' in R. Rose (ed.), *Electoral Behaviour: A Comparative Handbook* (New York, The Free Press, 1974), pp.515-516.

53. J.M. Bochel and D.J. Denver, 'Religion and voting: a critical review and a new analysis', *Political Studies,* vol. XVIII, No.2, June 1970, pp.205-219.
54. See Rose in Dogan and Rose, *op.cit.,* p.168.
55. *Glasgow Herald,* 11 March, 1970, 168-169.
56. Rose in Dogan and Rose, *op.cit.,* p.169.
57. The SNP victor in Clackmannan and East Stirlingshire, George Reid, is both a local man and a television personality; in addition the defeated Labour MP, Dick Douglas, had apparently offended some Labour supporters by his comments on the dispute between the miners and the Conservative Government. In Dundee East, where North Sea Oil issue may have contributed to the SNP's victory, the choice of an Englishman, George Machin, to contest the 1973 by-election met with criticism from Labour supporters in Dundee.
58. See R. Rose, 'The Voting Surveyed' in *The Times Guide to the House of Commons 1974* (London, Times Newspapers Ltd., 1974), pp.30-32.
59. I. McLean, 'The Rise and Fall of the Scottish National Party', *Political Studies,* Vol. XVIII, No. 3, September 1970, pp.357-372.
60. *Ibid.,* pp.364-366.
61. See M. Pinto-Duschinsky, 'Where have all the Liberals come from?', *The Times,* 25th February 1974; and Rose in Dogan and Rose, *op.cit.,* pp.515-516.
62. See Steed in Butler and Pinto-Duschinsky, p.389.
63. *The Scotsman,* 15 February 1974.
64. *The Scotsman,* 15 May 1974.

9. The Scottish Ruling Class: Problems of Analysis and Data

John Scott and Michael Hughes

Studies of economics and politics are invariably dissociated from sociological research and, as a consequence, the crucially important question of the overall distribution of power in society is fragmented and no overall picture emerges. This is particularly true for Scottish society and is something which is not of recent origin. Writing in 1824, Alexander Richmond noted exactly this situation and remarked that

> The theorists in political economy attach more importance to the aggregate accumulation of wealth and power than to the manner of its diffusion, or its effects on the interior of society. (1)

This chapter attempts to redress this situation by investigating the question of the existence of a ruling class in Scotland. Clearly, a full analysis of this question would require a consideration not merely of formal networks of social relationships and the 'aggregate accumulation of wealth and power', but also of the consciousness and cohesion of the dominant group and its effective participation in decision-making. The present chapter is a preliminary to such an analysis, and attempts an exploratory study of the formal structure of power. This will not only help to provide some knowledge about a totally neglected area, it will also help us to establish a conceptual framework which comes to grips with the phenomena of social stratification, relates them to the dynamics of the economy and the polity, and provides a basis for future research.

We propose to discuss such a framework and to illustrate its value with reference to the results of some pilot investigations. In the course of the chapter we aim not only to suggest an outline of the structure of power in Scottish society, but also to indicate some of the problems involved in collecting and using data on this subject.

The concept of a ruling class

The analysis of class, status and political power, although being a popular area of investigation for sociologists, shows a remarkable confusion of terminology and concepts. We do not wish to legislate vocabulary for other sociologists, even if this were possible, but we believe that a modified version of the framework proposed by Max Weber is perhaps the most fruitful approach to the subject. Employing Weber's framework, and seeing class, status and politics as aspects of the overall distribution of power in society, will enable us to present our own data, evaluate the published statistics, and outline the problem areas for future study. We are proposing that Weber's typology is a fruitful way of conceptualizing — that is, *describing* — these phenomena and we do not wish to preclude the *analytical* and *explanatory* utility of other frameworks — for example, the Marxian scheme.

Max Weber based his discussion of class, status and party on a typology of action, although this typology requires modification if it is to be adequate to Weber's own work. (2) The details of this typology need not detain us here, but certain essential points must be made. Weber's typology of action may be seen as a continuum running from *completely rational* action (end-rational or instrumental action) through *irrational* action (affectual and traditional) to *completely non-rational* action (ritual action). Clearly, these are all analytical constructs and any particular concrete course of action may combine all of them. Our main concern will be with the polar types. As Winch has indicated, (3) all human action, rational and non-rational, is rule-governed. Actions differ in terms of the nature of the rules: rational action is oriented towards systems of technically and economically efficient norms and is therefore 'instrumental', whilst non-rational action is oriented towards those norms characterised by Parsons as concerned with 'symbolic appropriateness'. (4) Conformity to these latter norms is *not* therefore instrumental but ritualistic or expressive.

It is our contention that the category of rational action is closely tied to economics and politics, whilst non-rational action relates to the notion of prestige or status. Our main concern in what follows is with rational action in the economy and polity, and we shall neglect ritual action. Briefly, we regard the norms involved in status as concerned with the way in which a person's social position is evaluated by others and the expression of this in terms of expectations about an *appropriate* life style. We do not intend to deny that there are value or non-rational elements involved in concrete political or economic activities. We are here making an analytical distinction between *aspects* of action.

Focusing, for present purposes, on rational action we may examine how Weber constructs the economic and political types of rational action. Economic action is seen as purposive action oriented to the attainment of 'utilities' through the use of peaceful means. On this basis Weber builds up his conception of the market as a structure of such self-interested rational acts and of 'class' as a particular constellation of market interests. (5) Political action, on the other hand, can be seen as that type of instrumental action which centres upon the attainment of goals through processes of decision-making. Weber sees this as comprising the institutional forms of bureaucracy and the state, which are based, ultimately, on the use of force.

Thus we have three major types of action — economic, political and ritual — and whilst these shade over into one another and have many intricate interrelationships in concrete systems of action, (6) they can be distinguished analytically and warrant further discussion. It may be recalled that for Weber class, status and party were all aspects of the distribution of power, and it is in this context that we propose to discuss our three types of action.

We propose that three major types of power may be distinguished: economic power based on an individual's relationship to the means of economic production, that social system which has the production of goods and services as its output; political power based on relationship to the means of political production, that social system with the production of 'decisions' as an output; and cultural power (7) based on relationship to the means of cultural production, that social system with the creation, change and maintenance of values and ideas as its output. The successful exercise of power thus represents a threat to mobilize the various economic, political and cultural resources at one's disposal in order to further one's interests in the face of opposition from others. Power, as a generalized form of social control, therefore, rests upon three bases. (8)

Any examination of social control through power must investigate each of these three 'dimensions'; that is, it must concern itself with class structures, political processes and status groups. We propose that an examination of the distribution of power in Scottish society may be made in such terms, although in the present paper we shall focus on the dimensions of economic and political power.

Given these Weberian distinctions, what meaning can be given to the idea of a 'ruling class'? A first preliminary to clarifying such an idea may be gained from a discussion of the notion of an 'elite' as it has recently been used by Giddens. An elite group comprises 'those individuals who occupy formally defined positions of authority at the head of a social organization or institution' (9) and the term 'elite' applies to either an elite group or a cluster of elite groups.

Giddens constructs a typology of elites in terms of two parameters: structure and recruitment. Elite recruitment may be regarded as 'open' when access to elite positions is available to people from a wide variety of backgrounds and where mobility is high; conversely it may be termed 'closed' when entry is restricted to certain social groups. The structure of an elite is analysed in terms of its social and moral integration: in terms of elite members having social contacts and relationships and sharing common ideas and values. (10) Cross-classifying these two dimensions yields a four-fold typology:

RECRUITMENT

	Open	Closed
High Integration	Solidary Elite	Uniform Elite
Low Integration	Abstract Elite	Established Elite

STRUCTURE

Figure 1.

A uniform elite is one in which a tightly-knit and cohesive group is able to restrict access to elite positions to the point where, ultimately, it is completely self-recruiting, totally closed to outsiders. In established elites recruitment is similarly limited but cohesion and solidarity are less than in the uniform elite. A solidary elite is found where the group is highly integrated but recruits itself from outside its own membership. Finally, an abstract elite is one in which recruitment is relatively open and the elite groups possess a low level of integration. (11)

Echoing Michels's claim that 'who says organization, says oligarchy', (12) Giddens argues that such elites are to be found wherever there are social organizations with formally defined authority systems. If this is the case then we should entertain the possibility, for example, that whilst some of the elites in any particular society may be uniform, others may be established: the structures of elite groups are *logically* independent of one another. Nevertheless, as Cohen has argued, (13) the institutional sectors of any particular society will exhibit a particular pattern of *interdependence* and therefore there are definite limits to their independent variability. We expect, in practice, to find a 'congruence' between the structures of the various elites, this congruence being most marked amongst the most strategic institutions. We are not proposing a naive equilibrium theory or suggesting that all elites will be of the same type, far from it. We are simply making two points: firstly, that each of the various elites limits and constrains the form of the other elites, certain elites being of greater significance in this respect; secondly, that in order to clarify the issues, an ideal typical limiting case may be constructed.

In the present chapter we shall discuss only the limiting analytical case in which the type of elite is the same in each of the three dimensions of economic, cultural and political power, although we relax this assumption in a later section in order to conceptualize 'sub-national' elites.

The question must be raised here of the relationship between the concepts 'economic elite' and 'class'. The former term is obviously broader in scope, referring to the purely *formal* analysis of economic power, and is hence merely descriptive. As such, it may refer to both Giddens' concepts of 'elite' and 'elite group'. To talk about the *dynamics* of economic power requires more substantive concepts, and 'class' is one such concept. Thus, not all economic elites are classes. We see classes arising in situations where the economic elite is based upon the operation of the market and the production and appropriation of surplus value.

We believe that there are certain inadequacies in Giddens' formulation and therefore propose to produce an alternative through critical discussion. Giddens constructs a fourfold typology of social control by combining his typology of elites with an analysis of 'effective power'. It would seem to us that in discussing structural forms of control it is out of place to discuss the actual process of decision-making; rather we would argue that it is only necessary to consider whether the power structure *as such* is centralised or diffused. (14) We therefore propose the typology presented in Figure 2.

	SYSTEM OF SOCIAL CONTROL	ELITE FORMATION	POWER DISTRIBUTION
1.	Ruling Class	Uniform	Centralised
2.	Governing Class	Established	Diffused
3.	Power Elite	Solidary	Centralised
4.	Leadership Groups	Abstract	Diffused

Figure 2. (15)

Giddens' typology of these four systems of social control is presented solely in terms of the *form* of the elites and their power rather than in terms of the *content* or *base* of their power and thus many significant problems creep into the analysis. For example, a ruling class is defined as a uniform elite with centralized power — nothing more than that. On this basis we could argue that the College of Cardinals is a ruling class and this clearly stretches the concept beyond reasonable bounds. For Marx, the question of the ruling class concerns the relationship between the class structure and the form and functioning of the state, the relationship between economic and political power. We therefore propose that the typology of social control should be taken as referring *only* to those situations in which each of the following three conditions are met:

(a) the analysis must be concerned solely with economic and political power; (16)

(b) the structure of elite formation is the same in both the economic system and the political system;

(c) there is a significant overlap in membership between the economy and the polity.

Thus, a ruling class may be said to exist where the economic elite is closed, highly integrated and takes the form of a 'class', where the political elite is closed and highly integrated, where there is a high concentration of power within each system, and where the members of the economic elite are, in large part, also members of the political elite. A governing class exists where both elites are rather less well integrated and where power is rather more diffused. (17) We may see the four systems of control as forming a hierarchy: the ruling class being the 'strongest' form of control and the pluralistic system of leadership groups being the 'weakest'.

We propose that this scheme is applicable to any level of analysis — national or sub-national — and in the next section we shall discuss the problems involved in applying the schema simultaneously to these two levels. A necessary preliminary to a discussion of a sub-national unit such as Scotland (18) is therefore an analysis of the political and economic environment within which the Scottish system is located.

Problems in the study of sub-national elites

Britain is not a totally autonomous unit since it is subject to international political and economic constraints. This is even more the case for Scotland. The Scottish system is a 'sub-national' unit operating in the overarching British 'national' system. As such it too possesses only a *relative autonomy:* the exercise of power in Scottish society is seriously limited and constrained by the environment in which it takes place. These environmental constraints are even more significant for the Scottish system than they are for the British system and it therefore follows that certain modifications to the schema must be made if we are to conceptualize the realities of the situation. We make these modifications through the parallel conceptions of the centre-periphery thesis of political power and the metropolis-satellite thesis of economic power. (19) Employing these ideas permits us to examine the question of whether sub-national elites are more or less autonomous centres of power or whether they are mere intermediaries between the national elites and the local community. The framework employed is presented in Figure 3.

	NATIONAL LEADERSHIP	LOCAL LEADERSHIP
POLITICAL LEVEL	Centre	Periphery
ECONOMIC LEVEL	Metropolis	Satellite

Figure 3.

In an attempt to come to grips with the problem of the 'underdeveloped' nations of the Third World, André Frank developed the notion of studying the economic relationship *between* a developed metropolis and the underdeveloped nation, seeing the latter as a satellite economy of the metropolis. Rather than seeing the underdeveloped nation as an isolated 'traditional' or 'feudal' society, we must realise that the only reason why one society is underdeveloped in relation to the other is because of the exploitative relationships of appropriation existing between metropolis and satellite. (20) Not only is this schema applicable to relations between developed and underdeveloped *nations,* it is also applicable to *regional* divisions within nations. It is our contention that Frank's framework is a useful way of viewing the relationship between the British and Scottish economies. We suggest that Scotland may be seen as a satellite of the London metropolis — and more specifically that the Glasgow-Edinburgh axis is the focus of the satellite and is, to a certain extent, a metropolis in relation to North-Eastern and Highland Scotland. (21)

The centre-periphery thesis has a similar origin but is generally used in the context of the kind of theory that Frank is criticizing: it is used as a political counterpart to the 'dual economy' theory. For instance, Davies argues (22) that the centre comprises the dominating mechanisms of urban politics whilst the periphery consists of the areas of society which are uninfluenced or unreached by the politics of the centre. It is thus generally used in studying 'modernizing' societies, and the periphery is equated with the traditional sectors — small communities lacking market mechanisms and based on ascriptive social relations.

We propose that the centre-periphery thesis be modified along the lines of Frank's schema. That is, any particular area may only be regarded as peripheral in relation to another, central, area: it is peripheral precisely *because* the other is central. We would argue that if this is *not* accepted then we cannot regard the two areas as parts of the same system — and if this is the case then the analogy of centre and periphery is inappropriate. We propose that Scotland may be seen, politically, as a periphery of the British centre. (23)

Thus we are arguing that London is both political *centre* and economic *metropolis,* whilst Scotland is a *peripheral satellite.* The question then arises of the specific mechanisms which constitute this relationship: what is the exact nature of the relationship between social control in Britain and social control in Scotland?

Mackenzie recognizes this geographical and sectional division in social control when he writes that (24)

It seems ... realistic to think in terms of a leadership sub-system based on the South Eastern 'heart-land', to which other sub-systems in part conceded their role of leadership, although they remained also partly in conflict with it.

Clearly we must examine the 'boundaries' of the various systems and their relative autonomy with respect to one another. Summarising his discussion of the Scottish political system James Kellas remarks that (25)

The Scottish system is both dependent and independent within the British system.

If we are to adequately approach the empirical measurement of the relative autonomy of Scottish elites we must build this perception into our previously established framework. Now clearly any of our four kinds of control — ruling class, governing class, power elite, and leadership groups — may occur at either the national or sub-national level, but certain combinations are more likely than others. An overall cross-classification would yield sixteen logically possible relationships between national and sub-national elites. The available empirical evidence would suggest that social control at the British level takes the form of a ruling class. (26) We are therefore concerned with only four of these possibilities. These are set out in Figure 4.

	NATIONAL STRUCTURE	SUB-NATIONAL STRUCTURE
1.	Ruling class	Ruling class
2.	Ruling class	Governing class
3.	Ruling class	Power elite
4.	Ruling class	Leadership groups

Figure 4.

Is there a ruling class in Scotland?

Any attempt to consider the question of the existence of a ruling class in Scotland must be rather tentative at the present moment since the available data are of limited value only. Official statistics tend to cover narrowly defined 'economic' factors and are not easily related to the theoretical categories of sociological analysis. Since there are no explicitly *sociological* studies in this area, it is necessary to use the somewhat limited data available in directories, biographies, membership registers, etc. (27)

In order to relate these data to our conceptual framework, we must formulate a set of operational definitions which will, as it were, bridge the gap between data and framework. We propose to use the term 'economic notables' to refer to the whole cluster of economic elites, and we operationally define the category as referring to all those individuals who are directors of the top manufacturing and retailing firms, banks, insurance companies, and investment trust companies. Our sample of 'top firms' was derived by extracting *all* those Scottish firms in the relevant categories of *The Times 1000.* (28) Our sample therefore includes such giants as Burmah Oil, Scottish and Newcastle Breweries, House of Fraser, The Weir Group, Anderson Mavor, The Distillers Company, The Scottish Amicable Life Assurance Company, The Scottish Widows' Fund and Life Assurance Society, The Royal Bank of Scotland, and less well known firms such as The Scottish Western Investment Company, The Scottish Eastern Investment Trust, The Low and Bonar Group, The Titaghur Jute Factory, Scottish and Universal Investments, and The American Trust Company. In total, the category of top firms comprised 69 companies. We use the term 'economic elite' to refer to those economic notables holding two or more directorships in these top firms. Thus, in relating these operational definitions to our conceptual framework, we are interested in the structure and recruitment of the economic notables; since, in practice, adequate data are not available, we shall focus on the narrower economic elite.

Similar distinctions can be made, with respect to political participation, between political notables and the political elite. Unfortunately, the data are even less satisfactory in this area (29) and so, without extensive research, it is impossible to use such distinctions. We shall therefore employ only the category of 'political notables'. In operational terms, then, our criteria for the existence of a ruling class refer to high integration and closed recruitment amongst both economic and political notables and a significant overlap of membership between the two.

The economic notables in whom we are interested are those in top positions in the commanding heights of the private sector of the economy. (30) We wish to examine the connections within the industrial and financial sectors and between the two. We shall also examine the extent to which this 'functional' division is reflected in the geographical separation of Glasgow and Edinburgh — a question of great importance in examining the metropolis-satellite thesis. (31)

The financial organisations upon which we shall focus are the major banks, insurance companies, and investment trust companies. We intend to show that the operations of these firms are shaped by the fact that there is no money market in Scotland — this is located in London, which exhibits both financial and commercial interests in close proximity to one another. Writing of Edinburgh, David Keir remarks that, (32)

> Edinburgh can be called the financial capital of Scotland yet it does not qualify to be a true financial centre. Though it is the seat of government for Scotland, and houses many financial institutions, it has never been a centre where risk capital could readily be raised for industrial projects. In part this has come about because Edinburgh has no money market, that is for short term obligations. (33)

Thus, any examination of Scottish financial firms is immediately concerned with the overarching 'British' system based on the City of London. The Scottish financial system can be seen as a differentiated sub-system of the British financial system, suited to the distinctive characteristics of Scottish trade and industry. Nevertheless, as many writers have argued, and as would seem to be apparent from Scotland's recent economic problems, these financial institutions have not always been well-attuned to the needs of Scottish industry and have frequently preferred investments outside the country, particularly in North America — and more recently in Japan — to indigenous industrial development.

Banks, insurance companies and investment trust companies have all been of importance in providing industrial finance. Perhaps the most characteristic financial institutions of the Scottish scene are the numerous investment trust companies. These trusts developed during the nineteenth century in order to finance developments overseas. (34) We estimate that today there are 49 such companies in Edinburgh, Glasgow, Dundee and Aberdeen, about half being located in Edinburgh. Our figures show that Scottish registered investment trust companies controlled assets totalling approximately £2,000 million, compared with the £2,600 million controlled by Scottish insurance companies. (35) Clearly, the directors of the top investment and insurance companies warrant the designation economic notables.

The industrial and merchandising sector (36) is very extensive in character, ranging from the heavy industries of the west — iron and steel, shipbuilding, machine tools, and textiles — to the more diverse industries of the east. Our category of economic notables includes all the directors of the major firms in this sector, regardless of the type of work carried out by the business. (37)

Table 1 gives basic figures on the distribution of directorships in 1972 for the 69 top Scottish firms. It shows that a total of 573 directorships were held by only 483 men and that there were 60 multiple directors. That is, of 483 economic notables, 60 formed the economic elite. In total, 150 directorships were held by members of the elite.

When these figures are examined by sector they show that financial firms are more likely to have multiple directors than are industrials. Of the 38 top industrial and merchandising firms, just under a half (17) had multiple directors; but amongst the top 31 financial firms, all but one are interlocked.

Table 1. The Distribution of Directorships (1972)

Number of directorships held	Number of men	Total number of directorships
1	423	423
2	38	76
3	17	51
4	4	16
5	-	-
6	-	-
7	1	7
Total	483	573

Table 2. The Distribution of Interlocks (1972)

Number of interlocked directors per company	Industrial and merchandising	Financial	Total
0	21	1	22
1-3	16	15	31
4-6	1	11	12
over 7	0	4	4
Total number of interlocked companies	17	30	47
Average number of interlocked directors per company	1.9	3.9	3.2

The figures in Table 2 show the number of interlocked directors per company and their distribution by sector. They show that whereas the interlocked industrial and merchandising firms have between one and three multiple directors (an average of 1.9 per company), financial firms are just as likely to have more than three. The average figure of 3.9 for financial firms covers up some significant differences within the sector: whereas investment trusts have an average figure of 3.1, insurance companies have an average of 4.4 and banks an average of 7.5 (38). Clearly, such bald figures must be interpreted with care, since interlocks *between* investment trusts, for example, may result in a relatively small number of people sitting on a large number of boards, and therefore producing a greater degree of interlock than would appear from the figures in Table 2. In order to investigate this possibility we carried out an analysis of the directorships of *all* Scottish banks, insurance and investment companies, and unit trusts.

Using the *Directory of Financial Institutions* (1973) as our source of data, we compiled an inventory of the financial companies registered in Scotland in 1972. This includes several companies which are subsidiaries of English and overseas companies. Further research is intended to analyse the relationship between wholly Scottish financial companies and non-Scottish owned companies. At present, however, this requires more data on shareholdings. The resulting 80 companies had a total directorate of 535, held by 342 individuals.

Perhaps the first observation to make is that, of these 342 directors, 56 were also in the economic elite of the main sample. This means that 93% of the economic elite were present as directors of financial companies. Similarly, 123 non-elite notables were on the boards of financial companies — 29% of the non-elite notables. Thus, an overlap between the main sample and the financial firms is evident. By combining these figures, we find that 37% of the economic notables held directorships in financial firms. Consequently, examining the presence of economic notables in the financial sector, we see that 52% of the directors of financial firms figure in the main (as sample 16% economic elite members, 36% non-elite notables). This significant overlap supports and further exemplifies our discussion of the importance of financial interests amongst the economic notables, and supports the conclusion that interlocking of directorships in the smaller and subsidiary firms consolidates the position found amongst top companies. A more detailed analysis of the financial firms will, therefore, provide further information on the distribution of power in Scottish society.

A general picture of the directorships shows that 54% were multiple directorships. (39) These were held by 28% of the directors, an average of 3 directorships per man. This indicates a high degree of integration between the financial firms, achieved through a significant minority of individuals holding multiple directorships. More detail on this integration can be gained from an examination of the various sub-sectors of the financial sector.

Investment trust companies are the most numerous, comprising 61% of all financial companies, and containing 49% of *all* directorships. They are tightly interlocked with one another and are extensively interlocked with other financial firms — contributing 57% of all multiple directorships (31% of all financial directorships). This propensity for investment trust companies' directors to hold more than one directorship gives the companies a central position in the interlocking of financial firms and the representation of their interests (63% of investment trust directorships are multiple directorships. There is an average of 3.4 multiple directorships per company. See Table 3).

Table 3. Financial Directorships (1972)

	Banks	Insurance Companies	Investment Trusts	Unit Trusts	Unit Trust Management	Total
Single Directorships	39	95	99	5	7	245
Multiple Directorships	45	46	165	21	13	290
					GRAND TOTAL	535

Insurance companies are the second largest sub-sector, comprising 20% of financial companies and having 26% of directorships. They are less well integrated than investment trusts, since they have fewer interlocks with other financial companies having 16% of the multiple directorships (an average of 2.9 multiple directorships per company). Banks occupy a similar position with 16% of the total directorships and 16% of multiple directorships. However, since the number of banks is half the number of insurance companies, they are more tightly integrated and interlocked. (40)

This brief overview of the situation indicates that investment trust companies play a key role in integrating the financial sector of the Scottish economy — but our data are not sufficiently detailed to assess the *precise* contributions made by the various companies, or the relative success they enjoy in representing their interests.

It is worth considering the size of funds controlled by the non-banking financial companies, although we do not have precise information on banking funds. Our figures suggest that funds are more thinly spread amongst the investment trusts than amongst insurance companies — approximately £2,000m. (42% of total Scottish non-banking funds) being held by 49 investment trust companies. The 16 insurance companies control approximately £2,600m. (54%). However, the differing degrees of integration characteristic of the two types of company imply that investment trust funds may not be any the less important as a resource, and that any analysis of economic power must take account of both size of funds *and* integration of firms with other firms. Unit trusts have a much smaller share of the cake with 4 companies holding £224m. (5% of non-banking funds).

So far, the picture that emerges from our analysis is one in which an economic elite of 60 men bring about an integration of the industrial and financial sectors of the Scottish economy. Our analysis suggests that there is a remarkably high degree of integration within the financial sector, and that the elite members who sit on the boards of financial companies are frequently to be found on the boards of industrial companies. The picture is, therefore, one of a partial differentiation of the economic notables into industrial and financial elite groups with an overall integration of these notables through the activities of a relatively small economic elite, oriented primarily by financial interests. (41)

Thus, we would argue that our evidence suggests the existence of either a solidary or uniform elite (see Figure 1), i.e. an economic elite with a high degree of integration. It may be argued against this, that a large number of individuals sitting on only one board (423) indicates quite a low degree of integration; but our separate analysis of all Scottish financial firms has shown that if we go beyond the top sixty-nine companies, we find a number of interlocks, involving these notables, amongst the smaller or subsidiary companies. We would conclude that our evidence gives reasonable grounds for the conclusion that the economic elite is either solidary or uniform.

We remarked earlier that the available data on political participation are even less satisfactory than those on economic activity, and we are therefore not able to present a full analysis of integration amongst political notables. Our procedure will be to examine a number of political organizations and to estimate the extent to which, within these, our economic notables are also political notables.

It is very difficult to obtain information on formal political participation at local and national level — for example as M.Ps, councillors, and office-holders in political parties. It is, of course, relatively easy to get unsystematic data showing that a small number of the members of the economic elite has engaged in national politics at ministerial level, or has held high posts in party administration. It is also possible to discover that a number of the elite comes from families which have traditionally been involved in Scottish politics. (42) Rather more systematic, but perhaps of slight significance to political power, is the fact that the economic elite includes 6 Justices of the Peace, 8 Deputy Lieutenants, and 1 Privy Councillor. Equally, the fact that the economic elite possesses, collectively, 11 knighthoods and baronetcies, 16 Orders of the British Empire (43) and 3 peerages, is a sign of *recognition* by the political centre, but is not really indicative of actual political power. We would suggest that such honours are more indicative of status — cultural power — than either economic or political power. (44)

Some time ago, Peter Worsley (45) suggested a distinction between what he called Politics I — the exercise of constraint in social relations — and Politics II — the specialized machinery of government. More recently, but in a similar vein, Ivor Crewe (46) has argued that political sociologists should move away from studying the social background of top political decision-makers and concentrate more of their attention on the less visible 'political' elites which operate 'behind the scenes'. In accordance with our earlier discussion of political power, we would accept the broader view of politics suggested by both of these writers and would define the category of political notables so as to include, not only participants in formal politics, but also those who are members of what Finer (47) has called the 'lobby'. We shall, therefore, discuss the relationship between three such groups which form a part of the Scottish political lobby and which therefore direct their attentions to influencing the decision-making processes of what Kellas (48) has termed the Scottish political system. The three groups we have selected are Edinburgh Chamber of Commerce, Glasgow Chamber of Commerce, and The Scottish Council (Development and Industry). (49)

Chambers of Commerce are regulated under Royal Charter and aim to represent the interests of commerce and industry at a number of levels. Their membership is drawn from the individuals, firms and associations located in their catchment area, but effective decision-making is in the hands of the directors and committee men. Most directors are elected by the individual and delegated members, and the elected directors generally nominate a number of additional directors. Much work is carried out by committees composed of both directors and ordinary members, the committees reporting back to the directorate. The Chambers see themselves as the 'organized voice' of commerce and industry, and therefore engage in a number of advisory, consultative and promotional activities with a number of other bodies. Both Edinburgh and Glasgow Chambers are represented on the Scottish Chamber of Commerce and, through this, on the Association of British Chambers of Commerce and the International Chamber of Commerce. They are also able to lobby local authorities and other official bodies and are thereby involved in various industrial promotion groups, transport consultative councils, and, recently, the Commissions on local government and constitutional reform. Their aims and activities together determine their particular policies, for example with respect to the promotion and stimulation of indigenous industrial development.

Our analysis of the membership of Edinburgh Chamber of Commerce shows that the economic notables who participate as members result in 44 *representations* of top firms. By *representation* we mean that an individual who is active in an organization may be said to *represent* all those firms with whom he is connected, regardless of the firm which officially *delegates* him. The *representation* of a firm, therefore, means the number of its directors who are in the particular political group. Our figures show that the members of the economic elite have a greater *representation* on the Chamber than their number amongst the economic notables as a whole would suggest:

out of 27 economic notables active on the Chamber, 9 are members of the economic elite. It appears that the presence of these elite members results in a greater *representation* of financial firms as compared with industrial and merchandising firms. Of the total of 44 *representations*, 23 are *representations* of financial firms by members of the economic elite. Those economic notables who are not members of the elite tend to *represent* industrial and merchandising firms rather than financial firms. We would conclude that the economic notables active in Edinburgh Chamber of Commerce come from a predominantly financial background (30 *representations* out of a total of 44) and that these financial *representations* tend to be concentrated in the economic elite. It would appear that the dominance of the financial element is reflected in this segment of the political lobby.

Turning to Glasgow Chamber of Commerce, we find that the directors and committee members reflect a similar pattern. Of a total of 12 *representations*, nearly a half (5) were elite *representations* of financial interests. Thus, whilst the Chamber shows an overall balance between the industrial and financial interests, not only are the financial *representations* mainly at the economic elite level, but the balance does not reflect the industrial bias in business in the west of Scotland.

An important result emerges from a comparison of the number of companies actually represented by economic notables on the Glasgow and Edinburgh Chambers with the potential number of top firms located in their catchment areas. These results are presented in Table 4. We take no account here of the number of *representations* per company; we are only analysing the *number of companies*. By Glasgow catchment area we refer to the Greater Glasgow area and the counties of Renfrewshire and Lanarkshire. The Edinburgh catchment area is Greater Edinburgh and the county of Midlothian.

Table 4. Top Companies Represented on Glasgow and Edinburgh Chambers* (1972)

	GLASGOW Potential	Actual	EDINBURGH Potential	Actual
Industrial and Merchandising	18	6	7	2
Financial	11	3	18	4
TOTAL	29	9	25	6

* Amongst directors and committee men only.

In the figures for 'potential' company representation by economic notables, the distinction can clearly be seen between the industrial west and the financial east of Scotland; a balance which is also present in 'actual' company representation. It is therefore significant that when account is taken of the number of times these firms are *represented*, the financial dominance is present in both Chambers — particularly at the economic elite level. Our data indicate that, amongst directors and committee men on Glasgow Chamber of Commerce, there is 1 *representation* of an industrial firm and 3 *representations* of financial firms by members of the economic elite, and that in Edinburgh Chamber there are 4 financial *representations* amongst elite members and no industrial *representations*.

Our comparison of Glasgow and Edinburgh Chambers shows that the economic notables are present in significant numbers amongst the political notables and that it is the financial members of the economic elite who produce a similar character in the two Chambers: the dominance of the financial interests amongst economic notables is reflected amongst political notables. A further conclusion pointed to by our data is that it is perhaps Edinburgh financial interests which are of greatest importance. An analysis of cross-representation shows that only one top Glasgow firm is *represented* by an economic notable on the Edinburgh Chamber — an industrial firm *represented* by a non-elite notable — whilst two Edinburgh top financial firms are *represented* on the Glasgow Chamber, both at the economic elite level.

Unlike the Chambers of Commerce, the Scottish Council (Development and Industry) has no Royal Charter. It is a registered company, limited by guarantee, having no share capital, and was formed in 1946 by the merger of the Scottish Development Council and the Scottish Council on Industry. Its finance comes from local authorities, companies, banks, trades unions, chambers of commerce, donations, and from public funds. Its aim is to promote the industrial and social development of Scotland, and it chooses specific policies which accord with this aim. It has looked recently to the upsurge in economic activity in Scotland and has produced various reports on strategies for the future. (50) The major concerns of the Scottish Council have been the steel and oil industries, and they have related the need for more investment in these areas to the position of Scotland in the E.E.C. A focus of its attention has been the attraction of English, North American and European, and most recently, Japanese firms to Scotland.

In order to promote these aims, the directors and committee members of the Scottish Council are represented on a number of bodies — for example, consultative councils for the Scottish Tourist Board and the Scottish Transport Group. Most importantly, the Council's activities are closely linked to those of the Scottish Office and it even appears as an agency of the Scottish Office in *A Handbook on Scottish Administration* (HMSO).

Thus, the Scottish Council operates at a rather higher level of the political system than the Chambers of Commerce, and it is therefore significant that economic elite participation at director and committee level is much higher than in either of the Chambers. Table 5 shows some comparative figures.

Table 5. Economic Elite Participation at Director and Committee Level (1972)

	Glasgow Chamber of Commerce	Edinburgh Chamber of Commerce	Scottish Council	Total
Economic Elite	2	1	12	15
Other Economic Notables	6	5	8	19
Total	8	6	20	34

The figures show that economic elite participation in the chambers of commerce is of about the same order: 25% of the economic notables in Glasgow and 17% in Edinburgh. In the Scottish Council there is a startling reversal of the figures, 60% of the politically active economic notables being members of the economic elite. Not only are more of the economic notables active in the Scottish Council than in the chambers of commerce, but also these notables are more likely to be members of the economic elite.

Our conclusions on the position of financial interests are borne out by our data on the Scottish Council. These data show that, out of a total of 37 *representations,* 27 are *representations* of financial interests — and 24 of these are at the economic elite level. Our data also show that none of the top firms outside the Glasgow–Edinburgh region is *represented* amongst directors and committee men of the Scottish Council — even though 15 of the top 69 companies are located outside the central belt. It is clear from our findings that the dominance of the financial sector operates through Edinburgh firms: there are 17 *representations* by Edinburgh firms amongst the 27 financial *representations.* Of these 17 *representations,* 15 are at the elite level.

Clearly our data have not enabled us to examine the question of the integration of the political notables directly, but we have produced some evidence on the relationship between the economic and political notables. The extensive involvement of the economic elite in formal and informal politics points to the existence of either a uniform or a solidary political elite, but further systematic research is obviously required. Our data suggest that the mode of social control in Scottish society takes the form of either a power elite or a ruling class. Before we can decide between these two possibilities, we must examine the evidence on recruitment to the economic and political elite.

Evidence on the recruitment of economic and political notables is perhaps the weakest, merely because many of these men do not appear in biographies and directories. We can, however, produce some evidence on the educational and family backgrounds of a number of the economic elite.

Of the members of the 60-strong economic elite upon whom we have information, 18 attended well-known English public schools (30% of the elite) and 10 attended independent Scottish schools (16%); thus, nearly half of the economic elite is known to have been educated in private, fee-paying schools. Of the members of the economic elite about whom we have information, 18 men went to Oxford or Cambridge University and 6 went to Scottish Universities. Thus, nearly a third of the elite is known to have attended Oxbridge, and more than one tenth is known to have received a university education outside Oxbridge. Our findings would suggest that the economic elite is recruited from an exclusive educational background. Our data could be explained in a number of ways: for example, it could be argued that those from an exclusive background are more likely to appear in directories and reference books. Nevertheless, it remains true that a large proportion of the economic elite *do* come from such a background; if anything, our figures are underestimates.

Further evidence on the exclusive background of members of the economic elite is shown by the family connections of the men. Systematic evidence on this is lacking, but we do have some evidence relevant to this. One source of evidence is the large number of family-owned or family-controlled firms amongst the top companies: our findings would suggest that about a third of the top industrial and merchandising firms falls into this category. These are firms which are known to have been built up by a particular family and which still have members of that family sitting on the board. This points not only to a basic continuity in the membership of the economic elite across several generations, but also, when taken in conjunction with our evidence on the interlocks between financial and industrial firms, strengthens our conclusions as to the high integration of the elite. Further evidence comes from the frequent appearance of ancestors of the present elite members in Scottish history. For example, in accounts of the Glasgow colonial merchants, many names of present day elite members appear. (51) The records on business history in Scotland and on local notables as M.Ps, Lord Provosts, etc. all point to the continuity of elite, and notable, membership. A final source of evidence is the family trees which can be constructed for certain families, and which show present day kinship links between members of the economic elite and connections with notables of earlier generations. (52)

The evidence which we have on recruitment, incomplete and unsystematic as it is, suggests a high degree of self-recruitment. And, as we have noted, our data tend towards an underestimation of this. This in turn would suggest that the economic elite is either uniform or established (see Figure 1). Taking this in conjunction with our conclusions on the *structure* of economic and political power, we may conclude that there is considerable evidence in favour of the proposition that social control takes the form of a ruling class.

We must now turn to a consideration of the relationship between economic and political power in Scotland and social control in Britain as a whole. Some evidence on this can be found in John Firn's (53) recent study of the ownership of industry in Scotland. His report shows that, taking Scottish manufacturing industry as a whole, in 1973, 50% of the plants employing more than 5000 employees were English-owned, only 21% being Scottish-owned. (54) Scottish-owned firms tended to be small plants with less advanced technology, and he concludes that

> The Scottish economy is firmly linked to that of the rest of the U.K. ... [and] it is no longer possible to assume ... that the majority of business decisions shaping the course and pace of economic development in areas such as Scotland are endogenous to the areas concerned. (55)

The consequence of such a situation is that a high proportion of all private capital invested in Scottish industry produces profits which tend to leave the country. This fact gives some corroboration to our view of the Scottish economy as a satellite of the London metropolis, but a full analysis would require figures on investment and capital flows — unfortunately such information is not available. A report by the Economist Intelligence Unit (56) concluded that it was virtually impossible to construct a Scottish Balance of Payments.

It would appear that the Scottish ruling class controls a relatively small amount of the total private investment in Scottish industry and, if our earlier interpretation is correct, this control is located in the Edinburgh financial institutions. Its control over public investment and spending is another matter, and one which, unfortunately, we cannot investigate here. Thus, if the Glasgow-Edinburgh axis is the focus of Scotland's satellite economy, Edinburgh is certainly the senior partner: a minor metropolis itself in relation to Glasgow industry. This can be illustrated by our evidence on regional interlocks based on the sample of top companies, presented in Table 6.

This table shows that in the case of both industrial and financial firms located in Glasgow, 33% of all interlocks were with Edinburgh financial firms. Clearly,

Table 6. Regional Interlocks in Top Companies (1972)

	Number of interlocks with all firms	Number of interlocks with Edinburgh financials	Number of interlocks with Edinburgh industrials	Number of interlocks with other Scottish firms
Glasgow industrial and merchandising firms	41	15	1	25
Glasgow financial firms	48	16	1	31

without an analysis of ownership patterns and the actual flow of capital, we cannot totally substantiate our thesis, but our findings are suggestive.

If we again turn to our study of all Scottish financial firms we find significant corroboration for this view. The distribution of financial companies between Edinburgh and Glasgow further illustrates Edinburgh's dominance in the financial sector: 53% of all the financial companies are located in Edinburgh, compared with 35% in Glasgow (12% are located in Dundee, Perth and Aberdeen). Similarly, looking at directorships, we find that Edinburgh-based financial companies account for 53% of all directorships, compared with 35% for Glasgow. Edinburgh companies are also more extensively interlocked with other financial companies, having 57% of all multiple directorships in the financial sector (Glasgow has 32%). (57) Tables 7 and 8 illustrate this.

Table 7. Regional Distribution of Companies (1972)

Number of Companies	Edinburgh	Glasgow	Other Scottish
Insurance	7	8	1
Investment Trusts	27	13	9
Banks	4	4	0

Table 8. Regional Distribution of Directorships (1972)

	Edinburgh	Glasgow	Other Scottish
Single Directorships	119	94	32
Multiple Directorships	165	93	32

Insurance companies are more evenly distributed between Glasgow and Edinburgh, but they represent a much greater proportion of the financial companies in Glasgow (29%) than in Edinburgh (17%). The location of banks regionally also favours Glasgow and Edinburgh equally (4 in each area), but, again, representing a greater proportion of Glasgow companies (14% compared with 10% in Edinburgh).

The regional variation in the distribution of multiple directorships in insurance companies and banks indicates that Edinburgh financial companies are highly integrated and interlocked, reflecting the impression given in our general overview. Half of the directorships in Edinburgh insurance companies are multiple directorships; this is 67% of all insurance company multiple directorships. On the other hand, multiple directorships in Glasgow insurance companies represent only 13% of insurance company directorships, and point to a much lower degree of interlock with other insurance companies and financial firms. The funds controlled by the Edinburgh insurance companies (c. £1,800 m.), 68% of all insurance company funds, indicate that they are by far the largest of the insurance companies. Glasgow insurance firms control only 16% of this amount (c. £402 m.). Combining this with our evidence on the degree of integration within Edinburgh insurance companies, we would suggest that Edinburgh is the dominant element in this sub-sector of Scottish finance.

Although the banks are equally distributed between Edinburgh and Glasgow, our data show a higher degree of integration and interlock for Edinburgh banks. In banking, 62% of multiple directorships are in Edinburgh. (58) This is further confirmation of the central position of Edinburgh within the financial sector, and this picture is even clearer when we note that two of the Glasgow banks are English subsidiaries. (59).

As we have argued earlier, investment trusts are perhaps the most significant vehicle for the integration and interlocking of financial companies. The regional distribution of investment trusts shows that Edinburgh contains 55% of these companies, compared with 27% in Glasgow. This situation is reflected in the distribution of investment trust directorships — Edinburgh companies having 57% of the total and Glasgow companies 25%. Similarly for multiple directorships, Edinburgh having 56% of the total and Glasgow having 29%. Both Edinburgh and Glasgow investment trust companies are tightly integrated with 62% of their directorships being multiple directorships. The distribution of funds completes this comparison. Edinburgh investment trusts control 59% of all Scottish investment trust funds, compared with Glasgow's 21%. (60)

Our data suggest that Edinburgh is the focal point of the Scottish financial system. For each type of firm we find Edinburgh to be the senior partner to Glasgow, in terms of both interlocks within and between financial sub-sectors, and by size of funds controlled. Edinburgh financial firms also display a much higher level of integration within and between the financial sub-sectors, suggesting a firm resource base for economic power. (61)

Conclusion

We have argued that there is, in Scotland, a ruling class centred upon the financial firms of Edinburgh, and that this ruling class has a relative autonomy with respect to the British ruling class. Scotland has a peripheral political system and a satellite economy and is subordinated to the metropolitan centre — London. We have tried to indicate some of the economic and political dynamics underlying this situation and to point to some of the problems of analysis and data involved in arriving at this picture.

We would emphasise that much research remains to be done. Our intention has been to point out the problems for future research. We have suggested only an outline; it is for future research to confirm this outline and to fill in the details.

REFERENCES

1. Alexander B. Richmond, *Narrative of the Conditions of the Manufacturing Population* and the Proceedings of Government which lead to the State Trials in Scotland, (New York, Augustus M. Kelley, 1971), p.1. The original book was published in 1824.
2. As originally pointed out in Talcott Parsons, *The Structure of Social Action* (Glencoe, The Free Press 1937).
3. Peter Winch, *The Idea of a Social Science* (London, Routledge and Kegan Paul, 1958). We use this formulation in order to sidestep the interminable discussion of the concept of 'rationality'.
4. Parsons, *op. cit.*, p.429 ff. Rex derives a similar notion from his discussion of Durkheim's work. See John Rex, *Key Problems of Sociological Theory* (London, Routledge and Kegan Paul, 1961), p.84.
5. See the excellent discussion of this in Julien Freund, *The Sociology of Max Weber* (London, Allen Lane The Penguin Press, 1968), pp.161-7.
6. c.f. Althusser's distinction between economic, political and ideological practice and Habermas' distinction between purposive rational action (the state and the economy) and symbolic interactionism (ideologies). See Louis Althusser, *For Marx* (Harmondsworth, Penguin Books, 1969), and Jurgen Habermas, *Towards a Rational Society* (London, Heinemann, 1971). See also the discussion of the interrelations of these types in Talcott Parsons, *The Social System* (Glencoe, The Free Press), p.69 ff.
7. Cultural power relates, for reasons which cannot be discussed here, to the notion of ritual action. We include this concept here in order to indicate its position within our general perspective.
8. This, of course, touches on the columinous literature on the concept and definition of 'power' and we would here mention only Peter Bachrach and Morton Baratz, *Power and Poverty* (New York, Oxford University Press, 1970). For a similar view on the three bases of power see John Urry, *Reference Groups and The Theory of Revolution* (London, Routledge and Kegan Paul, 1973), and the introduction to John Urry and John Wakeford, *Power in Britain* (London, Heinemann, 1973). We neglect here an alternative form of social control based upon the internalization of cultural values — authority. Such a system of control is based upon a belief in the legitimacy of the social order and is, clearly, tied to the ideas of ritual action and status. This is beyond our present scope, but we hope to discuss it in a later publication. For an earlier view see John Scott, 'Power and Authority: A Comment on Spencer and Martin', *British Journal of Sociology*, 24, 1, 1973.
9. A.C. Giddens, 'Elites in the British Class Structure', *Sociological Review*, 20, 3, 1972, p.348.
10. In practice we shall concentrate upon social integration, preferring to see moral integration as an aspect of cultural power. Nevertheless, as we employ the term, social integration implies a solidarity which necessarily involves certain 'normative' factors. See the discussion in Percy S. Cohen, *Modern Social Theory* (London, Heinemann, 1968), pp.135-138.

11. Giddens, *op.cit.*, p.351. These types of elite are fully explained in Giddens' article.
12. Robert Michels, *Political Parties* (Glencoe, The Free Press, 1958), p.418.
13. Cohen, *op. cit.*, Chapter 6. See also Alvin W. Gouldner, 'Reciprocity and Autonomy in Functional Theory', in Llewellyn Gross (ed.), *Symposium on Sociological Theory* (New York, Harper and Row, 1959).
14. We would emphasise that, in distinction to Giddens' use of these terms, we refer to the *institutional* structure of power — to what Giddens terms the 'institutional mediation of power'. Giddens uses these terms in relation to the 'mediation of control'.
15. We are not presenting a complete analysis of all the logically possible combinations of these variables. We are constructing a sociological typology of those ideal types which seem most useful.
16. As we have already noted, we are not discussing the dimension of cultural power. As Marx's discussion of ideology would suggest, a consideration of this should be involved in the concept of a ruling class — and, by implication, the other types of social control.
17. Our formulation says nothing *per se* about causal relations between the economy and the polity: it merely defines 'ruling class' and 'governing class' in terms of a structural isomorphism between economic and political elites.
18. In terming Scotland a 'sub-national' unit we are merely taking the national unit of 'Britain' as a convenient point of reference.
19. We would argue that the culture/subculture scheme runs parallel to these two theses.
20. See Andre Gunder Frank, *Capitalism and Underdevelopment in Latin America* (London, Monthly Review Press, 1967).
21. c.f., K. Buchanan, 'The Revolt Against Satellization in Scotland and Wales', *Monthly Review*, 19, 10, 1968. For a slightly different view see Ian Carter, 'The Highlands of Scotland as an Underdeveloped Region', in E. de Kadt (ed.), *Sociology and Development* (London, Tavistock, 1974).
22. Ioan Davies, *Social Mobility and Political Change* (London, Pall Mall, 1970), p.51 ff.
23. For a recent expression of this from a different point of view see M. Hechter, 'The Persistence of Regionalism in the British Isles 1885-1966', *American Journal of Sociology*, 79, 2, 1973.
24. W.J.M. Mackenzie, *Politics and Social Science* (Harmondsworth, Penguin Books, 1967), p.352.
25. James Kellas, *The Scottish Political System* (Cambridge University Press, 1973), p.18.
26. See the evidence in: Sam Aaronovitch *The Ruling Class* (London, Lawrence and Wishart, 1961); W. Guttsman, *The British Political Elite* (London, McGibbon and Kee, 1964); R. Miliband, *The State in Capitalist Society* (London, Weidenfeld and Nicholson, 1969); John Urry and John Wakeford, *op.cit.*
27. For some of the problems involved in using such sources see Colin Bell, 'Some Comments on the Use of Directories in Research on Elites', in Ivor Crewe, *The British Political Sociology Yearbook*, Vol. 1. (London, Croom Helm, 1974).

Our sources include *The Stock Exchange Official Yearbook* (1972), *The Times 1000* (1973-4), *The Directory of Directors* (1975), *Who's Who, Who Was Who, Who Owns Whom* (1973), *Kelly's Handbook, Burke's Peerage,* and *Burke's Landed Gentry*. Other sources will be noted where appropriate.

28. The categories used were 1000 largest U.K. industrial companies, 25 largest U.K. insurance companies, 50 largest U.K. investment trust companies, and all the Scottish clearing banks and large merchant banks. Our definition of a 'Scottish' firm was any firm with its registered office or head office in Scotland. Our category of 'directors' refers not only to 'ordinary' directors, but also to 'extraordinary' directors, presidents, and vice-presidents.

29. So far as we know, the only attempt to produce some data in this area is Dr. C.J. Larner's unpublished investigation of Scottish MPs in her paper, 'The Scottish MP since 1910: His Background and His Performance'.

30. Our procedure was to select the top firms from *The Times 1000* and to use *The Stock Exchange Official Yearbook* to obtain the names of their directors.

31. For a useful discussion of this relationship between Edinburgh and Glasgow see T.C. Smout, *A History of the Scottish People* (Glasgow, Collins, 1969), Chapter 15.

32. David Keir (ed.), *The City of Edinburgh (The Third Statistical Account of Scotland)*, Glasgow, Collins, 1966, p.572.

33. This situation has changed slightly in recent years with the growth of merchant banking facilities and of issuing houses, largely due to the impact of North Sea oil.

34. A major field of investment was the American railways, see R.E. Tyson, 'Scottish Investment in American Railways: The Case of the City of Glasgow Bank, 1856-1881', in P.L. Payne, *Studies in Scottish Business History* (London, Frank Cass, 1967). Other articles in this book are of interest. Studies of Scottish investment trusts and their overseas investments can also be found in: D.S. Macmillan, *Scotland and Australia* (Oxford, Clarendon Press, 1967), and W. Turrentine Jackson, *The Enterprising Scot* (Edinburgh, Edinburgh University Press, 1968).

35. Figures from *Directory of Financial Institutions* (1973).

36. 'Industrial' in the text is largely a residual term for non-financial firms and includes all types of merchandising companies. It comprises all strictly industrial firms and all holding companies with most of their interests in industrial firms. Our sample of top firms comprises 38 'industrial' and 31 'financial' firms.

37. Useful accounts of Scottish industry can be found in C.A. Oakley (ed.), *Scottish Industry* (Edinburgh, The Scottish Council, 1953). See also the various volumes of *The Third Statistical Account* – particularly the volumes on Aberdeen (1953), Edinburgh (1966) and Glasgow (1958).

38. The low overall average for financial firms is explained by the large number of investment trust companies present in the sample.

39. In contrast to the distribution of multiple directorships in our sample of top firms, where there are more single than multiple directorships.

40. The small number of banks (8) makes this analysis very tentative. For the same reason, Unit Trusts (4) are omitted from the discussion until more detailed data

can be obtained.
41. We make no reference here to their actual attitudes and values. We merely point to the predominance of participation in financial institutions amongst elite activities. The existence of many holding companies in the industrial and merchandising sector perhaps strengthens this conclusion.
42. For example, the participation of the Younger brewing family in national Conservative and Unionist politics and their continued involvement in the representation of Ayrshire constituencies.
43. 4 OBEs, 5 MBEs, 6 CBEs, 1 KBE.
44. For an interesting discussion of titles see S.N. Eisenstadt, *Social Differentiation and Stratification* (Illinois, Scott, Foresman and Co., 1971), p.48 ff.
45. P. Worsley, 'The Distribution of Power in Industrial Society', in P. Halmos, *The Development of Industrial Societies* (Sociological Review Monograph, 8, University of Keele, 1964).
46. I. Crewe, *op.cit.*, pp.16-18.
47. S. Finer, *Anonymous Empire* (London, Pall Mall, 1958).
48. Kellas, *op.cit.*
49. Our sources of information on these groups are the *Annual Reports* for the Scottish Council (1972-3) and Glasgow Chamber of Commerce (1972) and the *Year Book* for Edinburgh Chamber of Commerce (1973). As with company reports, problems of comparison arise because different organisations use different accounting periods. We are grateful to the Secretaries and Information Officers of the three organizations for providing us with this and other information.
50. See for example, the Nicoll Report (Scottish Council, 1973) and the recent account of the last international Forum on 'Scotland's goals' held at Aviemore: J. McGill, *Scotland's Goals* (Glasgow, Collins, 1974).
51. See T. Devine, 'Glasgow Colonial Merchants', in J.T. Ward, *Land and Industry* (Newton Abbot, David and Charles, 1971). See also, E. Gaskell, *Renfrewshire and Ayrshire Leaders* (Queenhithe Printing and Publishing Co., 1910, and G. Stewart, *Curosity of Glasgow Citizenship* (Glasgow, 1881).
52. See *Burke's Peerage* and *Burke's Landed Gentry*. Further evidence on exclusive backgrounds can be found in club membership and military service. The economic elite possesses, collectively, 9 memberships of well-known London clubs (Boodle's, Pratt's, Brooks', etc.), 8 men are members of the Western Club (Glasgow), and 17 are members of the New Club (Edinburgh). 7 men are members of military clubs, there are 3 DSOs, 3 MCs, and 14 men possess the Territorial Decoration (TD).
53. J. Firn, *The Scotsman*, October 30th, October 31st, and November 1st, 1973.
54. Firn defines as 'Scottish' any firm operating in Scotland. The definition of what is and what is not a Scottish firm is a thorny problem since it presupposes a definition of the Scottish economy — and no satisfactory definition is available.
55. *The Scotsman*, October 30th, 1973.
56. See: Economist Intelligence Unit, *The Economic Effects of Scottish Independence, Stage 1* (London, Economist Intelligence Unit, 1969).
57. Glasgow companies would appear to be more tightly integrated than Edinburgh

firms — but this is due to one particular Glasgow director who has 7 investment trust directorships in Glasgow but no other financial directorships in Glasgow.

58. This represents 60% of all Edinburgh bank directorships.
59. The banks in our sample are The Clydesdale Bank, The British Bank of Commerce, James Finlay Merchant Bank, and Clydesdale Bank Finance Corporation, in Glasgow, and The Bank of Scotland, The Royal Bank of Scotland, The National and Commercial Banking Group, and Scottish Agricultural Securities Corporation, in Edinburgh.
60. 20% is controlled by investment trusts outside the central belt. The figures for funds are:

Edinburgh investment trusts	...	approx. £1,172 m.
Glasgow investment trusts	...	approx. £ 421 m.
Other Scottish investment trusts	...	approx. £ 417 m.

61. Economic notables seem not to be aware of the precise details of the prominent position of Edinburgh in relation to the rest of Scotland. Instead, they focus on the London-Scotland relation and stress the need for greater autonomy and effective decision-making for Scottish industry. See, for example, the report of the First International Forum at Aviemore, *The Influence of Centralisation on the Future* (Edinburgh, Scottish Council, 1970). Such claims are frequently linked to a desire for a greater independence of the Scottish political system. We would argue that such a move may merely consolidate the dominance of Edinburgh financial firms within the Scottish economy. The real issue is that of the distribution of power *within* Scottish society.

Index

Aberdeen 16, 22, 30, 45, 54, 68, 69, 96, 109, 147, 173, 182
Aberdeen, Earl of 108, 122
Aberdeenshire 6, 63, 64, 70, 71, 86, 92, 93, 97, 99, 102, 103, 106, 108, 109, 114; *see also* North East
abortion 71, 146
agricultural improvements 6, 12, 86, 91, 92, 93, 94, 97, 101, 106, 112, 120
agricultural labourers 6, 7, 64, 65, 66, 70, 72, 79, 80, 86, 87, 88, 89, 90, 92, 93, 94, 95, 96, 98, 99, 100, 101, 102, 104, 105-22, 124, 127, 153
agricultural revolution *see* agricultural improvements
Alexander, Dr. 109
Alexander, William 114
Alford, Vale of 112
Alison, Dr. W.P. 13, 36, 41, 43
Allan, James 116
America, North 60, 173, 179
American Trust Company 172
Anderson Mavor 172
Angus 65, 86
Anti-Corn Law League 147
Arch, Joseph 109
Argyllshire 74
Arnott, Dr. Neil 13
Arran, 57, 77
artisans 100, 128ff, 132, 134, 136, 139, 141
atheism 145
Auchterless, parish of 113
Ayrshire 144

Banffshire 62, 63, 64, 66, 67, 68, 70, 71, 74, 75, 80, 81, 86, 106, 108, 111, 114, 125, 126
Bank of Scotland 188
Baptists 42
Barnes, George, M.P. 145
Baxter Bros. 21
Begg, Rev. Dr. James 25, 32, 65, 66, 122
Bendix, R. 128
Bentham, Jeremy 36
Berwickshire 63, 66, 67, 70
Best, Geoffrey 23, 128
Bird, Isabella 60

Boards of Health 39ff, 45f, 48, 53; *see also* epidemic disease; Infirmaries; Public Health Movement; sanitation
Bochel, J.M. & Denver, D.J. 165
bookbinders 130, 134, 141
bothy ballads 112, 113, 114, 121, 124
'bothy' system 16, 65, 66, 74, 75, 80, 97, 106, 108, 112, 115, 122, 125 *see also* 'chaumer' system
Brechin 40
British Bank of Commerce 188
brothels 57, 59ff, 69; *see also* prostitution
Brotherston, J.H.F. 41, 51
Broughty Ferry 45
Bruckley, parish of 124
Buchanan, J.L. 77
Building Societies 24, 25, 33, 129, 133
Burgh Police and Improvement Acts 19, 23
Burmah Oil 172
Burns, Robert 55
Butler, D. & Stokes, D. 158f

Cairnie, parish of 112
Caithness 65
Calvinism 3, 4, 5, 42, 43, 44, 47, 49, 162; *see also* presbyterianism
Campbell, Gordon, M.P. 160
capitalism 2, 6, 10, 36, 86, 144; *see also* labour force
Carr, E.H. 1, 42
Carter, Ian 6, 7
Catholic Socialist Society 145
Census, 1966 sample 148, 149, 153
Chadwick, Edwin 17, 22, 26, 43, 45
Chalkin, C.W. 18
Chalmers, Rev. Dr. Thomas 22, 36, 42
Chambers of Commerce 177-79
Chapel of Garioch, parish of 102
Chartism 22, 26, 145, 147
'chaumer' system 66, 67, 79, 80, 106, 112, 115, 122, 125
cholera *see* epidemic disease
church attendance 3, 22, 48, 71; *see also* religiosity
Church of Scotland 3-4, 41f, 52, 55, 61, 62, 71, 74, 76, 83, 145, 159 *see also* Calvinism; Free Church; kirk sessions; presbyterianism

INDEX

city missions 36, 43, 54
Clark, Dr. Gavin, M.P. 144
class consciousness 1, 4, 6, 7, 14-15, 16, 19, 20, 26, 47, 48, 49, 109, 127, 138, 143, 146f, 147, 148; *see also* Housing; social differentiation, process of
'clean toun' 7, 113f, 119; *see also* Horseman's Word, Society of
clergymen 42, 50, 54, 58, 61, 62, 70, 71, 83, 108, 112
Cluny, parish of 102
Clydesdale Bank 188
Clydesdale Bank Finance Corporation 188
Clydeside 28, 144, 148, 153
Coatbridge 46, 146
Cohen, Percy S. 168f
Communist Party 144
Congregationalists 42, 162
Connell, K.H. 73
Conservative Party 8, 146, 147, 148, 149, 150, 151, 152, 154, 156, 158, 159, 160, 161, 164, 165, 187
constituency boundaries 148, 152, 155
Co-operative Movement 7, 25, 33, 129, 130, 131, 132, 133, 137, 138
courtship 55f, 67, 69, 72f, 74-80; *see also* illegitimacy; marriage
Cramond, William 71, 72
Crawfurd, Lord 57, 77
Creech, William 57
Creighton, Charles 40, 44
Crewe, Ivor 152, 177
crime 5, 12, 17, 22, 23, 37, 61, 71, 131; *see also* drunkenness; prostitution
Crimond, parish of 89
crofters 6, 87ff, 92ff, 95, 96, 97f, 100ff, 119, 121, 144; *see also* farmers; landowners; ploughing
Cruden, parish of 102
Cullen, parish of 64

Dale, David 21, 36
Davies, I. 171
Dean of Guild 19
deferential traditionalism 105f, 109, 119ff
destitution 5, 13-14, 17, 20, 24, 26, 31, 33, 37, 38, 40, 41, 42, 46, 47, 48, 49; *see also* poor relief
Dewar, Duncan 106
Dilke, Sir Charles 13
Directory of Financial Institutions 173
Distillers Company 172
divorce 56, 146
Dollar 67
domestic industry 89

domestic servants 5, 37, 46, 58, 59, 60, 68, 69, 72, 79, 88, 93, 108
Douglas, Dick, M.P. 165
drunkenness 17, 37, 43, 47, 64, 77, 112, 131
Dumfries 39, 75
Dumfriesshire 63
Dunbartonshire 73
Duncan, Joe 113
Dundee 15, 16, 17, 18, 20, 21, 24, 25, 28, 30, 31, 34, 39, 40, 45, 46, 50, 60, 69, 145, 147, 159, 162, 165, 173, 182
Dunlop, John 61
Dwelling Houses (Scotland) Act, 1855 23

East Lothian 63, 66, 67, 68, 70, 106
Economist Intelligence Unit 181
Edinburgh 7, 9, 16, 17, 24, 25, 30, 33, 38, 39, 41, 43, 44, 57, 58, 59, 60, 61, 64, 68, 69, 81, 84, 85, 128ff, 139, 147, 171, 173, 178, 179, 180, 181ff, 188
Edinburgh and Leith Joiners Building Company Ltd. 33
Edinburgh Chamber of Commerce *see* Chambers of Commerce
Edinburgh Co-operative Building Company Ltd. 25, 129, 133
Edinburgh News 133
Edinburgh Savings Bank 129, 132, 139
Edinburgh Trades Council 130, 131, 133
Edinburgh Working Men's Building Association 25
education 2, 3, 4, 26, 29, 36, 41, 50, 56, 61, 63f, 72, 135, 137, 141, 143, 145ff, 163, 180 *see also* universities
Education Act of 1872 3
Education (Scotland) Act, 1918 145
Elgin 137
elites 2, 3, 4, 8, 9, 168-83; *see also* labour aristocracy
embourgeoisement 7, 105, 119, 134, 138; *see also* labour aristocracy; respectability
emigration 100, 119
employers 4, 15, 21, 22, 24, 25, 26, 31, 37, 59, 66, 76, 90, 100, 101, 105, 109, 114, 118, 119, 121, 134, 135, 136, 141, 143, 144
Engels, F. 78
engineers 130, 131, 135, 136, 141

INDEX

England – comparisons 1, 2, 3, 4, 5, 6, 8, 12, 16, 17, 19, 27, 38, 40, 43, 49, 62, 63, 91, 108, 109, 111, 118, 119, 121, 143, 145, 146; electoral politics 148-57, 161; municipal housing 145, 158, 179, 180, 181; London 8, 23, 24, 41, 52, 73, 144, 147, 153, 171, 173, 181, 183, 188; regions 118, 153f, 157ff, 164
epidemic disease 12f, 14, 17, 20, 22, 37f, 43-47, 49; bubonic plague 43f; cholera 5, 23, 37, 38ff, 47ff, 52, 53f; diarrhoea 39, 44; 'fever' 13f, 38, 44; influenza 44; smallpox 44; typhus and typhoid 5, 37ff, 43, 44, 47, 48, 49; venereal disease 5, 44, 57, 59, 60, 82; *see also* Boards of Health; Infirmaries; Public Health Movement; sanitation
Episcopal Church 3
Equitable Co-operative Society 25
Eskdalemuir, parish of 105, 106
Essex University Oral History Unit *see* Oral History
Europe 38, 63
European Economic Community 179
Evans, G.E. 119
Ewing, Winifred, M.P. 160

farm servants *see* agricultural labourers
farmers 64ff, 68, 73, 76, 79, 86, 89ff, 93-99, 101, 105f, 109f, 112, 114, 118f, 121, 124, 127; *see also* agricultural labourers; crofters; tacksmen
feeing markets 7, 64, 88, 98, 106, 108, 109, 110, 111, 112, 113, 116, 119, 121, 124
Fifeshire 65, 66
Finer, S. 177
Firn, John 181
First Book of Discipline 3
First World War 28, 63, 106, 110, 114, 147
Forfar 25
fishermen 39, 64, 68
Forth and Clyde Canal 46
Fotheringham, Peter 7, 8
Frank, Andre Gunder 170f
Free Church 4, 54, 65, 71f, 74f, 76f, 145; *see also* Calvinism; presbyterianism
Free Gardeners Society 129
Fyvie, parish of 124

Gaelic language 75, 77
Gallacher, William, M.P. 145
gambling 58
Garioch 112, 113, 124

Gauldie, Enid 4
General Elections, 1945-74 8, 148-61; *see also* parliamentary constituencies
Gerrard, Dr. 66
Giddens, Anthony 168ff, 185
Glasgow 9, 16, 17, 18, 23, 25, 26, 28, 30, 31, 35, 39, 45, 46, 50, 51, 53, 57, 60, 61, 64, 69, 137, 145, 147, 151, 152, 159, 163, 171, 173, 178, 179, 180, 181ff, 188
Glasgow Chamber of Commerce *see* Chambers of Commerce
Glasgow Landlords' Association 13
Glenmuick, parish of 102
Goldthorpe, John 105
Grange, parish of 125
Gray, Malcolm 6, 7, 119, 120
Gray, R.Q. 6, 7
Gray, Rev. A. 121
Greenock 30, 39, 69, 73
Greig, Gavin 117

Haddington 48, 92
Haddo Estates 108
Haddo House Association 71
Hardy, Keir 144, 145, 146, 148, 162
Harland & Wolff 163
harvesting 87, 88, 97
Health of Towns Association 26
Health of Towns, Select Committee on 23
Hebrides, The 68, 74, 75, 79, 80 *see also* Lewis, Isle of
Highlands 4, 6, 39, 60, 63, 64, 66, 70, 73, 74, 75, 76, 77, 80, 148, 171
Hole, James 22
holidays 110f
Horseman's Word, Society of 7, 114-18, 121, 125f *see also* 'clean toun'
horse-racing 57
House of Commons *see* Parliament
House of Fraser 172
housing – cellars 15, 34; evictions 12, 13; municipal 131, 147, 149, 158, 161; overcrowding 18, 19, 20, 26, 27, 30; slums and slum clearance 12, 13, 14, 15, 16, 17, 19, 20, 21, 23, 25, 26, 27, 65, 71; speculation 4, 17, 18, 19, 24, 26, 27, 29; tied cottages 21, 66, 70, 80, 122; *see also* class consciousness; crime; epidemic disease; rents; social differentiation; working class
Hughes, Michael 8, 9
Huntly, 102, 104

illegitimacy 5, 6, 55-59, 62-67, 69-83, 108, 126; *see also* courtship; marriage
immigration 12, 18, 100

INDEX

Independent Labour Party 146, 150
Infirmaries 37ff, 43, 48ff, 53, 57, 59, 68; *see also* epidemic disease
intemperance *see* drunkenness
Inveravon, parish of 64
Inverness 63, 74, 151
Inverurie 116
Ireland 73, 74, 79, 143; *see also* Northern Ireland
Irish Home Rule 144, 145, 146
Irish, the 31, 33, 61, 64, 69, 73, 74, 75, 79, 145, 162

James Finlay Merchant Bank 188
Japan 173, 179
Johnson, Dr. 78
Johnston, Russell, M.P. 151
joiners 129, 130, 131, 133, 135, 136, 137

Kavanagh, D. 105
Keating, Joseph 73
Keir, David 173
Keith, G.S. 89, 91
Keith Hall, parish of 89
Kellas, J.G. 1, 7, 8, 41, 171, 177
Kemnay 89
Kendall, Walter 148
Kennethmont, parish of 124
Kincardineshire 63, 64, 86, 94, 103, 106, 108, 114, 124, 125; *see also* North East
Kinnaird, Lord 24, 32
Kinnear, Michael 147
Kinnellar, parish of 102
Kirkcudbright 63
Kirkintilloch 46
Kirkmichael, parish of 64
kirk sessions 3, 4, 37, 55

labour aristocracy 7, 59, 69, 128-38, 139, 141; *see also* embourgeoisement; respectability
labour force 12, 16, 20, 21, 22, 31, 65, 80, 81, 86-102, 106, 108, 111, 113, 114, 119, 120, 122, 134, 154, 156f
Labour Party 8, 143, 144, 145f, 147, 148, 149, 150, 151, 152, 153, 154, 155, 156f, 157, 158, 159, 160, 161, 162, 163, 165; *see also* Scottish Labour Party Conference
labour services 88, 89; *see also* agricultural improvements
Lambie, David, M.P. 144
Lanarkshire 64, 70, 178
landlords *see* landowners
landowners 18, 21, 26, 29, 39, 55, 56, 57, 58, 86, 88, 89, 90, 91, 92, 94, 106, 108, 127

Leatham, James 109
legal profession 61, 143, 146
Leith 39, 69
Leslie, parish of 102
Lewis, Isle of 43, 55, 57, 75, 76, 77, 78, 79; *see also* Hebrides, The
Liberal Party 145, 146, 147, 148, 150, 151, 153, 157, 161, 164
'Lib-Labism' 146
Littlejohn, J. 105
Lloyd George, David 147
Lockwood, David 105, 106, 118, 121
Logan, William 60, 61
London *see* England
Longside, parish of 113
Lowlands 57, 62, 63, 65, 66, 70, 71, 72, 73, 75, 76, 79, 80, 92

Machin, George 165
Magdalene Institute 57, 58; *see also* prostitution
magistracy 37, 51, 52; *see also* town councils
marriage 5, 6, 7, 55f, 62, 66ff, 70f, 74-80, 83, 89, 98f, 100f, 108, 119, 129f, 143; *see also* courtship; divorce; illegitimacy
Martineau, Harriet 74
Marx, Karl 166, 169
masons 129, 130, 131, 133, 136
Maud, parish of 124
Mayhew, Henry 73
Mead, Richard 43-44
medical profession 38, 39, 41, 43, 44, 46, 48, 52, 56, 61, 67, 68, 81
Methodists 42, 162
Michels, Robert 168
Midlothian 64, 178
'Miller's Word' 116; *see also* Horseman's Word, Society of
mill-hands 60, 68
Milne, Johnny 113
miners 28, 39, 73, 109, 146, 156, 158, 165
Mitchell, Alex 112, 119
Model Lodging Houses 24, 32, 34
Monkland Canal 46
Monymusk, parish of 89
Moray 63, 86, 106, 108, 111, 114; *see also* North East
Musselburgh 57

McCaffrey, John 145
Macdonald, Alexander 146
Macgill, Patrick 73
Mackenzie, W.J.M. 171

INDEX   193

Mackintosh, J.P., M.P. 152
MacLaren, A.A. 4, 5, 22
McLean, I. 160
Maclean, John 144, 145

Nairn 86, 106, 108, 114
Nairn, Tom 144
nationalism 2, 8, 143, 144, 161, 162, 163; see also Scottish National Party
National and Commercial Banking Group 188
National Association for Social Science 24
New Deer, parish of 124
New Lanark 21
Newby, Howard 7, 105, 118, 121
North Briton 129
North East 62, 64, 67, 71, 79, 86-121, 122, 125, 127, 171
North Sea oil 160, 165, 179, 186
Northern Ireland 146, 150, 151, 163, see also Ireland

Oddfellows' Lodge 129, 130, 132, 139
Old Deer, parish of 92, 96
Old Statistical Account 91
Opinion Polls 149, 159, 161
Oral History 56, 59, 72, 74, 75, 78, 81
Orangeism 145, 146, 162, 163
Orkney & Shetland 60, 63, 64, 65, 67, 68, 73, 74, 75, 76, 77, 78, 79, 80
Owen, Robert 36
Oxfam 50

painters 130, 131, 136, 141
Paisley 16, 30, 39, 69
parish schools see education
Parliament 14, 15, 16, 23, 25, 26, 27, 29, 144, 149, 152, 154, 158
parliamentary constituencies —
  Aberdeen (South) 152, 153f, 156; Aberdeenshire (East) 151, 160; Aberdeenshire (West) 151; Angus (South) 151, 157, 160; Ayr 155, 156; Ayrshire (Central) 144; Ayrshire (North) 157; Argyll 151, 160; Banffshire 151, 160; Berwick & East Lothian 152, 156, 157; Caithness & Sutherland 151, 156, 157, 164; Clackmannan and East Stirlingshire 151, 160, 165; Coatbridge and Airdrie 156; Dunbartonshire (Central) 164; Dunbartonshire (East) 151, 152, 156, 164; Dunbartonshire (West) 156, 164; Dumfriesshire 156, 157; Dundee (East) 151, 160, 165; East Kilbride 164; Edinburgh — North 154, South 154, West 154, Pentlands 154; Galloway 151, 160; Glasgow — Blackfriars-Hutchesontown 145, Bridgeton 164, Camlachie 145, Cathcart 154, 156, 158, Central 164, Craigton 152, 158, 164, Govan 160, 164, Kelvingrove 152, 156, 164, Pollok 152, 164, Scotstoun 152, Woodside 152, 164; Hamilton 155, 160; Inverness 151; Kilmarnock 155; Lanark 152, 156; Moray & Nairn 151, 160; Paisley 155; Perth and East Perthshire 151, 156, 160; Stirling and Falkirk 155, 160; Stirlingshire (West) 160; Renfrewshire (East) 154f, 157; Renfrewshire (West) 152; Ross & Cromarty 151; Roxburgh, Selkirk & Peebles 151; Rutherglen 152, 155, 156; West Lothian 160; Western Isles 151, 160
parliamentary devolution 143, 144, 149, 152, 162
Parsons, Talcott 167
Paterson, William 137
peat 87-88, 92
Perthshire 63, 65, 69, 182
ploughing 64, 87f, 91f, 96f, 99, 106, 113, 115f; see also crofters
ploughmen see ploughing
Police 19, 20, 23, 31, 118, 119; see also crime; prostitution
Poor Law Amendment Act, 1845 41-42
poor relief 22, 36, 38, 40, 41, 48, 132, 133, 145; see also destitution
Post Office Directories 136, 141
poverty see destitution
presbyterianism 3, 4, 5, 32, 42, 64, 145, 146; see also Calvinism; Church of Scotland; Free Church
printers 129, 130, 135, 136, 141
Property Investment Association 25
prostitution 5, 23, 37, 55-62, 64, 69, 73, 78f, 81; see also crime; drunkenness
Public Health Movement 5, 13, 23, 26, 40, 41, 43, 47, 49, 52; see also epidemic disease; Boards of Health; sanitation

railways 111, 129
Rangers F.C. 163
'Red Clydeside' see Clydeside
Reform League 33
Reformation, the 55, 64, 81
Registrar General 59, 62, 63, 64, 65, 66, 68, 84, 148
Reid, George M.P. 165

INDEX

Reid, Jimmy 144
religion 1, 8, 56, 57, 64, 77, 143, 145ff, 147, 159, 161
religiosity 3, 37, 38, 42, 47, 48, 145, 159; see also church attendance
Renfrewshire 73, 178; see also Paisley
rents 4, 18, 22, 25, 26, 27, 29, 89, 91, 93, 95, 108, 133, 146; see also wages
respectability 7, 13, 15, 18, 57, 58, 69, 79, 128, 131, 132, 134, 138; see also embourgeoisement
Richmond, Alexander 166
Roman Catholic Church 3, 32, 74, 75, 145, 147, 159, 163
Rose, Richard 153, 158f, 159
Rosenberg, C.E. 48
Ross & Cromarty 63, 64, 67, 70, 74, 77
Ross, William 147, 163
Roxburghshire 70, 71
Royal Bank of Scotland 172, 188
Royal Commissions: on employment of women and children in agriculture 71; on Friendly and Benefit societies 24, 129; on housing 13, 14, 28, 130; on labour 109, 111
rural society 2, 4, 6, 9, 12, 59, 62-70, 72, 76-80, 86-102, 105-21, 135

Sabbath observance 77
St. Cuthbert's Co-operative Association 129, 130, 132, 133, 137, 138
sanitation 17, 19, 20, 21, 22, 23, 27, 28, 39, 43, 49; see also epidemic disease; Public Health Movement
Savings Banks 7, 25, 129, 132, 139
Scotsman; The 67
Scott, Messrs. J. & T. 129
Scott, John 8, 9
Scottish Agricultural Securities Corporation 188
Scottish Amicable Life Assurance Company 172
Scottish & Newcastle Breweries 172
Scottish and Universal Investments 172
Scottish Co-operative Wholesale Society 137
Scottish Council (Development and Industry) 9, 177, 179f
Scottish Eastern Investment Trust 172
Scottish Labour Party Conference 144, 162, 163
Scottish Miners Federation 28

Scottish National Party 8, 144, 147, 148, 149, 150, 151, 152, 156, 159ff, 162, 163, 165; see also nationalism; parliamentary devolution
Scottish Office 179; see also Ross, William
Scottish Studies, School of 75, 76, 81, 85
Scottish Tourist Board 179
Scottish Trades Councils 147; see also Edinburgh Trades Council
Scottish Trades Union Congress 144, 162, 163
Scottish Transport Group 179
Scottish Western Investment Company 172
Scottish Widows' Fund and Life Assurance Society 172
Scottish Workers Representation Committee 146
Scrymgeour, Edwin, M.P. 145
Seafield, parish of 64
self-help 13, 22, 24f, 128, 132
Shanin, T. 120
Shetland see Orkney and Shetland
shoemakers 130, 136, 139
Shop Stewards Movement 147, 163
shopkeepers 40, 52, 59, 132
Simon, John 22
Slaney, Richard 23, 33
Smiles, Samuel 2, 24, 128
Smillie, Robert 146
Smith, Adam 36
Smout, T.C. 4, 5, 6, 7
Snow, J. 44
social control 2, 4, 12f, 16, 20, 22, 23, 37, 47, 55, 65, 66f, 79, 114, 119, 169, 171, 181, 185
social differentiation, process of 15, 16-17, 20, 21, 22, 45, 46, 47, 48, 49, 51, 57, 61, 69, 72, 77, 86, 90, 92, 95, 97, 98, 105, 131f, 136ff; see also class consciousness; housing
Social Morality, Society for Promotion of 65
socialism 143, 144, 145, 163
Sproat, Ian, M.P. 152
Steel, David, M.P. 151
Stirlingshire 73
Strachan, Dr. J.M. 67-74, 77
Stranraer 61, 73
Strichen, parish of 104, 113
strikes & lockouts 25, 26, 28
Sunday Post 145
Sutherland 64, 65, 74

tacksmen 77, 87; see also crofters
Tait, Dr. 57, 59, 60, 61, 69
Tarves, parish of 102

Temperance Societies 36, 131; *see also* drunkenness
textile industry 16, 158
Thomson, Rev. Charles 65
tied cottages; *see* housing
Titaghur Jute Factory 172
Tomintoul 64, 75
Toulmin, David 114
town councils 17, 18, 27, 28; *see also* magistracy
trade 19, 38, 44, 46, 49, 50, 60, 141
trade unionism 7, 28, 108, 109, 111, 118, 119, 126, 129, 137, 143, 144, 146, 162, 179; *see also* labour force
Turriff 102
typhus *see* epidemic disease
Tyrie, parish of 96, 102

Udny 88
Ulster *see* Northern Ireland
unemployment 1, 12, 14, 19, 22, 26, 37, 38, 112, 132, 135, 144, 146
Unitarians 162
United Irish League 145
United Presbyterian Church 4
universities 1, 2, 82, 180

Valentine, James 68, 69
venereal disease *see* epidemic disease

wages 7, 13, 17, 21, 24f, 33, 88f, 90, 95, 105f, 108ff, 124, 129, 132ff, 137; *see also* rents
Wales 8, 64, 73, 121, 148, 150, 151, 152, 153, 155, 158, 159
Weber, Max 166ff
Weir Group 172
Wheatley, John, M.P. 145
Wick 65
Wigtownshire 63, 64, 67, 68, 70, 74, 80
Winch, Peter 167
witchcraft 116
working class – children 2, 37, 70, 135, 137; medical provisions 37ff, 47f; political behaviour 8, 20, 105, 119, 137, 143-61; radicalism 21f, 26, 28, 105, 143, 145, 147; *see also* class consciousness; housing; social differentiation
Worsley, Peter 177
Wright, Thomas 138

Zetland 63